PUBLICATIONS OF
THE MANCHESTER CENTRE FOR ANGLO-SAXON STUDIES

Volume 9

The Landscape Archaeology of Anglo-Saxon England

Traditional opinion has perceived the Anglo-Saxons as creating an entirely new landscape from scratch in the fifth and sixth centuries AD, cutting down woodland, bringing with them the practice of open field agriculture, and establishing villages. Whilst recent scholarship has proved this simplistic picture wanting, it has also raised many questions about the nature of landscape development at the time, the changing character of systems of land management, and strategies for settlement. The papers here seek to shed new light on these complex issues. Taking a variety of different approaches, and with topics ranging from the impact of coppicing to medieval field systems, from the representation of the landscape in manuscripts to cereal production and the type of bread the population preferred, they offer striking new approaches to the central issues of landscape change across the seven centuries of Anglo-Saxon England, a period surely foundational for today's rural landscape.

PUBLICATIONS OF
THE MANCHESTER CENTRE FOR ANGLO-SAXON STUDIES

ISSN 1478–6710

Published Titles

1. *Textual and Material Culture in Anglo-Saxon England: Thomas Northcote Toller and the Toller Memorial Lectures*, ed. Donald Scragg
2. *Apocryphal Texts and Traditions in Anglo-Saxon England*, ed. Kathryn Powell and Donald Scragg
3. *King Harold II and the Bayeux Tapestry*, ed. Gale R. Owen-Crocker
4. *The Place of the Cross in Anglo-Saxon England*, ed. Catherine E. Karkov, Sarah Larratt Keefer and Karen Louise Jolly
5. *Writing and Texts in Anglo-Saxon England*, ed. Alexander R. Rumble
6. *Anglo-Saxon Royal Diplomas: A Palaeography*, Susan D. Thompson
7. *Britons in Anglo-Saxon England*, ed. Nicholas J. Higham
8. *Edgar, King of the English 959–975: New Interpretations*, ed. Donald Scragg

The Landscape Archaeology of Anglo-Saxon England

edited by

NICHOLAS J. HIGHAM AND MARTIN J. RYAN

THE BOYDELL PRESS

First published 2010
The Boydell Press, Woodbridge

ISBN 978–1–84383–582–0

The Boydell Press is an imprint of Boydell & Brewer Ltd
PO Box 9, Woodbridge, Suffolk IP12 3DF, UK
and of Boydell & Brewer Inc,
668 Mt Hope Avenue, Rochester, NY 14620, USA
website: www.boydellandbrewer.com

A CIP catalogue record for this book is available
from the British Library

Papers used by Boydell & Brewer Ltd are natural, recyclable products
made from wood grown in sustainable forests

Papers used by Boydell & Brewer Ltd are natural, recyclable products
made from wood grown in sustainable forests

MIX
Paper from
responsible sources
FSC® C013604

Printed in Great Britain by
CPI Antony Rowe, Chippenham and Eastbourne

Contents

Illustrations

Plates

Figures

Tables

Contributors

Debby Banham, University of Cambridge

Stuart Brookes, University of London

Christopher Grocock, independent scholar

Nick Higham, University of Manchester

David Hill, University of Manchester

Richard Hoggett, NAU Archaeology

Catherine E. Karkov, University of Leeds

Carenza Lewis, University of Cambridge

Peter Murphy, English Heritage

Susan Oosthuizen, University of Cambridge

Stephen Rippon, University of Exeter

Tom Williamson, University of East Anglia

Acknowledgements

We are most grateful to the University of Manchester for financial support towards the management costs of the conference at Hulme Hall in 2007 and to the Medieval Settlement Research Group for providing funds for bursaries that allowed a number of postgraduate students to attend the conference. Organisation rested heavily upon the expertise and hard work of the staff of Hulme Hall. We are also grateful to the editorial committee of the Manchester Centre for Anglo-Saxon Studies for their championship of the volume, to the external reader who reviewed the papers and whose helpful comments have contributed greatly to the end product, and lastly to the professionalism and care for detail of Caroline Palmer and her colleagues at Boydell & Brewer.

Abbreviations

DB	Domesday Book
HE	*Bede: Historia Ecclesiastica Gentis Anglorum: Bede: Ecclesiastical History of the English People*, ed. Bertram Colgrave and R. A. B. Mynors (Oxford, 1969)
S	Peter H. Sawyer, *Anglo-Saxon Charters: An Annotated List and Bibliography*, Royal Historical Society Guides and Handbooks, 8 (London, 1968), with additions and revisions by Susan Kelly and Rebecca Rushforth, www.esawyer.org.uk
Stenton, *ASE*	Sir Frank M. Stenton, *Anglo-Saxon England*, 3rd edn (Oxford, 1971)

1

The Landscape Archaeology of Anglo-Saxon England: An Introduction[1]

NICK HIGHAM

This volume is one of a pair to emerge from a conference on the Landscape of Anglo-Saxon England hosted in 2007 by the Manchester Centre for Anglo-Saxon Studies (MANCASS) at the University of Manchester. It features exploration of the Anglo-Saxon landscape primarily via archaeological and/or art historical methodologies, leaving those approaches which are more specifically text and/or place-name based for the companion volume.[2] Naturally, this collection incorporates a wide spectrum of papers of different lengths and types, some dealing with quite specific issues or categories of data but some with major research questions and/or periods. Of course, it does not pretend to cover all aspects of the landscape of Anglo-Saxon England but it is hoped that it will mark a new stage in the development of our understanding, open up a series of research questions to wider discussion and provide a useful platform from which researchers will take the whole subject forward.

It is probably fair to say that more landscape archaeologists would see themselves as medievalists than either Romanists or prehistorians, but many have tended to focus primarily on the later Middle Ages, from *c.*1000 to the early sixteenth century. While there are several works of book length on the Roman landscape,[3] and then the later medieval,[4] there are remarkably few focusing exclusively on the Anglo-Saxon landscape.[5] Although, by their very nature, projects researching landscape archaeology tend to be multi-period in design, there is a tendency for the Anglo-Saxon period to be viewed either as the end-

1 My thanks to Martin Ryan for the care with which he has read and commented on early drafts of this introduction, which is much improved in consequence; needless to say, all remaining errors remain exclusively those of the author.

2 *Place-Names, Language and the Anglo-Saxon Landscape*, eds N. J. Higham and M. J. Ryan (Woodbridge, forthcoming).

3 As Richard Hingley, *Rural Settlement in Roman Britain* (London, 1989); Ken and Petra Dark, *The Landscape of Roman Britain* (Stroud, 1997).

4 As *The Countryside of Medieval England*, eds Grenville Astill and Annie Grant (Oxford, 1988); *Medieval Landscapes*, eds Mark Gardiner and Stephen Rippon (Macclesfield, 2007).

5 Della Hooke, *The Landscape of Anglo-Saxon England* (London, 1998), is the honourable exception.

point at which to close a project centred on the prehistoric and/or Roman landscape, or as an introduction to questions centred in the medieval.

Yet, conversely, the 'long Anglo-Saxon period' – from say 450 to 1100 – has long been seen as central to the ways in which we write the landscape history of England. A century ago, scholars believed it was the Anglo-Saxons who felled much of the wildwood and introduced the habit of living in villages – over and against the more scattered farmsteads of the pre-existing Celts (who had in any case mostly fled or been exterminated). Likewise, they believed that the Anglo-Saxons brought with them the ploughing of intermingled strips within shared fields, replacing pre-existing, much squarer 'Celtic fields'. By so doing, the Anglo-Saxons were setting out the open fields which were to dominate the English landscape until the enclosure movement of the sixteenth to nineteenth centuries. Placed beside the introduction and dissemination of Old English as a language, the conversion to Christianity and the formation of the nation state of England, these were developments which scholars viewed as fundamental to the making of England and which underpin the widely held belief that English history began not with Roman Britain but with the arrival of the Anglo-Saxons. In the late nineteenth century, it was widely believed that the peculiar genius of the English and the particular qualities of the institutions and society which they had created could be traced back to that event.[6] Such perceptions have dissipated since, of course, within the academic community but these models of historical development live on in popular esteem and have still to be confronted.

Central to this volume, therefore, are the nature, use and extent of woodland in the Anglo-Saxon period, the nature and development of Anglo-Saxon rural settlement and the inception and development of open fields. Many scholars exploring medieval settlement and agriculture have been drawn to the 'central province' – that region predominantly in the East Midlands but stretching from Northumberland to Dorset, where open fields and villages were most highly developed.[7] This introduction necessarily shares the same focus in part but it also introduces the several papers on very different aspects of the landscapes of Anglo-Saxon England which conclude the volume.

Woodland

The notion that virgin woodland was widespread in the Anglo-Saxon period remained dominant well into the twentieth century,[8] but was then gradually undermined by the findings of both palaeobotanists and landscape archaeologists. Analysis of pollen trapped in peat bogs developed as a research technique in

6 See for example John Richard Green, *A Short History of the English People* (London, 1892), pp. 1–28.

7 This is the preferred terminology of Brian K. Roberts and Stuart Wrathmell, *An Atlas of Rural Settlement in England* (London, 2000), fig. 10, p. 15.

8 See the widespread 'dense woodland' depicted on the map in R. H. Hodgkin, *A History of the Anglo-Saxons*, I (3rd edn, Oxford, 1952), facing p. 155.

Denmark but was taken up in Britain with the work of Harry Godwin.[9] He conducted much of his research in and around East Anglia, but explorations undertaken by the next generation of researchers shifted to the North and West, where deeper and more extensive peat deposits and lake sediments were concentrated,[10] which made it difficult to connect their results with the Anglo-Saxon landscape of the Lowland Zone. This work was also hamstrung initially by the absence of an absolute chronology, depending instead on the establishment of horizons common to numerous pollen diagrams (such as 'the elm decline'), but the emergence and gradual refinement of timescales based on the decay of carbon-14 eventually enabled the secure dating of cores and so provided a comparatively firm chronology. Traditionally, research has centred on prehistory,[11] since by its very nature, palaeobotany offers vegetation history across the *longue durée*, and the least disturbed peat and sediment deposits are necessarily deeper and so not the most recent. However, the last three decades have witnessed far greater attention being given to the first millennium AD. There has also been a concerted effort to access pollen data from more sites in Lowland Britain, so providing a spread of data more relevant to English history in particular. Although the spread of evidence remains patchy, with some areas quite poorly represented,[12] the pattern overall has been pulled together effectively by Petra Dark.[13]

In very general terms, it is now clear that Britain's woodlands were cleared very extensively across later prehistory. The Roman period witnessed the culmination of this process, with comparatively high levels of population in the Lowland Zone and extensive farming reducing tree cover still further. It is probably fair to say that the first 500 years AD saw the demise of any wild wood which had survived to that point, with surviving tracts of woodland (as the Weald) seriously impacted by grazing livestock, mining, metal working and charcoal burning. In the post-Roman era, some pollen diagrams suggest a reduction in the pressure of land use, with occasional local reforestation taking place, but within England only the immediate hinterland of Hadrian's Wall seems to have experienced large-scale regrowth of trees. Elsewhere, arable farming might vary against pasture, with drops in some areas comparable perhaps to that experienced in the fourteenth century following the Black Death, but in other places farming remained stable or even increased as a contributor of pollen. Outside

9 Harry Godwin, 'Pollen analysis and the forest history of England and Wales', *New Phytologist*, 39 (1940), 370–400.

10 In the Lake District and the Pennines: as D. Walker, 'The post-glacial period in the Langdale Fells, English Lake District', *New Phytologist*, 64 (1965), 488–510; Winifred Pennington, 'Vegetation history in the north-west of England: a regional synthesis', in *Studies in the Vegetational History of the British Isles: Essays in Honour of Harry Godwin*, eds D.Walker and R. G. West (Cambridge, 1970), pp. 41–79.

11 See, for example, *The Environment in British Prehistory*, eds Ian Simmons and Michael Tooley (London, 1981).

12 As Bruce Eagles, 'Evidence for settlement in the fifth to seventh centuries AD', in *The Medieval Landscape of Wessex*, eds Michael Aston and Carenza Lewis (Oxford, 1994), pp. 13–32, at p. 22.

13 Petra Dark, *The Environment of Britain in the First Millennium AD* (London, 2001).

particular localities there is a distinct lack of evidence for wholesale abandonment of the landscape, such as would be consistent with widespread population collapse in the fifth century. Rather, the pattern of the landscape continued to evolve, with cultivated fields, pastures, woodlands, hill-country, heaths and marshes all present and all in flux, each giving way periodically to another.

Archaeology has contributed massively to the vision of a comparatively full landscape before the 'Anglo-Saxon Settlement', with research particularly from the 1960s onwards providing evidence of large-scale prehistoric and/or Romano-British rural settlements and field systems. In combination, aerial archaeology and increasingly systematic archaeological exploration in advance of major new civil engineering works, including motorway construction, were responsible for a step-change in the rate of discovery across a significant proportion of England, particularly the lowlands but even parts of the uplands, which has amounted to a revolution in the number of sites known.

It rapidly became apparent that Lowland Britain in the Roman period was very heavily exploited indeed, with large numbers of rural settlements and complex, linear field systems predominating.[14] Some extensive systems and attendant settlements were later abandoned, as for example occurred in the vicinity of Sherwood Forest, and these are today only visible as cropmarks in cereals.[15] Some already ancient systems of banks and ditches were, however, still conditioning settlement and land use up to the seventh century and beyond, as at West Heslerton (N. Yorkshire), where the basic framework of the early Anglo-Saxon landscape was established in the Bronze Age,[16] and virtually all the better agricultural land in England was extensively occupied and used intensively. Therefore the Anglo-Saxon settlement occurred (whatever that phrase might mean) not in a heavily wooded environment where colonists needed to fell woodland to establish space to live and work the land, but in a farmed landscape in which settlements, fields, tracks, roads, pastures and managed woodlands were all pre-existing elements. This negates, of course, the vision of Anglo-Saxon pioneers clearing wild and uncultivated forests and, by so doing, sweeping away both the physical and moral bankruptcy of the Roman Empire, which was such a part of the English vision of their own history in the Victorian era. In fact, the extent of woodland left by AD 400 in what was to become England was arguably no greater than in 1900; although some secondary woodland undoubtedly developed thereafter, tree cover certainly did not predominate, as had earlier been supposed.[17] Anglo-Saxon England had an enormous appetite for timber as fuel,

14 J. Taylor, *An Atlas of Roman Rural Settlement in England* (York, 2007), pp. 23–54. Estimates of the total population pushed upwards towards five million in the 1980s but have since been scaled down to perhaps two million by more cautious authors, as David Mattingly, *An Imperial Possession: Britain in the Roman Empire* (London, 2006), pp. 356–7.

15 Derek Riley, *Early Landscape from the Air* (Sheffield, 1980).

16 Dominic Powlesland, 'Early Anglo-Saxon settlements, structures, form and layout', in *The Anglo-Saxons from the Migration Period to the Eighth Century*, ed. John Hines (Woodbridge, 1997), pp. 101–16.

17 See the seminal work by Oliver Rackham, *The History of the Countryside* (London, 1986), pp. 65–85.

for building and for a host of different crafts, as had all insular societies at least since the Bronze Age: with England's woodland already heavily exploited, there is every reason to suppose that stands of trees were both managed intensively and heavily exploited across the Anglo-Saxon period, as Christopher Grocock argues here.

Village and Farm

The assumption that the English habit of living in villages was imported from the Continent as part and parcel of the 'Anglo-Saxon Settlement' was barely questioned before the Second World War.[18] The first scholars to identify and begin to study deserted medieval villages (DMVs) were W. G. Hoskins, in Leicestershire, and Maurice Beresford, in Warwickshire,[19] both of whom were historians and interested primarily in the farmsteads such villages might reveal, their later medieval history and the story of their subsequent desertion. Early Anglo-Saxon foundation was simply taken for granted. The same preoccupations and assumptions characterise Beresford's classic monograph on the broader topic of medieval villages, and many later works of local history.[20]

In the early 1950s, Beresford joined forces with the archaeologist John Hurst to study these same topics via excavation of the DMV of Wharram Percy on the Yorkshire Wolds. With this project in hand, they then formed the Deserted Medieval Village Research Group (DMVRG), whose members attempted as systematic as practicable a survey of DMVs across England.[21] Their interest, however, began to switch towards processes of village formation on realisation that, contrary to their expectations, the village of Wharram Percy had not come into existence until after the Norman Conquest,[22] some 700 years after

18 See, for example, Hodgkin, *History of the Anglo-Saxons*, I, p. 174; F. M. Stenton, *Anglo-Saxon England* (Oxford, 1943), p. 285, envisaged village formation in the Trent valley beginning in the sixth century. The only settlement excavation which occurred pre-war was a series of small-scale, rescue-type digs by E. T. Leeds at Sutton Courtenay in advance of quarrying, which only revealed sunken-featured buildings and which he published in a series of articles entitled 'A Saxon village near Sutton Courtenay, Berks.', in *Archaeologia*, 73 (1923), 147–92; 76 (1927), 59–80; and 92 (1947), 78–94.

19 W. G. Hoskins, 'The deserted villages of Leicestershire', *Transactions of the Leicestershire Archaeological Society*, 22 (1946), 241–64; Maurice W. Beresford, 'The deserted villages of Warwickshire', *Transactions of the Birmingham Archaeological Society*, 66 (1945–46), 49–106; for an overview, see Beresford, 'A draft chronology of deserted village studies', *Medieval Settlement Research Group Annual Report*, 1 (1986), 18–23.

20 Maurice W. Beresford, *The Lost Villages of England* (London, 1954); for an exemplary local history discussing such issues, see Rowland Parker, *The Common Stream* (St Albans, 1976), p. 41.

21 The 1968 map which summarises these activities was published in Maurice W. Beresford and John G. Hurst, *Deserted Medieval Villages* (London, 1971), p. 66, but has been reproduced many times since.

22 *Wharram: A Study of Settlement on the Yorkshire Wolds*, ed. John G. Hurst (Leeds, 1979), Hurst, 'The Wharram Research Project', in *The Changing Past*, ed. N. J. Higham (Man-

the arrival of the Angles. In fact, the parish of Wharram Percy proved to have a far more complex settlement history than either Beresford or Hurst had anticipated.[23] This discovery challenged the most deeply entrenched assumptions regarding village origins and it was this, beyond all else, which set off a spate of village excavations across England from the very late 1950s onwards,[24] to test whether Wharram Percy was typical of English village formation or some sort of aberration. The results of these several projects generally supported the findings from Wharram Percy, confirming that villages were in many regions a comparatively late development in England and needed to be considered quite separate from the 'Anglo-Saxon Settlement' of the fifth/sixth centuries. This was despite the significant number of nucleated, fifth/sixth-century settlements which were being excavated on the Dutch coast, from which many Anglo-Saxon settlers were assumed to have derived.[25] In consequence of these findings, scholars have since taken on the task of unravelling far more complex understandings of Anglo-Saxon settlement history and archaeology than had hitherto been thought necessary.

The volume edited by David Wilson in 1976 signalled the first great leap forward for Anglo-Saxon archaeology, following a series of important excavations:[26] Philip Rahtz's contribution offered an oversight of Anglo-Saxon buildings excavated across the previous two decades, from which their architectural characteristics were beginning to emerge. Settlement layout as much as building style suggested that the settlements of the early Anglo-Saxon period

chester, 1979), pp. 67–74, and Hurst, 'The Wharram Research Project: results to 1983', *Medieval Archaeology*, 27 (1984), 77–111.

23 Colin Hayfield, *An Archaeological Survey of the Parish of Wharram Percy, E. Yorkshire. 1. The Evolution of the Roman Landscape* (Oxford, 1987).

24 See, for example, Philip A. Rahtz, 'Holworth medieval village excavation 1958', *Proceedings of the Dorset Natural History and Archaeological Society*, 81 (1959), 127–47; L. Still and A. Pallister, 'West Hartburn 1965', *Archaeologia Aeliana*, 45 (1967), 139–48; Maurice W. Beresford and John G. Hurst, *Deserted Medieval Villages* (Guildford, 1971); Guy Beresford, *The Medieval Clay-land Village: Excavations at Goltho and Barton Blount* (London, 1975); Lorna Watts and Philip A. Rahtz, 'Upton deserted medieval village, Blockley, Gloucestershire', *Transactions of the Bristol and Gloucestershire Archaeological Society*, 102 (1984), 141–54; J. Musty and D. J. Algar, 'Excavations at the deserted medieval village at Gomeldon, near Salisbury', *Wiltshire Archaeological and Natural History Magazine*, 80 (1986), 127–69; David Austin, *The Deserted Medieval Village of Thrislington, County Durham* (Leeds, 1989); Nicholas Higham and Terry Cane, 'The Tatton Park Project, Part 1: prehistoric to sub-Roman settlement and land use', *Journal of the Chester Archaeological Society*, 74 (1999), 1–61; Nicholas Higham, 'The Tatton Park Project, Part 2: the medieval estates, settlements and halls', *Journal of the Chester Archaeological Society*, 75 (2000), 61–133.

25 See the overviews offered by Malcolm Todd, *The Early Germans* (Oxford, 1992), pp. 62–79, and Helena Hamerow, *Early Medieval Settlements: The Archaeology of Rural Communities in North-West Europe 400–900* (Oxford, 2002).

26 *The Archaeology of Anglo-Saxon England*, ed. David M. Wilson (London, 1976): Wilson's 'Introduction' (pp. 1–22, at p. 1) stated his intention to replace G. Baldwin Brown's *The Arts in Early England* (London, 1903–37) as 'a corner stone of the study of Anglo-Saxon archaeology', to take account of the quantity of material excavated since that work was published.

needed to be viewed as quite distinct from later villages.[27] The exploration of early settlement therefore became a new area of research in its own right, with targeted excavations, for example, at Cowdery's Down and Chalton Down (both Hampshire), West Stow (Suffolk) and Catholme (Staffordshire),[28] and large-scale area stripping of whole settlements and their cemeteries at Mucking (Essex) and West Heslerton (N. Yorkshire).[29] These projects have slowly revealed much about the nature of settlements before and into the eighth century, which consisted almost entirely of combinations of surface-constructed, timber-framed buildings (halls) and sunken-featured buildings (SFBs).[30] There is little evidence for spatial demarcation, such as fences, within many settlements but West Heslerton has comparatively well-defined zones of activity, with manufacturing and habitation located in different areas of the site. Whether the limited range of building types and sizes owed more to British or Germanic architectural traditions has been much debated,[31] leaving some commentators to postulate accommodation occurring between the two traditions.[32] The absence of significant indicators of status between one early timber-framed building and another has encouraged the view that most were Anglo-Saxon farms devoid of much social distinction, but wealthier goods in some burials in the associated cemeteries – as at Mucking – may imply rather more social hierarchy than is indicated architecturally. With time, the post-in-hole style of early buildings gave way to post-in-trench and plank-in-trench construction, and some larger buildings were

27 Philip Rahtz, 'Buildings and rural settlement', in *Archaeology of Anglo-Saxon England*, ed. Wilson, pp. 49–98.

28 Martin Millett and Simon James, 'Excavations at Cowdery's Down, Basingstoke, 1978–81', *Archaeological Journal*, 140 (1984), 151–279; P. Addyman and D. Leigh, 'The Anglo-Saxon village at Chalton, Hampshire: second interim report', *Medieval Archaeology*, 17 (1973), 1–25; Stanley West, *West Stow: The Anglo-Saxon Village* (Ipswich, 1986), 2 vols; S. Loscoe-Bradley, 'Catholme', *Current Archaeology*, 59 (1977), 358–63; G. Kingsley and S. Loscoe-Bradley, *Catholme: an Anglo-Saxon Settlement on the Trent Gravels in Staffordshire* (Nottingham, 2002).

29 Helena Hamerow, *Mucking, Volume 2: The Anglo-Saxon Settlement* (London, 1993); the West Heslerton complex is not so far comprehensively published but see Powlesland, 'Anglo-Saxon Settlements, Structures, Form and Layout', pp. 101–16.

30 Jess Tipper, *The Grubenhaus in Anglo-Saxon England* (Yedingham, 2004).

31 Philip Dixon, 'How Saxon is the Saxon House?', in *Structural Reconstruction: Approaches to the Interpretation of the Excavated Remains of Buildings*, ed. P. Drury (Oxford, 1982), pp. 275–86; S. James, A. Marshall and Martin Millett, 'An early medieval building tradition', *Archaeological Journal*, 141 (1985), 182–215; Helena Hamerow, 'Anglo-Saxon timber buildings: the continental connection', in *In Discussion with the Past: Archaeological Studies Presented to W. A. van Es*, eds H. Sarfatij, W. Verwers and P. Woltering (Zwolle, 1999), pp. 119–28. The virtual absence in Britain of the aisled buildings which are so common along the continental side of the North Sea requires at least that we acknowledge a degree of accommodation by incoming Anglo-Saxons to different economic and/or social needs in their new habitat: Hamerow, *Early Medieval Settlements*, pp. 93–4.

32 That structures not dissimilar to SFBs have been identified in a securely Romano-British context implies that these two traditions were not entirely separate, even before 400, as one might expect in a highly fluid frontier zone running across northern Europe; the roadside Romano-British settlement at Monkton, Kent, is a case in point: Paul Bennett and John H. Williams, 'Monkton', *Current Archaeology*, 151 (1997), 258–64.

created.[33] A small minority of settlements from the late sixth century onwards have revealed massive buildings which have been interpreted as royal halls, of which by far the grandest is undoubtedly early-seventh-century Yeavering, the royal complex whose name is recorded by Bede.[34]

The evolution of settlement from later Roman Britain to the High Middle Ages has therefore become a fast-moving area of scholarly research, with particular interest focusing on the Anglo-Saxon period and with a significant number of settlement sites being excavated.[35] Perhaps the most important single project in the wake of excavations at Wharram Percy was that undertaken at Raunds (Northamptonshire) between 1977 and 1987, which featured a series of comparatively well-funded, large-scale, open-area excavations around the northern end of this small town in the Nene valley. The project explored the issue of settlement types across the whole medieval period, but focused particularly on the nature and chronology of village formation, which occurred here in the later Anglo-Saxon period. Pottery from the early and middle Anglo-Saxon periods in the Nene valley proved virtually impossible to differentiate, resulting in an unrealistically static vision of settlement pre-800, but numerous sites were identified by field-walking, with an overall density of 0.55 per km^2. Clearly, not all are likely to have been occupied at any one time, particularly as different sites had very different histories: the extensive early settlement at Furnells, for example, was abandoned by the later seventh century but then reoccupied as the site of an Anglo-Scandinavian farm in the later ninth century. A common factor across the several settlements explored was their dispersed pattern in the early- to mid-Anglo-Saxon period, but some grew in the ninth/early tenth centuries and began to develop into villages. So, for example, the Furnells Anglo-Scandinavian farm was overlaid in the tenth century by a new settlement using a regular plot system, which was interpreted as part of the reorganisation of the landscape associated with the English 'reconquest' of the Danelaw.[36]

A new model of settlement change was on offer from the early 1980s: on the basis of excavated sites across much of England, early Anglo-Saxon settlements were seen to be disproportionately associated with very well-drained locations which did not offer particularly fertile soils to farmers;[37] it was suggested that their abandonment and the shift of settlement to heavier soils was due to wholesale reorganisation of land use and the territories within which

33 Anne Marshall and Garry Marshall, 'A survey and analysis of the buildings of Early and Middle Anglo-Saxon England', *Medieval Archaeology*, 35 (1991), 29–43.

34 *HE*, II, 14; Brian Hope-Taylor, *Yeavering: An Anglo-British Centre of Early Northumbria* (London, 1977); *Yeavering: People, Power & Place*, eds Paul Frodsham & Colm O'Brien (Stroud, 2005).

35 See, for example, Christopher Taylor's *Village and Farmstead: A History of Rural Settlement in England* (London, 1983), which highlights ongoing change in the formation of the settlement landscape, and the several references to new work in the footnotes following.

36 Michel Audouy and Andy Chapman, *Raunds: The Origin and Growth of a Midland Village AD 450–1500: Excavations in North Raunds, Northamptonshire 1977–87* (Oxford, 2009), pp. 22–39.

37 As Chalton Down, which is on chalk downland, and Mucking, on sands and gravels.

farming operated, in or around the eighth century.[38] This model of settlement shift has had its critics,[39] but several recent studies support the notion that major change which might involve settlement relocation was occurring at about this period.[40] One possibility is that settlement relocation should be associated with the break-up of older systems of extensive lordship (sometimes known as 'multiple estates'[41]), the inception of smaller, separate estates, or manors, within the more closely defined land units which resulted, and the laying out of open fields, but it is noticeable that early Anglo-Saxon settlements do seem to sprawl across the landscape, so shift in time in any case. The whole issue of a step-change in settlement, the economy and land use across England in the eighth century is addressed in this volume by Stephen Rippon, and our understanding of 'multiple estates' and their social and economic rationale is taken forward by Stuart Brookes.

Recent research in this area has relied heavily on new archaeological strategies, such as systematic field-walking of arable land to pick up artefacts. Since the 1980s this has made a major contribution, particularly in the East Midlands and East Anglia where the incidence of ploughed land and of identifiable Anglo-Saxon pottery fragments – primarily Ipswich ware from the eighth/ninth centuries and St Neots ware from the mid-ninth century onwards – makes this strategy most effective. Field-walking has been particularly concentrated in Suffolk and Northamptonshire. Here large-scale campaigns have suggested that permanent settlement generally retreated from heavy clay land in the sub-Roman period, with early Anglo-Saxon settlements located very largely on river gravels and more free-draining soils. On the best agricultural lands of Northamptonshire, significant numbers of small early-Saxon sites have been identified by means of pottery scatters, away from medieval villages but within the open fields with which those were later associated. Their distribution necessitates that these settlements pre-dated the open fields. The absence of later Anglo-

38 C. Arnold and P. Wardle, 'Early medieval settlement patterns in England', *Medieval Archaeology*, 25 (1981), 145–9.

39 Helena Hamerow, 'Settlement mobility and the "Middle Saxon Shift": Rural Settlement and Settlement Patterns in Anglo-Saxon England', *Anglo-Saxon England*, 20 (1991), 1–17, arguing that mobility was inherent in early Anglo-Saxon settlements and that small-scale excavation may often only have identified part of a gradually shifting settlement.

40 As argued by John Newman, 'East Anglian kingdom survey – final interim report on the Southeast Suffolk Pilot Field Survey', *Bulletin of the Sutton Hoo Research Committee*, 6 (Woodbridge, 1989), 17–20; J. Moreland, 'The significance of production in eighth-century England', in *The Long Eighth Century: Production, Distribution and Demand*, eds I. L. Hansen and C. Wickham (Leiden, 2000), pp. 69–104.

41 Glanville R. Jones, 'Multiple estates and early settlement', in *English Medieval Settlement*, ed. Peter H. Sawyer (London, 1979), pp. 9–34: 'multiple estate' is the term used for a wide-scale territorial unit or estate made up of numerous communities in separate locations but sharing common facilities, such as grazing, each specialising in an aspect of agriculture and responsible for a particular aspect of the general food render to a central high status settlement, as grain, or cattle or sheep. The best recent discussion comes in Rosamond Faith, *The English Peasantry and the Growth of Lordship* (London, 1997), pp. 1–14.

Saxon pottery has been interpreted as evidence of their abandonment as part of 'a fairly fundamental reorganisation of settlement' across the seventh to tenth centuries,[42] when the inhabitants of these small settlements apparently moved to form villages within the same territories, perhaps located at what may already have been higher status and/or larger settlements.[43] Here, therefore, was evidence of settlement shift occurring across the early Anglo-Saxon period, then the occupation of what would eventually become the site of the medieval village in the second half of the Anglo-Saxon period, which then grew as population rose. Whether this was merely part of a long drawn-out process, or involved a degree of planning and direction from above, still seemed unclear, however, and this pattern has not so far been replicated away from the best agricultural terrain, on the poorer draining soils.

The recognition that dispersed Anglo-Saxon farmsteads might precede village formation has in turn given rise to very different perspectives on medieval settlement *per se*. Distinctive regional patterning of settlement and agricultural landscapes has been recognised since the sixteenth century. Lowland England divides between 'ancient' or 'woodland' landscapes, where towns, hamlets and isolated farms have long been the norm, both west and east of a 'central belt' or 'central province' of 'champion' country, which became, after the enclosure movement, 'planned' countryside, characterised by villages surrounded by regular, rectangular fields.[44] Settlement nucleation was far from omnipresent, clearly, but the identification of dispersed settlement preceding the villages of even the 'central province' brought with it the realisation that the medieval village was less the norm of medieval rural settlement that had traditionally been assumed, but rather just one development away from a more uniform and widespread pattern of dispersal. The need to research patterns of dispersed settlement which had on occasion given way to nucleation represented a fundamental shift for a research community hitherto focused almost exclusively on the village. Once again, the availability of reasonable quantities of early medieval pottery to field-walkers encouraged the exploration of these issues in the first place in Northamptonshire, where new work in the 1990s suggested that the process of nucleation was already well advanced by 850, as the culmination of processes across the eighth

42 David Hall, 'The late Saxon countryside: villages and their fields', in *Anglo-Saxon Settlements*, ed. Della Hooke (Oxford, 1988), pp. 99–122, at p. 120.

43 As Newman's survey in Suffolk, footnote 41, above; Royal Commission on Historical Monuments (England), *An Inventory of the Historical Monuments in the County of Northampton* (London, 1982), 4 vols; M. Shaw, 'The discovery of Saxon sites below fieldwalking scatters: settlement evidence at Brixworth and Upton, Northants.', *Northamptonshire Archaeology*, 25 (1993), 77–92; Tony Brown and Glenn Foard, 'The Saxon landscape: a regional perspective', in *The Archaeology of Landscape: Studies Presented to Christopher Taylor*, eds Paul Everson and Tom Williamson (Manchester, 1998), pp. 67–94. There has also been important work elsewhere: see, for example, Jill Bourne, ed., *Anglo-Saxon Landscapes in the East Midlands* (Leicester, 1996); G. Hey, *Yarnton: Saxon and Medieval Settlement and Landscape* (Oxford, 2004).

44 As Rackham, *History of the Countryside*, pp. 1–5; Roberts and Wrathmell, *Atlas of Rural Settlement in England*, p. 15, fig. 10.

century. These nucleated settlements were then thought to have been reorganised in association with the laying out of open fields.[45] The nature of the agricultural regime associated with these earlier nucleated settlements has so far not been explored effectively, but we do seem to have here an earlier phase of nucleation than had hitherto been recognised, in conjunction with the beginnings of a long and drawn-out process of agricultural reorganisation leading up to full-blown open fields.

From the 1980s, relocation of scholarly activity away from village-dominated areas towards regions with longer traditions of dispersed and/or mixed settlement patterns began to give rise to a variety of local projects in hitherto under-researched regions.[46] It also triggered the reorganisation of existing research networks, leading to the formation of the Medieval Settlement Research Group (MSRG) in 1987. The new agenda was pushed forward by Christopher Dyer, who headed up a major research project to explore the settlement history of four east-midland counties,[47] which concluded that the boundaries between different landscape types (as 'planned', 'woodland') were far less clear-cut than previously thought, but that in this area at least there was a tendency for dispersed settlement to give way during the later Anglo-Saxon period to nucleated villages as population rose, with or without lordly coercion being a factor. This project identified areas where further research on the interface between dispersal and nucleation might be fruitful and led directly to the so-called 'Whittlewood Project'.

Whittlewood straddles the Buckinghamshire/Northamptonshire border within the 'central province' – which is of course generally dominated by villages – but was selected for detailed study as being a sub-region which was more diverse than surrounding areas, with a mix of villages, hamlets and isolated farms. Within Whittlewood, the project revealed that Romano-British settlement died away in the fifth century, leaving the area virtually unoccupied until around 600 and increasingly wooded. This was an area available for colonisation, therefore, in the mid-Anglo-Saxon period, when a series of dispersed settlements was established. Village formation seems not to have begun before *c.*850–1000. Nucleated settlements either developed at existing occupation sites or at settlements only founded in this same period.[48] No evidence was found of older dispersed farmsteads being abandoned in association with a movement of population to new nucleated settlements. While some villages developed via in-filling between originally separate but closely contiguous farms, bringing into existence polyfocal settlements,[49] full-scale nucleation generally failed to occur

45 Brown and Foard, 'The Saxon landscape: a regional perspective', pp. 67–94.

46 As Christopher Gerrard with Mick Aston, *The Shapwick Project, Somerset: A Rural Landscape Explored* (Leeds, 2007), although this does actually centre on the formation of a medieval village.

47 Carenza Lewis, Patrick Mitchell-Fox and Christopher Dyer, *Village, Hamlet and Field: Changing Medieval Settlements in Central England* (Manchester, 1997), focusing on Leicestershire, Northamptonshire, Buckinghamshire and Bedfordshire.

48 Richard Jones and Mark Page, *Medieval Villages in an English Landscape: Beginnings and Ends* (Macclesfield, 2006).

49 As initially discussed by Taylor, *Village and Farmstead*, p. 131.

where early farmsteads were comparatively widely scattered; instead the separate farmsteads merely developed into larger, but still separate settlements. Even where villages did form, no evidence of planning was identified; rather, early layout went on to influence the topography of later villages and very different plans resulted. The result was a mix of idiosyncratic nucleation and dispersal, much as is now visible.

Interpretation of Whittlewood took account of different settlement histories in surrounding areas, and assumed interaction between local inhabitants and their neighbours. So the limited processes of nucleation identified here were assumed to have been influenced by more pronounced processes in the champion countryside on all sides, but mediated in this locality by the well-wooded nature of the landscape and the thinness of its population throughout the mid- to late-Anglo-Saxon period. That the outcomes here differed from those at Raunds is probably in part at least explicable by reference to the history of occupation and land use, and variable environmental conditions, all of which clearly were different at these two locations. Therefore, a comparatively localised modelling of Anglo-Saxon settlement history seems now to be called for, that recognises the differences between numerous sub-regions of England and depends on the interaction of a number of factors. Some areas remained comparatively open as agricultural land from the Roman period onwards; some were already more wooded; some experienced a degree at least of reforestation during the sub-Roman period; others were characterised by heathland or by wetlands, most of which had already developed in prehistory. While Whittlewood may well be characteristic of the more wooded areas of the East Midlands, the picture of settlement reorganisation emerging at Raunds and elsewhere in Northamptonshire may well be typical of more continuously open landscapes in the region, where agriculture was still widespread across the early Anglo-Saxon period.

One of the key methods of investigation used in the Whittlewood Project was the use of test pits dug within currently occupied settlements. This has the advantage of enabling researchers to explore the archaeology not just of failed settlements, as can be undertaken at DMVs, but also of more successful ones. Patterns of artefact retrieval – particularly pottery – allow the chronology of a settlement to be explored, not just in terms of the overall occupation or abandonment of a site but more particularly via comparison between different parts of a single later nucleation. It is this technique that has in recent years been applied in the CORS project by Carenza Lewis and a team based at Cambridge University,[50] to further explore rural settlement archaeology across the Anglo-Saxon period in six of the eastern counties of England, and which forms the basis of her contribution to this collection. An important outcome is the identification of significant numbers of villages forming at settlements already occupied in the mid-Anglo-Saxon period.

Further west, the archaeological exploration of changing settlement patterns has been much affected by the scarcity of dateable artefacts. At Tatton

[50] Standing for 'Currently Occupied Rural Settlement'.

(Cheshire), a large, sub-Roman timber structure with ancillary buildings all laid out within a fenced enclosure was virtually without finds. The immediate site was abandoned for several centuries, but a timber-framed hall-type building was constructed, arguably in the late Anglo-Saxon period, which marked the beginning of a new phase of occupation that led to the development of a large hamlet in the twelfth and thirteenth centuries. Successive reoccupation of the site was arguably associated with the presence of a local road and a small spring capable of providing a supply of water sufficient for a small settlement, but other occupation sites existed within the township throughout the Middle Ages.

At Shapwick (Somerset), several small settlements, some with their own fields, pre-dated the laying out of two open fields and the formation of the main village in the late Anglo-Saxon period. Thereafter the settlements were abandoned and ploughed over but the memory of their earlier existence was preserved in field names,[51] implying a complex history of settlement. There was a progressive intensification of nucleation, in combination with the laying out and perhaps extension of open fields, within the later Anglo-Saxon period.

The old assumptions regarding early medieval rural settlements are, therefore, dead and buried and no one within the academic community now accepts that incoming Anglo-Saxons brought with them the habit of dwelling in villages. Early settlements consisted of timber-framed buildings (halls) and SFBs. Settlement relocation was comparatively commonplace leading to the successive abandonment of sites, until the mid-Anglo-Saxon period when the medieval landscape began to take shape, with later village sites beginning to come into use. Thereafter, the growth of settlements was a significant factor, in some areas at least, with increasing regularity within some settlements beginning to emerge in the Viking Age. Anglo-Saxon settlement archaeology has emerged as a major aspect of study capable of absorbing a great deal of scholarly energy over the next few decades.

Fields

It will have become obvious by this point that the discussion of village formation is not easily divisible from that of open field inception, since villages and their fields were so closely interdependent across the Middle Ages that it has often been assumed that their origins were interlinked. However, these two aspects of the landscape have long been the subjects of distinct literatures, which need to be explored within their own terms, and the extent to which their inception is associated remains in question.

The study of field systems began significantly earlier than that of settlement. Indeed, an awareness of and interest in open fields goes back beyond the nineteenth century to the main phase of enclosure, in the eighteenth, when they were widely considered an anachronism in need of replacement. From the later

51 Gerrard with Aston, *The Shapwick Project*, p. 974.

nineteenth century onwards, for three-quarters of a century, it was assumed that open fields were introduced by the Anglo-Saxons in the sub-Roman period, alongside villages.[52] The modern study of open fields rests, however, on Howard Gray's 1915 monograph, *English Field Systems*, which distinguished six different regional types.[53] He assumed that the origins of these different types were ethnic, with the dominant town-field style of the North and West even being termed 'Celtic'. He viewed the 'Midland System', appearing primarily in what is now termed the 'central province', as the best-developed exemplar, reflecting most purely the land-use practices of Anglo-Saxon immigrants. It was this type of field system which rapidly came to dominate study of the subject, emerging as the standard from which others were assumed to have deviated.

The characteristics of the 'Midland System' were two or (more usually) three large open fields which were cultivated in long, narrow, intermingled strips according to a set of rules regarding crops grown and the timetable for annual activities (such as the release of livestock into the open field). Such fields encompassed a high proportion of the land available to the manor. An annual rotation was adhered to by which one field per year was removed from cultivation as fallow, and the authority by which to manage the system was invested in a manorial court capable of levying fines on those breaking the rules.

Scholars sought reasons for the intermingling of narrow strips of ploughland, explaining it variously in terms of co-aration (shared use of a plough),[54] the sharing out of collectively cleared ('assarted') land,[55] partible inheritance of previously integral fields by co-heirs,[56] risk avoidance by sharing different soil types among peasant farmers,[57] and/or its origins in primitive share holding[58] as opposed to private property. Several of these scholars were also beginning to study the morphology of field systems in some detail, with the Orwins for example focusing on Laxton and 'getting their boots on' to relate its magnificent seventeenth-century estate maps to the surviving landscape. They were, however, far more interested in the mature and comparatively well-documented system of open field agriculture, as practised in and after the thirteenth century, than in its early development.

As with the nucleation of settlement, the chronology of open field development has increasingly become an issue. That it was a consequence of Anglo-Saxon immigration was an early assumption that found a measure of support in the lawcode of King Ine of the West Saxons, *c.*700, which made reference

52 The seminal study was that of Paul Vinogradoff, *Villeinage in England* (Oxford, 1892).

53 Howard Gray, *English Field Systems* (Cambridge, Mass., 1915).

54 Frederick Seebohm, *English Village Community* (1890); C. S. Orwin and C. S. Orwin, *The Open Fields* (3rd edn, Oxford, 1967; 1st edn, 1938).

55 First proposed by T. A. M. Bishop, 'Assarting and the growth of the open fields', *Economic History Review*, 6 (1935), 26–40.

56 Gray, *English Field Systems.*

57 Donald McCloskey, 'English open fields as behaviour towards risk', *Research in Economic History,* 1 (1976), 124–70; McCloskey, 'The prudent peasant: new findings on open fields', *Journal of Economic History*, 51 (1991), 343–55.

58 J. M. Kemble, *The Saxons in England* (London, 1849).

to shared land (*gedelland*) growing 'common crops or grass'.[59] The general assumption that their inception was early was, however, challenged by Joan Thirsk in the 1960s. She argued that open fields had a longer and more complex history than hitherto suggested: regional variations, she suggested, derived less from the inadequate replication of the 'Midland System' elsewhere than from arrested development of the overall process in some areas, in which case the 'Midland System' represented the furthest development of the system, so a comparatively late stage of progression, rather than the starting point.[60] For her and many others, the principal driver for change was demographic growth, which was (and still often is) seen as a constant (broadly) of the period 700–1300:[61] it encouraged the sub-division and intermingling of strips under the pressure of partible inheritance, and communal assarting to bring new land under cultivation. The result was a contraction of pasture land, leading in turn to a crisis in the supply and maintenance of oxen (the tractors of the age) and so growing pressure to make efficient use of arable land for grazing as well, on the margins, the stubble and the fallow. The result was widespread imposition of overall manorial control of the landscape and its exploitation as a means of managing scarce resources by imposing a strict rotation of arable and pasture, with recognised times by which the harvest should be completed. For Thirsk, therefore, open fields only reached their furthest development in the twelfth and thirteenth centuries, emerging from quite humble beginnings in the Anglo-Saxon period.

This 'late' model found a degree of support in the work of landscape archaeologists, who were, of course, finding evidence of dispersed early Anglo-Saxon settlements overtaken by the open fields associated with nucleated villages of the High Middle Ages. If Wharram Percy, for example, did not come into existence until the twelfth century, then surely nor did the open fields with which it was associated. It was becoming quite clear, therefore, that open fields had not been introduced, at least in their more developed form, by Anglo-Saxon colonists in the fifth and sixth centuries.

The two issues of chronology and causation held centre stage thereafter. In a thoughtful review of the evidence, Harold Fox generally endorsed Thirsk's model but preferred an earlier date for their inception, seeing open fields already well down the developmental road by the tenth century, driven by the problems which Thirsk had identified and particularly a growing shortage of pasture.[62] At the same time, Bruce Campbell noted a correlation between types of tenure

59 *Die Gesetze der Angelsachsen*, ed. F. Liebermann, I (Halle, 1903), pp. 88–123, cap. 42; the quoted translation is from *English Historical Documents*, I, ed. Dorothy Whitelock (2nd edn, London, 1979), p. 403.

60 Joan Thirsk, 'The common fields', *Past and Present*, 29 (1964), 3–29; Thirsk, 'The origins of the common fields', *Past and Present*, 33 (1966), 142–7.

61 See, for example, Peter Fowler, *Farming in the First Millennium AD: British Agriculture between Julius Caesar and William the Conqueror* (Cambridge, 2002), pp. 16–18, who suggested four to five million at the close of the Roman period dropping sharply thereafter, then (p. 17) 'a long, slow rise in population over the half-century or so to 1086'.

62 H. S. A. Fox, 'Approaches to the adoption of the Midland System', in *The Origins of Open-Field Agriculture*, ed. Trevor Rowley (London, 1981), pp. 64–111, at p. 88.

and the nature of regional open field systems which he felt to be significant, arguing that social and tenurial factors should be recognised as potential causes of the differences displayed by open fields in different parts of the country.[63] Approaching these issues from a more geographical and less 'English' perspective, Robert Dodgshon reminded his audience that sub-divided fields are virtually universal across Britain in the Middle Ages and are largely blind to issues of land tenure, occurring as often on lands held by unfree tenants as by free. He argued that they were created because rising population, expanding lordship and growing seigneurial rights all pressured local communities to define their property and resource access more closely than had been necessary at an earlier date.[64] Eric Kerridge, however, challenged aspects of this explanation, arguing that population growth and partible inheritance were not of themselves significant factors capable of explaining the inception of open fields, which resulted from an expansion in the number of farms rather than population *per se*.[65] He associated open fields rather with a switch from extended to nuclear families, large-scale colonisation of the landscape, the decline of personal slavery and the 'hutting' of slaves to become unfree peasants, and shifts in tenurial status as lordship replaced kinship as the dominant social relationship. As the population rose so the number of slaves fell, but numerous previously free tenants became progressively less free, leading to the massing together of similar tenurial holdings and the formation of intermingled strips, managed and cultivated by an increasingly amorphous village community. It was the proliferation of small and intermixed holdings which then drove forward the formation of full-blown open fields, since their cultivation required the pooling of oxen as plough beasts, shared rotation and communal management of grazing. Some open fields were laid out from scratch while others were remodelled, so as to make efficient use of the land.

Since the 1980s, the initiative has increasingly been seized by archaeologists. Chris Taylor was prepared to accept an extended chronology for open field formation,[66] given the late development of many villages which had been excavated to that point. However, David Hall's studies of ridge and furrow led him to identify a complex history of open field development specific to the East Midlands, with much longer strips sometimes preceding those which commonly appear on post-medieval maps. Although this gave general support to the Thirsk model, Hall favoured inception of the initial laying out of open fields in the region of study in the eighth and/or ninth centuries, with subsequent replanning in many instances.[67] A mid- to late Anglo-Saxon starting point for open fields

[63] B. M. S. Campbell, 'Commonfield origins: the regional dimension', in *The Origins of Open-Field Agriculture,* ed. Rowley, pp. 112–29.

[64] R. Dodgshon, *The Origins of British Field Systems: An Interpretation* (London, 1980).

[65] E. Kerridge, *The Common Fields of England* (Manchester, 1992), pp. 17–49.

[66] C. Taylor, 'Archaeology and the origins of open-field agriculture', in *The Origins of Open-Field Agriculture*, ed. Rowley, pp. 13–22.

[67] David Hall, 'The origins of open-field agriculture: the archaeological fieldwork evidence', in *The Origins of Open-Field Agriculture*, ed. Rowley, pp. 22–38; Hall, 'The late Saxon

has since gained ground, particularly in the East Midlands; here the research projects led by Dyer have generally favoured the appearance of nucleated settlement in the later Anglo-Saxon period in association with extended open field systems (in response to the same factors which Thirsk had earlier identified), spreading by emulation after the Conquest to areas where the pressures were less.

The umbilical cord linking nucleation with the inception of open fields is, however, increasingly open to question, with recent work in Northamptonshire (above) suggesting that villages were coalescing by 850, much earlier than the appearance of open fields, which emerge here in the ninth and tenth centuries.[68] The complexity of this history and the strength of links between open field and village formation is therefore an ongoing area for discussion, which is explored in this volume by Susan Oosthuizen, with particular reference to the South-East Midlands.

A rather different approach was taken by Tom Williamson in 2003. He started his important study of medieval field systems with the observation that areas which adopted the 'Midland System' did not have the highest population densities in England either at Domesday or in the later Middle Ages, so population growth makes little sense as the overriding factor in explaining open field development. Nor does nucleation of settlement necessarily align with the geography of strong lordship, undermining another central feature of the Thirsk model and its derivatives (above). Williamson directed attention instead to a variety of alternative factors, such as marked regional differences in the distribution of woodland which are visible already by 1086, and which – on the evidence of place names – were present across much of the Anglo-Saxon period. The geography of woodland coincides inversely with that of the 'Midland System', with far less in 'champion' areas than elsewhere.[69] That said, this lack of woodland, and the extension of open fields in many instances to township boundaries, does not seem to have markedly expanded the amount of food available within these communities, hence the unexceptional population densities which characterise areas in which the 'Midland System' was adopted. Rather, Williamson argues, different types of open field system represented particular responses by farmers to challenges posed by subtly different combinations of soil, climate and topography; broad regional landscape types are best explained very largely through environmental factors. Extensive open fields were adopted where there was little woodland but an abundance of meadowland capable of maintaining oxen without much further grazing,[70] where there were clay soils, so the need for

countryside: villages and their fields', in *Anglo-Saxon Settlements*, ed. Della Hooke (Oxford, 1988), pp. 99–122, at pp. 108–20.

68 Brown and Foard, 'The Saxon landscape: a regional perspective', pp. 67–94.

69 Tom Williamson, *Shaping Medieval Landscapes: Settlement, Society, Environment* (Macclesfield, 2003), pp. 28–61; Roberts and Wrathmell, *Atlas of Rural Settlement in England*, fig. 24, p. 31.

70 It is noticeable that meadowland is measured in some shires at Domesday in terms of the number of plough-teams it was capable of sustaining, while elsewhere it was in acres.

a heavy plough, and where there were comparatively few locations suitable for settlement, predisposing farmers to share settlement sites where, for example, a water supply was available. A rising population would certainly have pushed farmers towards heavier lands and the adoption of the larger ploughs and plough teams necessary to cultivate them, which were used co-operatively to gain the necessary efficiencies. A certain level of population was needed for extensive open fields to become viable, and that had still not been achieved by 1066 in many areas of the North West,[71] for example, but the factors influencing the style of farming adopted were far more complex and subtle than had previously been realised.[72] Williamson's contribution to this volume builds on this major work, with important suggestions for how we read the landscape in the Anglo-Saxon period, the different regions into which it was divided, and its connections to the various incomers of the sub-Roman period. His current (unpublished) research using GIS as a tool to re-examine Northamptonshire's landscape will further transform our understanding of the relationship between open fields and the settlements from which they were managed and cultivated.

To an extent, the elephant in the room when it comes to explaining the advent of open field agriculture is the adoption of the heavy plough. With some reservations, it is generally agreed that the standard plough of the Roman period in Britain was an ard or light scratch plough, which cultivated the land without turning over a furrow, was often used to cross-plough rectangular fields and which could be pulled by a pair of oxen.[73] How Romano-British peasants cultivated heavy soils is not entirely clear but abandonment of much of the heavier clay-based terrain in the fifth century concentrated agriculture on the better-drained sands and gravels of the river valleys – as is widely confirmed both by place-name studies and archaeological field-walking. Here, the scratch plough was at its most effective and it seems fair to see it, therefore, as the standard type in use around 600.[74]

If we switch to the opposite end of our time period, the heavy plough which was in widespread use in the High Middle Ages had already been introduced by the mid-eleventh century; this was illustrated as if the norm in some but not all the late-Saxon illuminated manuscripts explored by Catherine Karkov in this volume, and in the Bayeux Tapestry, but how much earlier it came to be used

71 N. J. Higham, *A Frontier Landscape: The North West in the Middle Ages* (Macclesfield, 2004), pp. 46–55.

72 Williamson, *Shaping Medieval Landscapes*, pp. 180–4.

73 Fowler, *Farming in the First Millennium AD*, pp. 182–204. The stock illustration of a Romano-British ard is a bronze model of around AD 100 from Piercebridge (Durham), illustrated by Fowler as plate XXV. There was also, however, a heavy plough available in the Roman period, and the presence of ridges underlying, for example, several forts on Hadrian's Wall suggests that some sort of plough capable of turning a furrow was available in Britain even in the Iron Age.

74 It was the type excavated at Sutton Hoo: *Bulletin of the Sutton Hoo Research Committee*, 4 (1986), ed. Martin Carver, fig. 30 on p. 46.

remains in doubt.[75] The general assumption that it was adopted to deal with heavier soils which were only being recolonised in the mid-Anglo-Saxon period or later seems reasonable, although there is very little direct evidence available. Peter Fowler has argued for the shift from ard to mould-board plough occurring as late as the tenth to eleventh centuries, largely on the basis of ards represented in illuminated manuscripts as late as the eleventh century,[76] but such inclusions could easily have resulted from illustrators copying from much earlier originals, since they were notoriously conservative in their use of exemplars, as David Hill points out. That said, finds of Anglo-Saxon share fragments so far discovered in England all seem to derive from ards and all come from tenth- or eleventh-century deposits,[77] seeming to confirm that the shift to the heavy plough was not universal much before 1086.

It would certainly help us to make sense of the history of the Anglo-Saxon landscape if widespread adoption of the heavy plough could be shown to have coincided with the beginnings of villages and the reorganisation of their field systems. Whenever it occurred, though, the adoption of the heavy plough necessarily influenced the whole pattern of agricultural life. It required a plough-team around four times bigger than the paired oxen used to pull an ard. Such was probably beyond the resources of most peasants, so it encouraged co-operation. At the same time, the new plough was capable of cultivating far more land in a season than the ard, and far more than a peasant would either normally have available or need. This new technology would, therefore, have encouraged farmers to group together to assemble a plough-team, and to divide their agricultural land in such a way that it equated to the contribution each was making – hence the appearance of the bovate and the oxgang as standard units of land tenure. It is easy, therefore, to suppose that joint plough-teams encouraged the intermingling of strips, as the Orwins suggested. The need to manage the new and far more co-operative farming that resulted can only have encouraged farmers to live in close proximity, hence reorganisation of settlement as well as the land which surrounded it. The adoption of the heavy plough was arguably, therefore, a major stimulus for change in the countryside, although precisely what form change would take in each locality depended also on a variety of other factors.

We are discussing, therefore, something which amounts to a revolution in the way the rural landscape operated in the Anglo-Saxon period, the repercussions

75 John Langdon, 'Agricultural equipment', in *The Countryside of Medieval England*, eds Astill and Grant, pp. 88–9. The Bayeux Tapestry plough occurs in the lower border beneath activity depicted in France, so might represent agricultural activity across the Channel. However, the designer, who is generally thought to be Anglo-Saxon, is unlikely to have been so discerning as to ignore scenes local to Canterbury, unless a pre-existing illustration was available to him. However, the fact that the animal pulling the plough is a single ass does open the door to speculation.

76 Fowler, *Farming in the First Millennium*, pp. 198–204.

77 Grenville Astill, 'Agricultural technologies in medieval England', in *Medieval Farming and Technology: The Impact of Agricultural Change in Northwest Europe*, eds Grenville Astill and John Langdon, I (Leiden, 1997), pp. 193–224, at p. 201.

of which worked out differently in different regions. It is still generally assumed that it was population growth that drove the shift onto heavier ground but an alternative offered here by Debby Banham is that it was in part at least a shift to wheat as a staple of the Anglo-Saxon diet that precipitated the change. Cereal crops in the Roman period included both bread and spelt wheat types, barley, rye and oats, of which spelt and barley had been the staples in late prehistory, but bread wheat dominated after the fourth century, with rye, barley and oats also being grown, alongside flax and hemp.[78] The shift from barley bread to wheat meant that Anglo-Saxon farmers were increasingly placing rather different demands on the landscape than had their ancestors, and changes may well have been necessitated by the change in taste.

Beyond the 'Central Province'

There were other issues which also impacted on the Anglo-Saxon countryside, beyond the interfaces between woodland, settlement and fields. From the seventh century onwards, this was an increasingly Christian landscape, with Christianity no longer just a religion of whatever substrate British community that remained but taken up by the elite. Churches and monasteries were founded by royal families and other members of the secular and clerical elite, often with considerable lands attached. The conversion to Christianity had a profound impact on the ways in which the landscape was organised, with the abandonment of many pre-existing burial sites in favour of new cemeteries. These would eventually focus on churches, but there was a convergence of burial and settlement already from the seventh century, even where no church so far existed. This change was particularly marked in the South and East. Richard Hoggett's paper provides us with new insights as to the impact in East Anglia and proposes that we recognise that conversion had a more profound impact in the seventh century down through society than has often been recognised. Indeed, was conversion to Christianity a factor in the shift towards more nucleated settlements in some areas in the mid-Anglo-Saxon period? Thereafter, church foundation eventually caught up with nucleation and churches proliferated in the more prosperous areas in the later Anglo-Saxon period, to the point where most if not all estates had their own church. The gradual erosion of the rights and responsibilities of some of the early minster churches in favour of local, manorial foundations, and growing demands from the church on its tenants and parishioners, arguably played an important role in the evolution of the countryside across the late Anglo-Saxon period.[79]

Hoggett's study of the Christianisation of the East Anglian landscape lies outside the 'central province' to the east. Right on the very edge of this landscape, the coast provides a truly marginal space which was exploited by man

[78] Summarised by Fowler, *Farming in the First Millennium AD*, pp. 212–13.

[79] For discussion, see Faith, *The English Peasantry and the Growth of Lordship*; John Blair, *The Church in Anglo-Saxon Society* (Oxford, 2005), particularly p. 291 ff.

for a variety of purposes. Peter Murphy offers a review of important new evidence of shoreline activity primarily in the mid-Anglo-Saxon period, including evidence of fish-trapping. This has come to light as a consequence of recent work co-ordinated by English Heritage, to explore the archaeology of coastal exploitation before parts of this fragile environment are lost to the sea. It is interesting to note that activity seems to be focused on the same period which witnessed the development of markets and the appearance of 'productive sites', which arguably reflect the reawakening of trade in the middle of the Anglo-Saxon period. That such fish traps were intended to produce a saleable surplus therefore becomes an interesting possibility.

It is important to remember, also, that by the mid-Anglo-Saxon period English cultural and political dominance had reached parts of the far west, including Shropshire, Cheshire and Lancashire, where rather different landscape developments were occurring. Here on the margins of England there never had been large-scale enclosure systems delimiting the countryside; Romano-British settlement had been characterised by dispersed, enclosed settlements, and such arguably continued in the sub-Roman period, though perhaps with less emphasis on ditched enclosure. Pre-Christian, Anglo-Saxon burials are absent and the survival of 'eccles' place names in some numbers suggests that British Christianity survived into the seventh century, only then to be 'converted' to Catholicism in the age of Wilfrid and Theodore, losing previous cultural associations in the process.[80] This is a countryside which was thinly populated, particularly in Lancashire and the uplands of Cumbria, with a comparatively high incidence not only of woodland but also of lowland mosses and heathland. Manorialisation did occur pre-Conquest south of the Mersey, but further north Domesday Book reveals a very different style of organisation, with hundredal manors to which outlying free tenants owed limited services.

All in all, therefore, this volume brings together a wealth of new research on the physical evidence for the Anglo-Saxon landscape, ranging from the results of archaeological excavations to illuminated manuscripts and from field-walking to aerial archaeology. The papers presented here are written by scholars who are individually at the very cutting edge of the subject and responsible for the way that it is moving forward. This is a vibrant area of study which will not stand still in the foreseeable future but will continue to develop, as new research tests the models which have been formulated, develops them further or pushes onwards towards new horizons. Whether the reader is interested primarily in rural settlement, in open field and other types of field systems, in woodland, or in the shoreline, there is something engaging in what follows. The conference from which this volume has emerged was highly stimulating, well attended and buzzing with ideas. It is my hope that this collection of essays can put over something of the excitement that was shared at the event.

80 Stephen Bassett, 'How the West was won: the Anglo-Saxon takeover of the West Midlands', *Anglo-Saxon Studies in Archaeology and History*, 11 (2000), 108–18; N. J. Higham, 'Britons in northern England in the early Middle Ages: through a thick glass darkly', *Northern History*, 28 (2001), 5–25.

2

Barriers to Knowledge: Coppicing and Landscape Usage in the Anglo-Saxon Economy

CHRISTOPHER GROCOCK

The purpose of this paper is to explore some of the implications of the use of coppiced wood – hazel, rowan, willow and so forth – for our understanding of the exploitation of the landscape in the Anglo-Saxon period. The discussion is informed by the author's experience in reconstruction archaeology. Much raw data was obtained from experience as Project Director of the Bede's World Museum in Jarrow, and was illuminated and informed by discussion with a number of suppliers of material to the project, notably Jonathan Howe, of Stockbridge, Hampshire, who was largely responsible for bringing coppiced rods to the site in its first three years before more local sources could be found.[1] Initial presentations of this material to a number of local history societies, and particularly in a lecture arranged in 1996 by the now sadly defunct Mayo Abbey Project (in the Republic of Ireland), sparked off some useful reaction and comment, and helped to shape the conclusions presented here. The author is particularly indebted to Joe Brett, of the Mayo Abbey Project, for the chance to share these ideas and find them both challenged and corroborated, all of which has added to the process of refinement. Latterly the opportunity to revisit the findings made at Jarrow has been provided through activity at Butser Ancient Farm, where discussions with Simon Jay, the farm manager, and Steve Dyer have proved extremely fruitful, and of course conversations with delegates at MANCASS in the spring of 2007 afforded further help.

Contemplation of any 'traditional' English landscape such as may still be seen all over England reveals a variety of land usage. As well as arable areas under regular cultivation, there are spaces set aside for meadow, bordered with hedgerows, and on steeper slopes or land which is less suitable or not needed for such purposes, woodland is seen – no less managed, and functioning in the medieval period for a multiplicity of uses, including providing pannage for pigs, fuel for heating, cooking and artisan activities, and construction materials of various kinds.

1 www.coppice-products.co.uk is an invaluable source of information on the basic processes and products of present-day coppicing.

Plate II.1. Standing coppice at Henley, West Sussex.

Coppicing – whether from stools or by pollarding – is one of the many activities that may have gone on in such wooded areas in the landscape with such regularity that they were unremarkable – and hence escaped notice in many of the written records (Pl. II.1). At the same time, these activities undoubtedly made considerable demands not only on the allocation of land, but also in terms of human activity. Earlier studies, notably that of Roland Bechmann,[2] established the value of coppiced woodland in the Middle Ages: he discusses the existence of *bois revenants* or *bois de vente* cut at regular intervals, and, more relevant for the early medieval period, *silvae palariae* which were 'frequently mentioned' for providing stakes.[3] He claims that the Roman term *silva caduca*

2 Roland Bechmann (tr. Katharyn Dunham), *Trees and Man: the Forest in the Middle Ages* (New York, 1990) (originally published as *Des arbres et des hommes. La forêt au moyen-âge* (Paris, 1984)).

3 Bechmann, *Trees and Man,* p. 202. He has used Du Cange's *Glossarium mediae et infimae Latinitatis* (Niort-Mondon, 1886) as the source for the terms *silua palaria*, *caduca* and *concida.*

lasted into the early medieval period,[4] with the term *silva concida* coming into greater use later on.[5] According to Bechmann:

> the Romans divided the forests into three types. Those intended to produce firewood were subjected to annual cuts and were called *silua caedua*[6] (forests to cut) or *siluae minutae*. These woods also provided props for the vines and, according to Pliny the Elder, were cut every eight years for the chestnut tree, and every eleven years for oak.[7]

Thus there seems to have been a variety of activity based on differing time-scales: the annual requirement for fuel meant that some woods were subject to intensive usage, while other timber products – for agriculture and construction – were the result of a longer 'production cycle'. Bechmann goes on to contrast an earlier medieval term, *talea*,[8] with *bannum*,[9] or *foresta*,[10] in the Anglo-Norman period.[11] According to Meiggs,[12] Columella described coppice only as a means of producing stakes for vines, but from his admission that it was a common form of silviculture this implies that there were other markets. Coppice could produce fencing, poles and firewood as well as stakes and props, and the market was sufficiently large to encourage the peasant as well as the large-scale landowner. Hazel coppicing produces a stark landscape, but quickly regrows and is ready for cutting again within seven years.

4 In Jan Frederik Niermeyer, *Mediae Latinitatis Lexicon Minus* (Leiden, 2nd revised edn, 2002); *silua caduca* only refers to 'mortmain' – something passed down by inheritance – and according to the *Oxford Latin Dictionary*, the term *ligna caduca* found in Varro, *Lingua Latina*, 66.6 means 'fallen wood' which can be collected in the fields.

5 *Thesaurus Latinae Linguae*: *concido* III.1 means 'chop up', especially in a culinary sense, not referring to woods. Du Cange *concisa/concides* refers to *Salic Laws* tit. 18.4: *si quis concisam uel sepem alterius capulauerit uel incenderit ...*, and then refers to it taking over from *silua caedua* as 'bois taillée'. This appears to be the source of Bechmann's argument.

6 For example Cato, *De Re Rustica*, 1.7; Varro, *De Agricultura*, 1.7.9, 1.23.6; Columella 3.3.1.

7 Pliny the Elder, *Historia Naturalis*, 17.141–51 gives detailed instructions on the planting of willow, reed, chestnut and oak for providing props.

8 Or *tallia, talia, talgia, taillia.* In Niermeyer this is rendered as 'pruned tree' from 'AD 718, 761'; Du Cange explains *tallea* as '*species tigni, materiae, uel Scandula*' (whence *taille*, or harvest-tax).

9 Niermeyer translates *bannus* 14 as 'forest authority' from 'AD 896, 890, 1024', which indicates an earlier continental usage for this term.

10 Niermeyer, *forestis, -a, -ia* from AD 648 (Merovingian charters) with the sense 'area denied to common easement and reserved to the king'; see also entry 6, where it is a general term for 'woodland' (but with few citations).

11 Bechmann, *Trees and Man*, pp. 202–3. Perhaps the change occurred under Christian influence: Ronald Edward Latham, *Medieval Latin Word-list* (Oxford, 1965), suggests that *caduca* has a sense of 'transitory', in opposition to *eterna* in a Christian sense, from the seventh century onwards; Latham gives *concides* in the sense of ' a barrier of felled trees' from the twelfth century. Niermeyer lists the terms *concides, concites – bois taillis –* coppice-wood.

12 Russell Meiggs, *Timber and Trees in the Ancient Mediterranean World* (Oxford, 1982), pp. 268–9, with refs to Martial, 10.79, 7.28.1–2; Pliny the Younger, *Epistulae*, 3.19; and Pliny the Elder, *Historia Naturalis*, 16.173–8.

Turning to the Anglo-Saxon world, we may note Rackham's comment that:

> the distribution of wooded and non-wooded areas in Anglo-Saxon England was, in the main, not the work of the Anglo-Saxons ... there is very little evidence of extension of woodland at the time of the transition.[13]

Using linguistic evidence, Della Hooke further noted that:

> the presence of woodland in the Anglo-Saxon period is often shown by the distribution of the *lēah*-term, a term which originally meant 'woodland' but was later applied to clearings within wooded areas.[14]

However, she made no specific reference beyond this to coppicing or its impact on the landscape, despite examining the documentary sources in considerable detail.[15]

Rackham also noted a charter, dated 866, of Burgred, king of Mercia, which granted a regular supply of:

> pasture for 70 pigs in that wooded common ... which the country-folk call Wulfferdinleh [Wolverley, Worcestershire] and five wagons full of good rods (*uirgis*) and every year one oak for building ... and wood ... for the fire as necessary.[16]

Rackham comments that:

> Wolverley was one of the most wooded parts of England, where woodland management should have been slow to penetrate. Yet the regular large-scale supply of rods as well as timber and firewood, from a wooded common presupposes not merely coppicing but compartmented wood-pasture.[17]

Rackham also notes another impact on the landscape made by this activity: an incidental side-effect of coppicing is woodland flowers – such as primroses and violets.[18]

13 Oliver Rackham, *Ancient Woodland: its History, Vegetation and Uses in England* (London, 1980), p. 131.

14 Della Hooke, 'The Anglo-Saxon landscape', in *Field and Forest: An Historical Geography of Warwickshire and Worcestershire*, eds Terry R. Slater and Peter J. Jarvis (Norwich, 1982), pp. 79–104, at p. 83 (with a note to Albert Hugh Smith, *English Place-Name Elements II* (Cambridge, 1970) pp. 18–22).

15 Della Hooke, 'Early medieval estate and settlement patterns: the documentary evidence', in *The Rural Settlements of Medieval England: Studies Dedicated to Maurice Beresford and John Hurst*, eds Michael Aston, David Austin and Christopher Dyer (Oxford, 1989), pp. 9–30.

16 Rackham, *Ancient Woodland*, p. 134, n. 206: W. de Gray Birch, *Cartularium Saxonicum*, 3 vols (London, 1885–93), no. 513, = S212.

17 Rackham, *Ancient Woodland*, pp. 134–5; I take 'compartmented wood pasture' to refer to a system of dividing the land up into small areas or 'parcels' in which discrete areas are set aside and protected from grazing stock so that timber products can be obtained from them.

18 Rackham, *Ancient Woodland*, pp. 79–81.

There is also some limited evidence for coppicing from contemporary continental sources of the same period. Hans-Jürgen Nitz cites the *capitulare de uillis*, where section 62 mentions *forestarii* and *lignaria*, 'which can be translated as places for wood working, timber and fuel yards from which *materia* (timber) and, for example, *facular* (torches) and *axilae* (shingles) had to be supplied to the centre'.[19] Other medieval landscape studies examined, whether their focus is on the Anglo-Saxon world or a continental one, make no specific reference to the use made of woodland.[20]

The calculations set out in the discussion that follows were developed during a three-year period from 1993 to 1996 while the author was engaged as Project Director of the Bede's World Museum in Jarrow. One of the main purposes of this project was to establish a site where experimental archaeology could be carried out in an artificially 'recreated' landscape with features which might have been identifiable in a Northumbrian landscape some 1300 years ago.[21] The site at Jarrow is now relatively well established, though difficulties with contaminated soils and the exposed location have slowed the growth of flora and particularly of the trees which were envisaged by the designers. These difficulties were even more apparent during the first years of the project, and the challenge of implementing the vision of what the site ought to look like was hampered by the reality of the locale and the handicaps imposed by the in-built factors mentioned above. Nevertheless, through sheer hard work and determination, those involved were able to turn a mud patch, shaped from river dredgings, into something akin to an Anglo-Saxon landscape to coincide with the formal opening of a new museum building in the summer of 1996.

In the course of this work, the demand for coppiced material was very high, and since there were no on-site resources for it, it had to be brought in from outside. In modern terms, a considerable outlay in capital was involved; in an early medieval context we were made to ponder what allocation of labour would have been necessary, not only in *using* the material for various tasks on site, but in *obtaining* it in the first place. Many of the lessons were learned the hard way; had we been real Anglo-Saxons, I think grandpa would have put us right straight away! One of the most difficult lessons to be learned from experimental

19 Hans-Jürgen Nitz, 'Settlement structures and settlement systems of the Frankish central state in Carolingian and Ottonian times', in *Anglo-Saxon Settlements*, ed. Della Hooke (Oxford, 1988), pp. 249–74, at pp. 266–8. The reference is taken from *Die Land güterordnung Kaiser Karls des Grossen*, ed. K. Gareis (Berlin, 1895).

20 From a later period, see *Town and Country in the Middle Ages: Contrasts, Contacts and Interconnections*, eds Kate Giles and Christopher Dyer (Leeds, 2005) which offers no contribution on woodland *per se*; Christopher Dyer, *Hanbury: Settlement and Society in a Woodland Landscape*, Dept of English Local History Occasional Papers, 4th series, 4 (London, 1991), has on pp. 22–5 discussion of the agricultural economy of the Hanbury estates – but makes no mention of woodland.

21 There is a fine website illustrating the work done at Bede's World: www.bedesworld.co.uk; cf. also Peter J. Fowler, 'Farming in early medieval England: some fields for thought', in *The Anglo-Saxons from the Migration Period to the Eighth Century: an Ethnographic Perspective*, ed. John Hines (Woodbridge, 1997), pp. 245–68.

archaeology is the range of expertise which has to be brought to bear on a project, none being superior to the rest. This was particularly true in two aspects: first, the seasonal availability of coppiced material, and second, its 'shelf-life' once it was cut. These have an important bearing on any theoretical reconstructions of past landscape usage. So far as the seasonal availability is concerned, it is important to remember that in order to cause least harm to the parent tree, wands are cut in the 'dormant' period after the sap has stopped rising and before it recommences in the spring; as a result, they are available mainly during the late autumn, winter and early spring. Once they are cut, their flexibility begins to wane as the natural seasoning process takes place; in practice, it was found at Bede's World that anything up to 25% of the material (delivered at any one time from a considerable distance away in a quantity which made delivering it worthwhile for the supplier) was unusable as wands to be woven because there was not enough labour to deploy them before they became brittle. This was particularly the case during a dry spring in 1995. The wood had other uses – even as firewood – but it was noticeable that, in an ideal situation, a regular supply of freshly cut wands would have been much more suitable for construction purposes and less wasteful in all respects. More recently, the author has been able to discuss some of these observations from Bede's World, first made in the 1990s and since reviewed in desk studies, with ongoing experience from the Butser Ancient Farm project in Hampshire; here, in a less exposed and less saline location, it has been noted that the seasoning process is much less rapid, and wands cut several months previously and laid in long wet grass (away from sun and wind) were still in the main suitable for weaving into a hurdle in February 2007 in time for the Manchester conference in April.[22]

Despite the obvious artificialities of the Bede's World project, the work carried out there was nevertheless useful, and two specific areas of activity were valuable in producing relevant data in respect of coppiced material. These were, first, fencing, and second, building works. It is a well-known country dictum that fencing exists not to keep animals in but to keep animals out. This is a reality of rural life reflected back as far as the *Laws of Ine*, 42:

> [Be đam þæt ceorlas habbađ land gemæne 7 gærstunas.]
> Gif ceorlas gærstun hæbben gemænne ođđe oþer gedálland to tynnane, 7 hæbben sume getyned hiora dæl, sume næbben, 7 etten hiora gemænan æceras ođđe gærs, gán þa þonne þe đæt geat agan, 7 gebeten þam ođrum, þe hiora dæl getunedne hæbben, þone æwerdlan þe đær gedon sie; abidden him æt þam ceape swylc ryht swylce hit kyn sie.
>
> §1. Gif þonne hryđera hwelc sie þe hegas brece 7 ga in gehwær, 7 se hit nolde gehealdan se hit ođđe ne mæge, nime se hit on his æcere mete 7 ófslea, 7 nime se agenfrigea his fel 7 flæsc 7 đolie þæs ođres.
>
> (If commoners have a common meadow or other – partible – land to fence, and some have fenced their portion and some have not, [and cattle get in] and eat up their common crops or their grass, then those who are responsible for

22 Particular thanks are due to Simon Jay, farm manager at Butser.

Plate II.2. Fence-building at Bede's World, Jarrow.

the opening shall go and pay compensation for the damage which has been done to the others, who have enclosed their portion. They [the latter] shall demand from [the owners of] the cattle such amends as are fitting.)[23]

Even in its earliest phases of development, the farm site at Bede's World (known as *Gyrwe* from the Old English name for the place) had a mixture of animal and arable farming, combining livestock and succulent plants in a small area – so immediate fencing was required. This took the form of fencing woven *in situ* and portable hurdles (Pl. II.2); any hedging planted on *Gyrwe* would take years to grow (though a hedging programme was begun in the third year of the project). From the experience gained in carrying out this work, a tentative summary can be established of the land requirements needed to supply coppiced material for a site such as this and of equal extent. It goes without saying that all the assumptions made in the discussion which follows can be challenged, but they have been refined through discussion and debate on a number of occasions with the various parties mentioned in the introduction,[24] and may be taken as a fairly secure starting-point.

23 Cited in *The Laws of the Earliest English Kings*, ed. Frederick L. Attenborough (Cambridge, 1922), p. 49.

24 See above, p. 23.

Summary of land requirements, Gyrwe

- Fencing on *Gyrwe*, 1.2m high on average, uses 60 rods of 4m to make a 3m (10') length
- This equates to 20 rods average per metre – the number varies slightly depending on the thickness of rods used and their overall length
- These rods take 7 years to grow
- The completed fence lasts 7 years

In addition to these figures based on the actual use of material, further estimates can be made about the likely productivity of a woodland area. Thus:

- 15 rods average are produced by each stool (productive tree) in 7 years
- Thus 1.3 stools per metre of fence is a fair estimate

This enables a simple table to be drawn up which incorporates the figures and permits some conclusions about land requirements to be arrived at, as shown in Table 2.1. Now, if we take this as an example, it is possible to arrive at a rough estimate of the amount of work going on in coppicing and the extent of land needed for it. In Table 2.1, the extent of hazel woodland required to supply 3000m of fencing on an annual basis comes to 163,800m^2, which is 16.4 hectares or 40.5 acres (1 hectare = 10,000m^2 = 2.471 acres).

This can be compared with the actual amounts achieved at Bede's World between early summer 1994 and August 1996 – which we can count as two years since periods of work were intermittent. Here a construction rate of approximately 750m of fence per year was achieved, with a target of 2000–2250m to complete the site. Even assuming enough material was required for 1000m per year, the total length would necessitate a minimum area of woodland ready to coppice of 2600 stools occupying 6m^2 each, or 15,600m^2, which would not be ready for coppicing again for six or seven years. At Jarrow it was also found (perhaps because of the coastal location and the nature of the site itself) that the fences became rotten before 7 years were up – and on a visit to the site in 2001 I was not surprised to see that every section of fence I had been personally acquainted with from 1993–96 had been replaced. In addition, damage to fencing by livestock has to be taken into account.

This enables the possible land usage total to be refined a little more. If, for example, 2000m of fencing must be constructed every three years, then the approximated figures of 1.3 stools at 6m^2 per stool need to be multiplied by 670 (the number of metres to be built each year on a rolling cycle); this produces a figure of 5226m^2 as a bare minimum needed, and none of this coppice would be productive for a further seven years. The actual area required would almost certainly be far in excess of this figure.

It must be borne in mind that many permanent barriers (i.e. thick hedging) might have been used in a real Anglo-Saxon landscape, and it would (for obvious reasons) have been more established and developed than *Gyrwe* was in its formative years. In addition such hedgerows may also have been the source of

Table 2.1 Hazel usage at Bede's World and possible land requirements

Number of rods required per metre of fencing	20
Rods produced per stool (average)	15
Stools of hazel required per metre of fence	1.3
Land required to grow each stool	6m^2
Length of time required to grow each stool	7 years
Land required to produce a metre of fence annually	54.6m^2

The estimated 20 rods required per metre come from 1.3 stools; each stool needs 7 years to grow. About 55m^2 of land would be needed for coppice to produce a metre of fence on an annual basis.

material suitable for weaving and wattle (especially in the form of 'sun shoots' which grow from the base of established trees), but nevertheless the calculations serve to indicate the impact on woodland management of even a relatively small site. It should also be noted that these calculations do not include the demand on the woodland areas for material for building work, to which we may turn next.

The second major activity at Bede's World which involved considerable demands for coppiced material was building work. As is the case at other sites where experiments in reconstruction archaeology have encompassed the creation of buildings, such as at Butser and West Stow, specimen buildings based on the ground-plans of known archaeological examples have been constructed on *Gyrwe* using appropriate technologies (i.e. no power tools).[25] It may be noted that there was nothing unusual about the techniques used in the Anglo-Saxon period: from an earlier period, the house of Romulus was supposedly 'made of wattle and daub with a thatched roof,'[26] and at Inchtuthil: 'the standard form of construction seems to have been wattle and daub within a timber framework … the volume of timber required for Fendoch and Inchtuthil was very considerable,' Meiggs mused, 'and it would be interesting to know how the supply was organized.'[27] This issue remained a key one in the economy of Anglo-Saxon England, and beyond: as Bechmann noted:

> wood remained for a long time the dominant element in English construction and Viollet-le-Duc noted that the framework of monuments of the Middle Ages in England was distinguished by their richness and the large size of the lumber-wood.[28]

25 Susan Mills, '(Re)constructing Northumbrian timber buildings: the Bede's World Experience', in *Northumbria's Golden Age*, eds Jane Hawkes and Susan Mills (Stroud, 1999), pp. 66–72; see also www.bedesworld.co.uk.

26 Meiggs, *Timber and Trees*, p. 219.

27 Meiggs, *Timber and Trees*, pp. 178–9.

28 Bechmann, *Trees and Man,* p. 159.

Plate II.3. 'Thirlings A' under construction at Bede's World, Jarrow.

The construction of the building 'Thirlings A' has been outlined by Susan Mills, curator of Bede's World when the work was carried out.[29] In addition to large timbers (50-year-old oaks) used in the main framework, the internal panels were made of woven material. This activity used complete lengths of hazel or other coppiced material (approximately 3m) for the vertical pieces, while off-cuts and shorter sections could be used for the horizontal rods woven in. It was noteworthy that some of the panel sections – whose dimensions were defined by the framing of the building, itself based on the excavated post-holes[30] – left very little room for this activity; in some cases only one upright could be inserted, and the horizontal pieces had to be 'sprung' against the oak posts, while at the very top of the panels, either thin material was threaded through or a small gap was left for filling in with daub at a later date (Pl. II.3). At Butser Ancient Farm, in the reconstruction of the timber-framed Roman villa (based on the excavated example at Sparsholt) the framing in the upper works is mostly rectangular, and the opportunity was taken to experiment with weaving in both a horizontal and vertical manner. The panels left exposed give an indication of the technique used in completing this part of the building (Pl. II.4).[31]

[29] See above, n. 25.

[30] Mills, '(Re)constructing Northumbrian timber buildings', p. 69; Colm O'Brien and Roger Miket, 'The early medieval settlement of Thirlings, Northumbria', *Durham Archaeological Journal*, 7 (1991), 57–91.

[31] Illustrations of the completed buildings at Bede's World may be seen on the museum's website, www.bedesworld.co.uk/academic-buildings.php; see Plates 1 and 2 in Hawkes and Mills (eds), *Golden Age of Northumbria*.

Plate II.4. Reconstruction of Sparsholt Roman villa, Butser Ancient Farm.

As with fencing and hurdle production, a calculation to estimate the amount of material required for a building such as 'Thirlings A' may be drawn up as follows. First, there are five fairly broad spaces between the post-holes on the ends, and a further eleven down each side; one on each of the long sides was left unfilled except for the areas above the doors. An estimated average of five vertical rods was needed for the end sections (the middle sections reach a height of approximately 5m at the centre) and three for each panel on the long sides. This gives a total requirement of 110 rods for the vertical sections. For the horizontal sections an average of 50 rods of varying thickness to complete each metre of panelling, with 4 pieces of material taken from each whole rod, gives an approximate figure of 50/4 per metre of whole coppiced rods. Thus for 'Thirlings A' as a whole, approximately 1285 rods have been used (see Table 2.2).

In addition, experiments have been carried out with 'replicas' of smaller structures, in particular a *Grubenhaus* based on an excavated example from New Bewick which made extensive use of coppiced material in its sides (shown under construction in Pl. II.5),[32] and a circular building loosely based on a supposed goose-house from a Devon site which was little more than a basket on a large scale. For a *Grubenhaus* which has sides approximately 2.5m in height to the apex of the roof, and is approximately 5m in length, the same type of simple calculation can be employed as was used in working out the material needed

32 Tim Gates and Colm O'Brien, 'Cropmarks at Milfield and New Bewick and the recognition of *grubenhaüser* in Northumberland', *Archaeologia Aeliana*, 5th series, 16 (1988), 1–9.

Table 2.2 Coppiced material needed for reconstructing building 'Thirlings A' at Bede's World

	Length in metres	Number of rods
Vertical rods		
20 side panels @ 3 rods		60
10 end panels @ 5 rods		50
Total rods used vertically		110
Horizontal rods		
50 required per metre height of each panel, each divided into 4 pieces; 12.5 required per metre length		
20 side panels @ 2.2m	44	550
10 end panels @ 5m	50	625
Total metres	94	
Total rods used horizontally		1175
Total rods		1285

for building fences in Table 2.1, viz. 30 rods per metre produce a woven area of 1.2m^2; thus for each side of 12.5m^2 a total of 312.5 rods – doubled to take account of both sides. When additional material for the ends is also included (planks were used in the Bede's World example) the total begins to approach 1000 rods – not far short of those needed for the much larger 'Thirlings A'.

A final aspect of 'demands on the landscape' in the broadest sense of that term is the labour required, and to this we may now turn. We should note that making fences is not a particularly skilled job: at Bede's World a variety of personnel including teams of volunteer office workers (BT) and young people (Prince's Trust) were involved in this work, and as an approximation, one hour of steady activity was needed to build 1m of fence on average, providing the material was in place ready to use.

As a step up from this, hurdle-making takes more skill and harder hands. Volunteers engaged in this work needed much more training and closer supervision, and two-and-a-half to four hours of labour per hurdle were required. The other lesson which was learned in the early years was the lack of suitable material in the vicinity of Jarrow in the quantities required. Most of the hazel used from 1993 to 1996 had to be brought from woodlands in southern England and this raises two questions: namely, the seasonality of the coppicing process and the logistics of moving the material to the place where it was to be put to use.

At the present time, the cutting season is said to begin at Bonfire Night and lasts until the sap starts rising (so early November until the end of March); this is done for the sake of the tree, so as not to harm it.[33] We might assume

[33] Verbal communication from John King, coppicer in Hampshire.

Plate II.5. Replica of *Grubenhaus* at New Bewick under construction at Bede's World, Jarrow.

that similar considerations were taken into account in the Anglo-Saxon period, though there is no evidence one way or the other that the author has been able to trace. Certainly general or unskilled labour would have been better used in food production outside of the period between late autumn and early spring.

Logistics is a further issue. At Bede's World the main problem was ensuring that economic volumes were ordered to be transported, given that the only regular supply was some 300 miles away (coppicing is now more common in the locality, and just two or three new specialists are sufficient to supply Bede's World's relatively modest needs). A single delivery in 1994–96 provided enough material for some twelve weeks' work with the available labour, and took the supplier approximately two weeks to cut.[34]

However, with volunteer labour there was a decided reluctance to work during adverse weather, and in warm weather much of the material was unusable within five to six weeks at the very outside. It would have been preferable to have had a regular supply – small quantities cut, transported and put in place – possibly with an allocation of labour to each part of the operation. Problems were also posed by different species having different characteristics – additional variation being caused by purpose or use, soil types and growing conditions, which vary

34 This represented between 1500 and 2000 rods per delivery.

the time between cuttings.[35] The material came from both coppice and coppice clearance (i.e. woods being brought back into use), which also introduces a variable, for as Bechmann noted, 'in young woods, the proportion of live tissues is much larger than in older woods'.[36]

The time taken to cut and prepare coppiced rods also varies, depending on the weather, terrain and the skill of the worker. At Wispers School, Haslemere, in the early spring of 2007, the author coppiced a maximum of 40 rods per hour; this involved cutting the rod and then trimming it and tidying up. It goes without saying that it is much more efficient to cut rods in a clear space which has been coppiced regularly than it is to hack through overgrown areas; fine material for weaving and hurdle-making is also provided by 'sun shoots' or suckers which grow from the base of a tree and are common in hedgerows, but which take more time to cut and collect.[37]

Transport in early medieval style might have included a mule or horse, and the time taken would clearly depend on the distance travelled. It would be an interesting experiment to see how many bundled rods could be transported by a single pack animal this way; carrying rods tied in bundles of ten gives a limit of twenty per person over medium distances. Thus, including transport, each metre length of completed woven fence or panel in a building might easily represent four hours of labour, albeit unskilled.

We may conclude this brief discussion as I began, with an observation from an earlier scholar. Bechmann asserted that 'Towns needed forests first for firewood and second for construction timber,' and further, that '... wood wasn't economized and the greatest part of all construction, from cottages to fortified castles, was in wood'.[38] But we may contrast this with the *Laws of Ine*, 43, which seems to make it clear that misuse of timber was a serious matter:

> [Be wude bærnete.]
> Đonne mon beam on wude forbærne, 7 weorđe yppe on þone đe hit dyde, gielde he fulwite: geselle LX scill., forþamþe fyr biđ þeof.
>
> § 1. Gif mon afelle on wuda wel monega treowa, 7 wyrđ eft undierne, forgielde III treowu ælc mid XXX scill.; ne đearf he hiora má geldan, wære hiora swa fela swa hiora wære; forþon sio æsc biđ melda, nalles đeof.
>
> (If anyone destroys a tree in a wood by fire, and it becomes known who did it, he shall pay a full fine. He shall pay 60 shillings, because fire is a thief. §1. If anyone fells a large number of trees in a wood, and it afterwards becomes known, he shall pay 30 shillings for each of three trees. He need not pay more, however many there may be, because the axe is an informer and not a thief.)[39]

35 Bechmann, *Trees and Man*, p. 203.
36 Bechmann, *Trees and Man*, p. 211.
37 The author is indebted to Simon Jay at Butser Ancient Farm for pointing this out.
38 Bechmann, *Trees and Man*, pp. 141, 161.
39 *Laws of the Earliest English Kings*, ed. Attenborough, p. 51.

Fencing and building have been the main considerations of this paper, but there were also many other uses to which woodland material could be put. Bechmann reminds us that 'Most containers which were not meant to hold liquids used these (interlacing) techniques: baskets, trugs, hurdles, and mats for cheeses. The flexible branches of several bushes or trees were used – willow, rush, hair-grass, hazel, and especially osier.'[40] In construction work, 'Hurdles were also used as planking on building-sites. In the miniatures one can see these elements that were used to constitute ramps or work floors on the scaffoldings.'[41]

Cut wood was also employed to produce charcoal, useful above all in iron-making, but suitable for other purposes too. To produce one ton of refined iron over 65m^3 of wood was needed. Given that a good coppice produces about 84m^3 per hectare every sixteen years, one can understand the impact on the forests of all the human activities consuming this fuel.[42]

It seems likely that there was a great deal of activity going on in the Anglo-Saxon landscape which was so banal (and banausic) as to escape the attention of the written sources. A significant element of this will have been woodland exploitation. Given this likelihood, it is possible that a good deal of the land sometimes identified in archaeological studies as 'scrub' was, in fact, some kind of coppice.

40 Bechmann, *Trees and Man*, p. 196.
41 Bechmann, *Trees and Man*, p. 197.
42 Bechmann, *Trees and Man*, p. 153.

3

Landscape Change during the 'Long Eighth Century' in Southern England*

STEPHEN RIPPON

Introduction: Challenging the Midland-Centric Focus of Medieval Landscape Studies

England's is a rich and varied landscape. A fifteenth-century traveller making the journey from Exeter in the South-West, to Oxford in the South Midlands, and then across to Ipswich in East Anglia would have witnessed a wide variety of countrysides, with scattered farmsteads and small hamlets set within predominantly enclosed fields around Exeter, the 'champion' countryside of villages surrounded by vast open fields in the Midlands, and another area of dispersed settlement and a predominantly enclosed fieldscape across in the southern part of East Anglia (Fig. 3.1). The origins of this broad tripartite division in landscape character, which was first described by the antiquarian John Leland in the mid sixteenth century,[1] have been much debated, with old ideas that villages and open fields were brought across the North Sea by Early Anglo-Saxon migrants being rejected in favour of current views that they were an indigenous development of the mid ninth to twelfth centuries.[2]

A wide variety of explanations have been put forward as to why this central zone of England – which Brian Roberts and Stuart Wrathmell have called the

* I would like to thank Brian Ayers, Richard Brunning, Alan Hardy, Helena Hamerow, Michael Metcalf and Peter Murphy for their help in researching this paper. Derek Gore kindly commented on an earlier draft.

1 The best edition of John Leland's itineraries remains Lucy Toulmin Smith, *The Itinerary in Wales of John Leland in or about the years 1536–1539* (London, 1906). The areas that he described as 'champion' countryside have been mapped by G. Slater, 'The inclosure of common fields considered geographically', *Geographical Journal*, 29.i (1907), 35–55.

2 For examples of migrationist views see H. L. Gray, *English Field Systems* (Cambridge, Massachusetts, 1915) and W. G. Hoskins, *The Making of the English Landscape* (London, 1954). For examples of the currently predominant view that villages date from around the tenth century see Christopher Taylor, *Village and Farmstead* (London, 1983) and Christopher Dyer, *Making a Living in the Middle Ages. The People of Britain 850–1520* (London, 2003); for a survey of recent comment, see the Introduction to this volume.

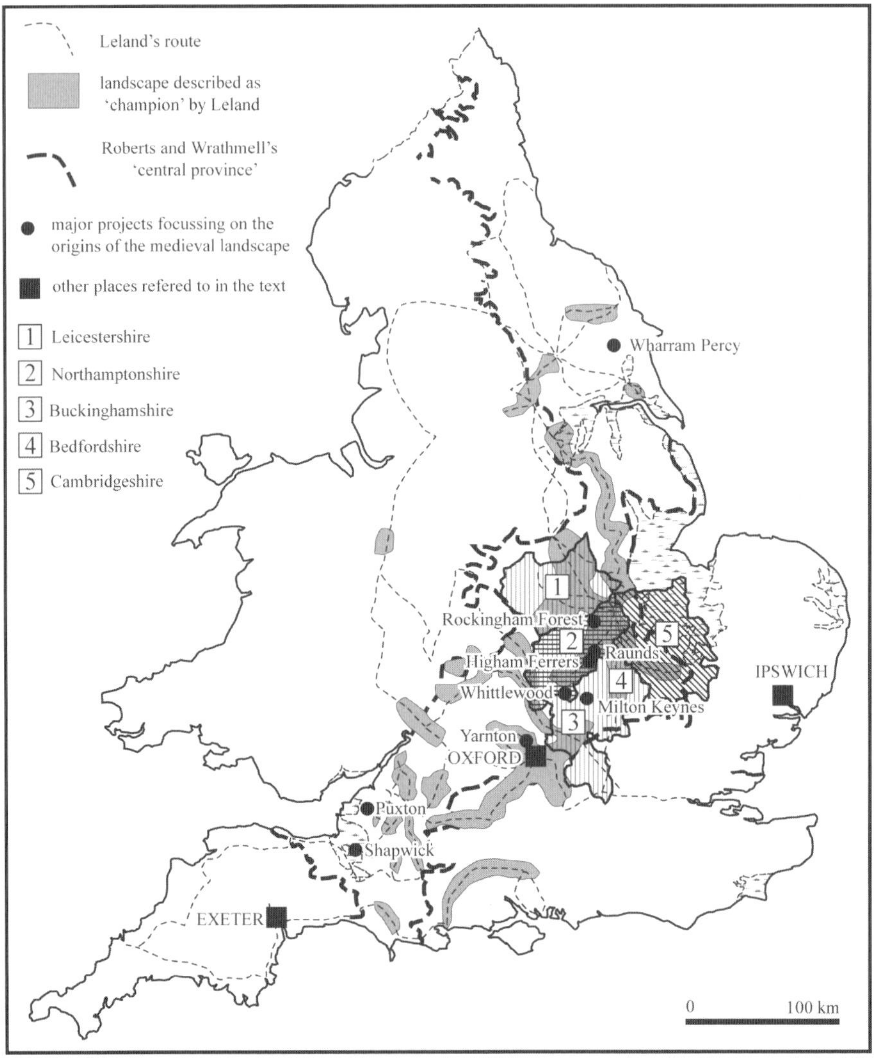

Figure 3.1. The 'central province' of England, characterised by nucleated settlement, as mapped by Brian Roberts and Stuart Wrathmell, *An Atlas of Rural Settlement in England* (London, 2000). This broadly corresponds with areas of 'champion' countryside described in the mid-sixteenth-century itineraries of John Leland and mapped by G. Slater, 'The inclosure of common fields considered geographically', *Geographical Journal*, 29(i) (1907), 35–55. Major recent projects that have examined the origins and development of the medieval landscape have showed a marked bias towards this central zone.

'central province'[3] – saw the development of champion countryside characterized by settlement nucleation and open fields. These include rising population and the restructuring of resources within landed estates which, in the context of an expanding economy and the increased burdens that an emerging English state placed upon landowners, encouraged the reorganization of agriculture in order to increase production. In a number of recent studies, there is a more or less explicit assumption that the central zone saw the development of villages and open fields because this was the most socially and economically advanced region, with areas to the east and west being somewhat less well developed (Fig. 3.2).[4] Della Hooke, for example, suggests that 'if the dominant land use of such areas [of dispersed settlement] was pastoralism, and there was an abundance of woodland and waste, there would be little incentive for massive reorganization of earlier settlement and field systems'.[5] Carenza Lewis, Patrick Mitchell-Fox and Chris Dyer claim that 'the areas where the nucleated village was the dominant form of settlement in the middle ages, appear to have had consistently higher proportions of arable land in cultivation in 1086, which is likely to reflect a long standing bias towards cereal cultivation'.[6] Roberts and Wrathmell have even provided a schematic representation of how the idea of villages and open fields may have originated in the East Midlands and then spread out to the rest of their 'central province', leaving the South-East and South-West of England – regions that they suggest had greater amounts of woodland – untouched by this transformation of the landscape (Fig. 3.2). Whilst Tom Williamson has challenged the idea that villages and open fields were created in response to cultural factors such as a greater population density, his suggestion that it was the nature of soils and extent of meadowland in the 'central province' that led to settlement nucleation and the creation of open fields still perpetuates the very Midland-centric emphasis of the debate into the origins of regional variation in medieval landscape character:[7] all too often, the focus of attention is on how circumstances in this one part of the country may have led to changes there, rather than questioning what was going on at the same time in adjacent regions which did not see the development of villages and open fields. Were areas such as the South-East, the South-West and the West Midlands simply remote, backward regions that in this great era of agrarian innovation were passed by?

One of the problems in addressing this question is that there has been such a marked bias in archaeological research towards the origins of villages and open

3 Brian Roberts and Stuart Wrathmell, *An Atlas of Rural Settlement in England* (London, 2000).

4 These ideas are discussed in a series of recent studies: Carenza Lewis, Patrick Mitchell-Fox and Christopher Dyer, *Village, Hamlet and Field* (Manchester, 1997); Brian Roberts and Stuart Wrathmell, *Region and Place* (London, 2002); Tom Williamson, *Shaping Medieval Landscapes* (Macclesfield, 2003); and Stephen Rippon, *Beyond the Medieval Village: The Diversification of Landscape Character in Southern Britain* (Oxford, 2008).

5 Della Hooke, *The Landscape of Anglo-Saxon England* (London, 1998).

6 Lewis, Mitchell-Fox and Dyer, *Village, Hamlet and Field*, p. 198.

7 Williamson, *Shaping Medieval Landscapes,* and see his *The Transformation of Rural England* (Exeter, 2002) and *England's Landscape: East Anglia* (London, 2006).

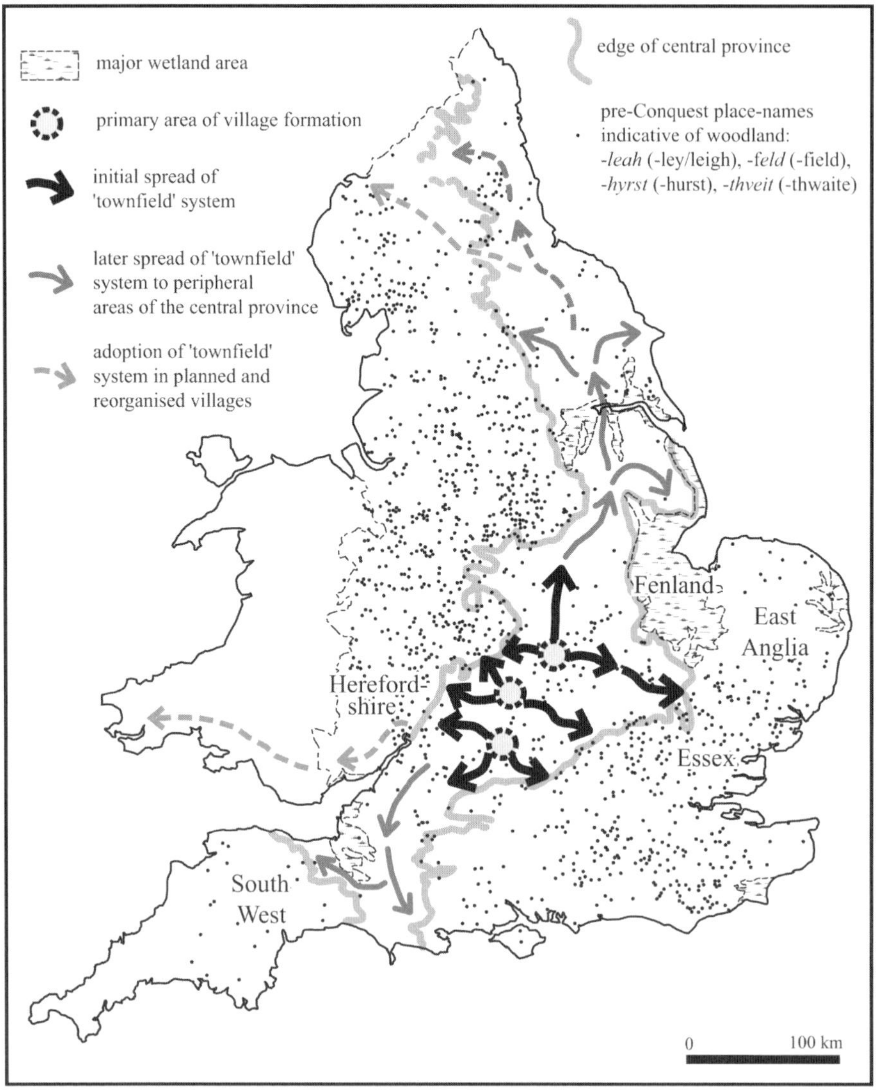

Figure 3.2. Roberts and Wrathmell's model for the spread of villages and open fields from the East Midlands to the rest of their 'central province' (*Region and Place*, fig. 5.11). Their mapping of pre-Conquest woodland suggests that the areas beyond the 'central province' – such as Essex and Herefordshire – were less well developed.

fields at the expense of regions that saw other forms of landscape (Fig. 3.1).[8] Since the 1950s, the attention of both historians and archaeologists has been increasingly drawn to the visually impressive, and somewhat poignant, remains of deserted medieval villages and this led to a growing corpus of excavations, of which the most famous is Wharram Percy in Yorkshire, that provided the training ground for a generation of medievalists.[9] The urban expansion of Milton Keynes in Buckinghamshire and Higham Ferrers in Northamptonshire, and the planned expansion of gravel quarrying at Raunds in Northamptonshire and Yarnton in Oxfordshire, were all preceded by extensive programmes of survey and excavation in what had been champion countryside.[10] Research projects have similarly focused in areas characterized by villages and open fields. Gerrard and Aston have recently published a ten-year study of the classic village and open field parish of Shapwick in Somerset, while Lewis, Mitchell-Fox and Dyer studied the four East Midland counties of Bedfordshire, Buckinghamshire, Leicestershire and Northamptonshire, which led to the Whittlewood Project on the borders of Buckinghamshire and Northamptonshire.[11] Hall has had a long-term research interest in Northamptonshire, while Foard has surveyed Rockingham Forest in the north of the county, producing a remarkable reconstruction of the extent of common fields over an area of some 572 square kilometres.[12] Oosthuizen's recent work in Cambridgeshire is once again concerned with a landscape characterized by villages and open fields,[13] and this author's attempt

8 This is discussed further in Stephen Rippon, 'Understanding the medieval landscape', in *Fifty Years of Medieval Archaeology*, eds Roberta Gilchrist and Andrew Reynolds (Leeds, 2009), pp. 227–54.

9 Maurice Beresford and John Hurst, *The English Heritage Book of Wharram* (London, 1990).

10 Robert A. Croft, *The Changing Landscape of Milton Keynes* (Aylesbury, 1993); A. Hardy, B. M. Charles and R. J. Williams, *Death and Taxes: The Archaeology of a Middle Saxon Estate Centre at Higham Ferrers, Northamptonshire* (Oxford, 2007); Stephen Parry, *Raunds Area Survey* (Oxford, 2006); Gill Hey, *Yarnton: Saxon and Medieval Settlement and Landscape* (Oxford, 2004).

11 For the Shapwick project see Christopher Gerrard with Mick Aston, *The Shapwick Project, Somerset. A Rural Landscape Explored*, Society for Medieval Archaeology Monograph 25 (Leeds, 2007); for the Midlands Settlement Project see Lewis, Mitchell-Fox and Dyer, *Village, Hamlet and Field*; and for the way that this led to the Whittlewood Project see Christopher Dyer, 'The Medieval Settlement Research Group Whittlewood Project', *Medieval Settlement Research Group Annual Report*, 14 (1999), 16–17; Richard Jones and Mark Page, 'Characterising rural settlement and landscape: Whittlewood Forest in the Middle Ages', *Medieval Archaeology*, 47 (2004), 55–83; and Richard Jones and Mark Page, *Medieval Villages in an English Landscape* (Macclesfield, 2006).

12 David Hall, 'Fieldwork and fieldbooks: studies in early layout', in *Villages, Fields and Frontiers: Studies in Rural Settlement in the Medieval and early Modern Periods*, eds B. K. Roberts and R. E. Glasscock (Oxford, 1984), pp. 115–32; David Hall, *The Open Fields of Northamptonshire* (Northampton, 1995); Glenn Foard, 'Medieval woodland, agriculture and industry in the Rockingham Forest, Northamptonshire', *Medieval Archaeology*, 45 (2001), 41–97; Glenn Foard, David Hall and Tracey Partida, 'Rockingham Forest, Northamptonshire: the evolution of a landscape', *Landscapes*, 6.ii (2005), 1–29.

13 Susan Oosthuizen, 'Saxon commons in south Cambridgeshire', *Proceedings of the Cambridgeshire Antiquarian Society,* 82 (1993), 93–100; Susan Oosthuizen, 'Medieval greens

to study landscapes characterized by dispersed settlement on the North Somerset Levels ended up finding a medieval village and open field at Puxton where there is now just a small hamlet and a scatter of isolated farmsteads.[14] Even within allied disciplines such as historical geography, it is villages that have drawn most attention for it is substantial, nucleated settlements that are most amenable to the techniques of plan analysis that have become so popular since the work of Thorpe and Roberts.[15] Villages and open fields are also relatively simple forms of landscape: the management of a regularly arranged, two- or three-field system in Somerset, with its strips, furlongs, rotational cropping and communal fallowing, was essentially the same as that in the East Midlands. The far more irregular field systems in areas such as the South-West and the South-East, with a predominance of closes but also small areas of open field, formed a far more complex landscape and a more daunting one to study. Indeed, ever since Gray suggested that 'the early field system of few English counties is so difficult to describe as that of Essex',[16] landscape historians and archaeologists appear to have been far more comfortable with studying the predictable villages and open fields of champion countryside.

The rest of this paper, however, will challenge two central pillars of this Midland-centric tradition of landscape research: that the development of villages and open fields can be understood simply by studying the areas in which they were created, and that this was a process that started no earlier than the mid ninth century.[17] Instead, it will be argued that the changes seen in areas such as the East Midlands were part of a more general phase of innovation across large parts of southern England, and that the eventual formation of villages and open fields was just one regional variation on a far broader theme. It will also be argued that this process of landscape transformation has a far longer history than is commonly assumed, that it began in a period which archaeologists have traditionally referred to as 'Middle Saxon' (*c.*650–*c.*850) and historians have recently called 'the long eighth century' (the late seventh to early ninth centu-

and moats in the central province: evidence from the Bourne valley, Cambridgeshire', *Landscape History*, 24 (2002), 73–88; Susan Oosthuizen, 'The roots of the open fields: linking prehistoric and medieval field systems in West Cambridgeshire', *Landscapes*, 4 (2003), 40–64; Susan Oosthuizen, 'New light on the origins of open-field farming', *Medieval Archaeology*, 49 (2005), 165–95; Susan Oosthuizen, *Landscapes Decoded: The Origins and Development of Cambridgeshire's Medieval Fields* (Hatfield, 2006); Susan Oosthuizen, 'The Anglo-Saxon kingdom of Mercia and the origins and distribution of common fields', *Agricultural History Review*, 55.2 (2007), 153–80.

14 Stephen Rippon, *Landscape, Community and Colonisation: the North Somerset Levels During the 1st to 2nd Millennia AD* (York, 2006).

15 H. Thorpe, 'The village greens of County Durham', *Transactions of the Institute of British Geographers*, 15 (1949), 155–80; B. K. Roberts, *The Making of the English Village* (London, 1987); B. K. Roberts, 'Dating villages: theory and practice', *Landscape History*, 14 (1992), 19–30.

16 Gray, *English Field Systems*, p. 387.

17 A recent overview that assumes a tenth- to eleventh-century date for village origins is David Stocker, *England's Landscape: The East Midlands* (London, 2006).

ries), when there were significant social, political and economic changes right across North-West Europe.[18]

Society and Landscape in the 'Middle Saxon' Period

This author's realization that changes in the rural landscape during the 'long eighth century' were more significant than previously recognized came when trying to understand palaeoenvironmental sequences (recording the preserved plant remains within cores taken from peat bogs) in the Devon landscape.[19] This is, however, a problematic period to study. Whilst the early medieval period as a whole (the early fifth to the mid eleventh centuries) suffers from a scarcity of archaeological evidence and documentary sources compared to preceding and later centuries, the 'Middle Saxon' period is particularly ill-understood: 'the period from around the end of the seventh century to the ninth century has tended to suffer in the eyes of researchers through its relative lack of easily identifiable material remains … and its lack of an easily understandable social structure'.[20] Particularly, diagnostic features of the 'Early Saxon' period – such as burials furnished with grave goods and sunken featured buildings – generally disappear, and with relatively few documentary sources there is a danger that the few documented figures, such as Offa, can assume an exaggerated importance simply because more is known about them than about their undocumented contemporaries.[21] What is clear, however, is that this was a period when there were significant changes in society, and if various disparate strands of evidence are drawn together, then the late seventh to early ninth centuries can be seen as a dynamic period of great change.

Although old concepts of a heptarchy of seven kingdoms forming around this time, comprising Wessex, Mercia, Northumbria, East Anglia, Essex, Kent and Sussex, are now seen as outdated – Lindsey, for example, can probably be added to the list with its 7000 hides in the Tribal Hidage placing it on a par

18 L. Hanson and C. Wickham, eds, *The Long Eighth Century: Production, Distribution and Demand* (Leiden, 2000); Chris Wickham, *Framing the Early Middle Ages* (Oxford, 2005).

19 R. M. Fyfe, A. G. Brown and S. J. Rippon, 'Mid to Late-Holocene vegetation history of Greater Exmoor, UK: estimating the spatial extent of human-induced vegetation change', *Vegetation History and Archaeobotany*, 12 (2003), 215–32; R. M. Fyfe, A. G. Brown and S. J. Rippon, 'Characterising the Late Prehistoric, "Romano-British" and medieval landscape, and dating the emergence of a regionally distinct agricultural system in South-West Britain', *Journal of Archaeological Science*, 31 (2004), 1699–714; R. M. Fyfe and S. J. Rippon, 'A landscape in transition? Palaeoenvironmental evidence for the end of the "Romano-British" period in South-West England', in *Debating Late Antiquity*, eds R. Collins and J. Gerrard (Oxford, 2004.), pp. 33–42; S. J. Rippon, R. M. Fyfe and A. G. Brown, 'Beyond villages and open fields: the origins and development of a historic landscape characterised by dispersed settlement in South-West England', *Medieval Archaeology*, 50 (2006), 31–70.

20 Hardy, Charles and Williams, *Death and Taxes*, p. 191.

21 David Hinton, *Archaeology, Economy and Society: England from the Fifth to the Fifteenth Century* (London, 1990), 42.

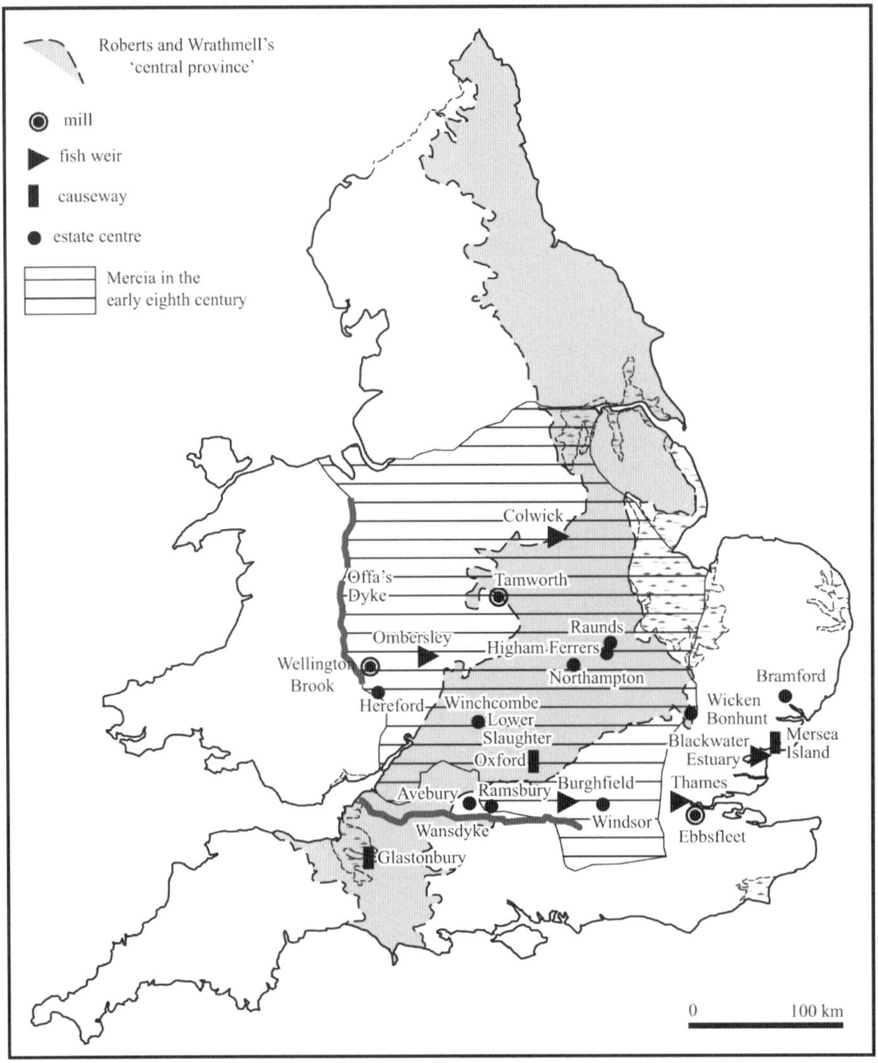

Figure 3.3. Examples of major investments in landscape management and estate centres dating to the 'Middle Saxon' period. Note how they show no correspondence to either the 'central province' as mapped by Roberts and Wrathmell, or the kingdom of Mercia in the early eighth century (based on David Hill, *An Atlas of Anglo-Saxon England* (Oxford, 1981), fig. 42.

with the East Saxons and South Saxons[22] – it is clear that there were significant developments at this time including the formation of relatively stable political entities.[23] The Augustinian church became well established and, through grants of land by successive rulers of these several kingdoms, various monasteries were starting to control significant areas of the landscape, a fact reflected in the investment they started to make therein (Fig. 3.3). For the kings, bishops and the emerging aristocracy, wealth was largely based upon holding landed estates and these were managed through centres such as Kingsbury in Old Windsor (Berkshire) where an eighth-century corn mill with three waterwheels was fed by a leat over 1km long, 6m wide, and 3.6m deep.[24] At Tamworth a mid-ninth-century or earlier mill, with a leat probably some 500m long, was constructed at 'a favourite residence of the Mercian royal household'.[25] An even earlier horizontal mill, this time powered by tidal water, has recently been recorded at Ebbsfleet in Kent and dendrochronologically dated to 691–92, while another mill is recorded at Chart in Kent in a charter of 762.[26] In Mercia, a series of strongholds was constructed and maintained in the eighth century by the *weall-geworc* and *burh-bot* of the *trinoda* (*trimoda*) *necessitas* (i.e. borough work) 'from which no-one could be excused and which had become obligatory in the Mercian kingdom by the mid eighth century'.[27] Along with other obligations, such as bridge-work – another indication of increased investment and activity in the countryside – these burdens that fell on the landowning class would have been a major incentive to increase the intensity and efficiency with which the countryside was exploited. One of the strongholds was presumably at Hereford, where two large corn-drying ovens dating to the eighth century, sealed beneath the later town defences, are testimony to the production and control of surplus

22 Kevin Leahy, 'The formation of the Anglo-Saxon kingdom of Lindsey', *Anglo-Saxon Studies in Archaeology and History*, 10 (1999), 127–33.

23 S. Bassett, *The Origins of Anglo-Saxon Kingdoms* (Leicester, 1989); Christopher Scull, 'Social archaeology and Anglo-Saxon kingdom origins', *Anglo-Saxon Studies in Archaeology and History*, 10 (1999), 17–24; Simon Keynes, 'Heptarchy', *The Blackwell Encyclopaedia of Anglo-Saxon England*, eds M. Lapidge, J. Blair, S. Keynes and D. Scragg (Oxford, 2001), p. 233; Wickham, *Framing the Early Middle Ages*.

24 D. Wilson and J. Hurst, 'Medieval Britain in 1957', *Medieval Archaeology*, 2 (1958), 183–5; J. M. Fletcher, 'Tree ring chronologies in the 6th to 16th centuries for oaks of southern and eastern England', *Journal of Archaeological Science*, 4 (1977), 335–52; D. J. Schove, 'Dark age tree-ring dates AD 490–850', *Medieval Archaeology*, 23 (1979), 219–23; G. Astill, 'An archaeological approach to the development of agricultural technologies in medieval England', in *Medieval Farming and Technology*, eds G. Astill and J. Langdon (Leiden, 1997), pp. 193–223.

25 Philip Rahtz and Robert Meeson, *An Anglo-Saxon Watermill at Tamworth: Excavations in the Bolebridge Street Area of Tamworth, Staffordshire, in 1971 and 1978* (London, 1992), p. 1.

26 Brigitte Buss, 'Ebbsfleet Saxon mill', *Current Archaeology*, 183 (2002), 93; Martin Welch, 'Anglo-Saxon Kent', in *The Archaeology of Kent to AD 800*, ed. J. H. Williams (Woodbridge, 2007), pp. 187–248; Alan Hardy, pers. comm., April 2008; S25.

27 R. Shoesmith, *Hereford City Excavations Volume 2: Excavations on and Close to the Defences* (London, 1982), p. 13.

agricultural goods.[28] Tamworth was another of these Mercian strongholds and, along with Winchcombe, it has evidence for undated fortifications that pre-date the tenth-century defences of Æthelflæd.[29] At what was to become another Mercian town, Northampton, the substantial timber and then stone halls built to the east of St Peter's church are suggestive of another royal estate centre that, judging from the scale of the buildings, was able to call upon significant resources.[30] A late-eighth or early-ninth-century iron-working site at Ramsbury, which became the seat of the newly created bishopric of the West Saxons in 909, was another probable villa regalis, drawing its iron ore from up to 30km away.[31] Note how this emergence of major estate centres, which commanded considerable resources, seems to be found in both Mercia and Wessex, and both within (e.g. Northampton, Tamworth) and without (e.g. Hereford, Ebbsfleet) England's central zone (Fig. 3.3).

The enclosure at Kings Meadow Lane in Higham Ferrers (Northamptonshire) may be another estate centre, as the large amounts of Ipswich Ware imported from East Anglia are suggestive of a high status site.[32] There is other evidence for enclosures dating to this period, such as Lower Slaughter in Gloucestershire where a possibly manorial enclosure next to the parish church dates from the eighth century.[33] The phenomenon of ninth- and tenth-century manorial enclosures is well known – such as Faccombe Netherton in Hampshire, Trowbridge and Yatesbury in Wiltshire and Goltho in Lincolnshire – whereas Draper has highlighted the importance of settlements with '-bury' place names, suggesting many were 'Middle Saxon' estate centres that may have been the catalyst for settlement nucleation, such as the '-bury' at Avebury which may actually refer to a manorial enclosure rather than the 'Late Saxon' *burh* postulated by Pollard and Reynolds.[34] Other 'Middle Saxon' enclosures include Bramford in Suffolk,

28 R. Shoesmith, *Hereford City Excavations Volume* 2; Alan Thomas and Andy Boucher, *Hereford City Excavations Volume 4: 1976–1990. Further Sites and Evolving Interpretations* (Hereford, 2002).

29 David Hill, 'The eighth-century urban landscape', in *Aethelbald and Offa: Two Eighth-Century Kings of Mercia*, eds David Hill and Margaret Worthington (Oxford, 2005), pp. 97–102; Gareth Williams, 'Military obligations and Mercian supremacy in the eighth century', in *Aethelbald and Offa: Two Eighth-Century Kings of Mercia*, eds Hill and Worthington, pp. 103–10.

30 John H. Williams, Michael Shaw and Varian Denham, *Middle Saxon Palaces at Northampton* (Northampton, 1985).

31 Jeremy Haslam, 'A Middle Saxon iron smelting site at Ramsbury, Wiltshire', *Medieval Archaeology*, 24 (1980), 1–68.

32 Hardy, Charles and Williams, *Death and Taxes*, p. 198.

33 D. Kenyon and M. Watts, 'An Anglo-Saxon enclosure at Copsehill Road, Lower Slaughter: excavations in 1999', *Transactions of the Bristol and Gloucestershire Archaeological Society*, 124 (2006), 73–110.

34 J. Fairbrother, *Faccombe Netherton: Excavations of a Saxon and Medieval Manorial Complex* (London, 1990); A. H. Graham and S. M. Davies, *Excavations in Trowbridge, Wiltshire, 1977 and 1986–1988* (Salisbury, 1993); Andrew Reynolds, 'Yatesbury', *Current Archaeology*, 171 (2000), 113–18; Guy Beresford, *Goltho: The Development of an Early Medieval Manor c.850–1150* (London, 1987); Simon Draper, *Landscape, Settlement*

Raunds in Northamptonshire and possibly Wicken Bonhunt in Essex (the plan of which is unfortunately incomplete).[35] Once again, this phenomenon seems to be found across much of southern England, both within the 'central province' and without.

There are other examples of great works in the 'Middle Saxon' period that reflect the resources – both in terms of materials and manpower – at the disposal of major landowners (Fig. 3.3). These include a series of impressive infrastructure developments such as causeways that have been known about for some time across the Thames at Oxford and linking Mersea Island to the mainland of Essex,[36] and another example that has recently been identified linking Glastonbury and Street in the Somerset Levels which dates to between the late seventh and the early ninth centuries,[37] and which was presumably constructed by Glastonbury Abbey. Other examples of major infrastructure developments of this period are frontier works such as Offa's Dyke and perhaps the Wansdyke that Reynolds and Langlands have recently argued may have marked the frontier between Wessex and Mercia at around the same time.[38]

It is not clear whether the Mercian fortresses at Hereford, Tamworth and Winchcombe contained much settlement other than a royal estate centre (see above) but there is growing evidence in eastern England for occupation as early as the eighth century beneath a number of medieval towns (e.g. Canterbury and Norwich).[39] In addition to the development of estate centres and the expenditure of resources on major infrastructure developments, there are other indications of the production of an agricultural surplus and increased economic activity generally during the 'Middle Saxon' period in the form of a series of major coastal/estuarine trading settlements – with 'wic' place names – at Southampton (*Hamwic*), London (*Lundenwic*), Ipswich and York, along with numerous lesser

and Society in Roman and Early Medieval Wiltshire (Oxford, 2006); Joshua Pollard and Andrew Reynolds, *Avebury: The Biography of a Landscape* (Stroud, 2002), p. 204.

35 Andrew Reynolds, *Later Anglo-Saxon England: Life and Landscape* (Stroud, 1999), pp. 141–4; A. Boddington, *Raunds Furnells: The Anglo-Saxon Church and Churchyard* (London, 1996); Keith Wade, 'A settlement site at Bonhunt Farm, Wicken Bonhunt, Essex', in *The Archaeology of Essex to AD 1500*, ed. David Buckley (London, 1980), pp. 96–102.

36 Brian Durham, 'Archaeological investigations at St Aldgates, Oxford', *Oxoniensia*, 42 (1977), 83–203; P. Crummy, J. Hillam and C. Crossan, 'Mersea Island: the Anglo-Saxon causeway', *Essex Archaeology and History*, 14 (1982), 77–86.

37 Based on radiocarbon dates 1250±50 BP (670–920 cal AD) from a wooden pile beneath the causeway, and 1320±50 BP (640–850 cal AD) from a strand deposit overlying the causeway: Richard Brunning, pers. comm., April 2008.

38 David Hill and Margaret Worthington, *Offa's Dyke* (Stroud, 2002); Andrew Reynolds and Alex Langlands, 'Social identities on the macro scale: a maximum view of Wansdyke', in *People and Space in the Early Middle Ages AD 300 – 1300*, eds W. Davies, G. Hassall and A. Reynolds (Turnhout, 2006), pp. 13–44.

39 Paul Bennett, Alison Hicks and Mark Houliston, 'Canterbury Whitefriars: "The Big Dig"', *Current Archaeology*, 185 (2003), 190–6; Brian Ayers, 'How Norwich began', *Current Archaeology*, 170 (2000), 48–51; Brian Ayers, 'The urban landscape', in *Medieval Norwich*, eds Carole Rawcliffe and Richard Wilson (London, 2004), pp. 1–29.

landing places around the coasts of Essex and Kent.[40] Within the hinterland of these 'emporia' there is other evidence for the growing importance of markets at this time. In various parts of eastern and southern England, metal detecting has produced large amounts of material from particular locations, which has given rise to the term 'productive sites'.[41] These have been interpreted as market places, and the complex of eighth-century pits recently excavated at Dorney, on the north bank of the Thames in Buckinghamshire, has been interpreted in a similar way due to the character of its pottery assemblage and lack of evidence for permanent structures.[42] In most cases these trading sites lie on the edges of kingdoms – Dorney, for example, is on the contested boundary between Mercia and Wessex, and Ipswich on the border between East Anglia and Essex – as do most of the very rich burials that are so characteristic of the early seventh century: Taplow, for example, is just upstream of Dorney; Sutton Hoo is close to the boundary of East Anglia and Essex (and near the trading site at Ipswich), while Prittlewell overlooks the Thames Estuary which formed the boundary between Essex and Kent.[43] All these 'wics' and other 'productive sites' would have been consumer sites both in terms of their populations being non-agriculturally productive, and their use of raw materials in craft activities such as smithing, textile production, bone/horn/antler working and jewellery manufacturing. Along with the goods that were traded with the Continent, this once again illustrates how productive the countryside was becoming.[44]

The eighth century also sees the increased circulation of coinage in the form of silver sceattas, the early form of pennies.[45] The distribution of many types is largely limited to the kingdoms within which they were produced, such as Series H and W in Wessex and Series R in East Anglia – suggesting that in part they are another reflection of increasing royal power and the economic hinterlands of their respective emporia. Others are found more widely, indicating that they

40 Keith Wade, 'Anglo-Saxon and medieval Ipswich', in *An Historical Atlas of Suffolk*, eds David Dymond and Edward Martin (Ipswich, 1989), pp. 158–9; John Naylor, *An Archaeology of Trade in Middle Saxon England* (Oxford, 2004).

41 John Newman, 'Wics, trade and the hinterlands – the Ipswich region', in *Anglo-Saxon Trading Centres: Beyond the Emporia*, ed. M. Anderton (Glasgow, 1999), pp. 4–23; Katharina Ulmschneider, *Markets, Minsters and Metal-Detectors: The Archaeology of Middle Saxon Lincolnshire and Hampshire Compared* (Oxford, 2000); Tim Pestell and Katharina Ulmschneider, eds, *Markets in Early Medieval Europe: Trade and 'Productive' Sites, 650–850* (Macclesfield, 2003).

42 Stuart Foreman, Jonathan Hiller and David Petts, *Gathering the People, Settling the Land. The Archaeology of the Middle Thames Landscape: Anglo-Saxon to Post Medieval* (Oxford, 2002).

43 Stephen Rippon, 'Focus or frontier? The significance of estuaries in the landscape of southern Britain', *Landscapes*, 8.i (2007), 23–38; Rippon, *Beyond the Medieval Village*, Fig. 5.2.

44 Jim Leary, *Tatberht's Lundenwic. Archaeological Excavations in Middle Saxon London* (London, 2004); Gordon Malcolm and David Bowsker, *Middle Saxon London: Excavations at the Royal Opera House 1989–99* (London, 2003).

45 Stewart Lyon, 'Anglo-Saxon numismatics', *British Numismatic Journal*, 72 (2003), 58–75.

were used in cross-border trade.[46] The quantity of sceattas found in rubbish deposits, on floor surfaces or simply as stray finds certainly suggests that they were in daily use, and in the 'productive sites' 'we are beginning to see the characterisation of quite a large number of Middle Anglo-Saxon places where coinage was regularly changing hands'.[47] So this is the prevailing view of the 'Middle Saxon' period: one that saw the emergence of increasingly stable and powerful kingdoms and monastic institutions, and a growing economy that was both stimulated by and sufficient to support increasing numbers of non-agriculturally productive people, including those in substantial coastal trading sites and inland markets. What is missing from this picture, however, is an understanding of the rural landscape that ultimately supported these other sectors of society.

Settlement Nucleation and Village Origins

The one aspect of the rural landscape in the 'Middle Saxon' period that is well known is the way in which the majority of excavated 'Early Saxon' settlements and cemeteries appear to have been abandoned around the late seventh century, in what has been called the 'Middle Saxon shuffle', as sites on lighter soils and higher ground were deserted in favour of richer soils in the valleys.[48] The idea of a sudden shift in settlement has been called into question, with Hamerow observing that many extensively excavated fifth- to seventh-century settlements show signs of having shifted their location over time, and that, as many settlements have not been completely investigated, their final phases may lie beyond the edge of the excavations.[49] At Bishopstone, for example, Mark Gardiner has observed that an isolated building to the south of the main settlement of post-

46 David Hinton, *Archaeology, Economy and Society: England from the Fifth to the Fifteenth Century* (London, 1990), Fig. 3.3; D. M. Metcalf, *Thrymsas and Sceattas in the Ashmolean Museum Oxford*, I (London, 1993); Newman, 'Wics, Trade and the Hinterlands', pp. 4–23; D. M. Metcalf, '"As easy as A, B, C": the mint places of early sceatta types in the South-East', *British Numismatic Journal*, 71 (2002), 34–48; D. M. Metcalf, 'Monetary circulation in England, *c*.675–*c*.710: the distribution patterns of series A, B, and C – and F', *British Numismatic Journal*, 74 (2004), 1–19; D. M. Metcalf, 'The first series of sceattas minted in Southern Wessex: series W', *British Numismatic Journal*, 75 (2005), 1–17; John Naylor, 'Mercian hegemony and the origins of series J sceattas: the case for Lindsey', *British Numismatic Journal*, 76 (2006), 159–70.

47 Hinton, *Archaeology, Economy and Society*, p. 54; Mark Blackburn, '"Productive sites" and the pattern of coin loss in England 600–1180', in *Markets in Early Medieval Europe*, eds Pestell and Ulmschneider, pp. 20–36.

48 e.g. Mucking in Essex, West Stow in Suffolk, Bishopstone in Sussex, Chalton in Hampshire: C. Arnold and P. Wardle, 'Early medieval settlement patterns in England', *Medieval Archaeology*, 25 (1981), 145–9; John Moreland, 'The significance of production in eighth-century England', in *The Long Eighth Century: Production, Distribution and Demand*, eds Hanson and Wickham, pp. 69–104.

49 Helena Hamerow, 'Settlement mobility and the "Middle Saxon shift": rural settlements and settlement patterns in Anglo-Saxon England', *Anglo-Saxon England*, 20 (1991), 1–17; Helena Hamerow, *Early Medieval Settlements: the Archaeology of Rural Communities in North-West Europe 400–900* (Oxford, 1996).

built halls has trench-built foundations and so is likely to be of 'Middle Saxon' date.[50] Mucking can also be reinterpreted as having seen occupation into the eighth century. The eastwards migration of the settlement has already been demonstrated by Hamerow, and if the site is placed in its wider context we see that from the fifth to the seventh centuries the focus of occupation shifted at least 1.2km, this being the distance from the centre of fifth-century occupation which includes the Linford Quarry site to the west of the main Mucking excavation, as far as the 'North Ring' site, excavated in 1978 separately from the main Mucking campaign, where the occupation is dated to the late seventh century.[51] It is also significant that a few sherds of Ipswich Ware were found within the latest excavated features, which if Blinkhorn's re-dating is correct takes the occupation of the settlement into the eighth century, as does the discovery of two early-eighth-century *sceattas* from immediately beyond the edge of the excavations (the precise location is not known).[52] Whether the settlement at Mucking was abandoned in the eighth century, or simply continued slowly migrating across the hillside, is unclear though at some stage it was replaced by an open field.[53]

West Stow has also produced small amounts of Ipswich Ware, suggesting its occupation extended into the eighth century, when it too was abandoned.[54] It was not alone in failing to survive beyond the eighth century. Elsewhere in East Anglia a series of extensive field-walking surveys and a long history of metal detectorists reporting their abundant finds have contributed to an emerging picture of dispersed settlement associated with fifth- to seventh-century material being replaced by fewer settlements associated with 'Middle Saxon' Ipswich Ware.[55] That these Ipswich Ware scatters are usually found in association with parish churches raises an important issue: did settlement coalesce around an existing church, or was the church added later to a pre-existing settlement? Archaeological and documentary evidence from across England suggests that

50 Gabor Thomas, 'Bishopstone: in the shadow of Rookery Hill', *Current Archaeology*, 196 (2005), 184–90.

51 The main excavations at Mucking are well known: see Helena Hamerow, *Excavations at Mucking, Volume 1: the Anglo-Saxon Settlement* (London, 1993). The other excavations in this area are less well known: for the Linford Quarry see K. Barton, 'Settlements of the Iron Age and pagan Saxon burials at Linford Essex', *Transactions of the Essex Archaeological Society*, 3rd series, 1.ii (1962), 57–102; for the North Ring see D. Bond, *Excavation at the North Ring, Mucking, Essex: A Late Bronze Age Enclosure, East Anglian Archaeology*, 43 (1988), 45–51.

52 Paul Blinkhorn, '"Of cabbages and kings": production, trade and consumption in Middle Saxon England', in *Anglo-Saxon Trading Centres: Beyond the Emporia*, ed. Anderton, pp. 4–23. I would like to thank Helena Hamerow and Michael Metcalf for the information about these sceattas.

53 Rippon, *Beyond the Medieval Village*, Fig. 5.12.

54 Stanley West, *West Stow, the Anglo-Saxon Village*, *East Anglian Archaeology*, 24 (1985).

55 e.g. Peter Wade-Martins, *Fieldwork and Excavation on Village Sites in Launditch Hundred, Norfolk*, *East Anglian Archaeology*, 10 (1980); Alan Davison, *Six Deserted Villages in Norfolk*, *East Anglian Archaeology*, 44 (1988); Alan Davison, *The Evolution of Settlement in Three Norfolk Parishes*, *East Anglian Archaeology*, 49 (1990).

burials within minster churches started in the eighth century as the earlier trend for kings to be buried within churches trickled down to the lower levels of society.[56] Churchyard burial for the whole population is generally thought to have begun much later, perhaps around the tenth century, when former minster territories started to disintegrate in the face of manorial churches developing to serve the wider local community, forcing people to bring their dead to these central locations: this led to the abandonment of scattered rural cemeteries and 'the tenth century may have been the first time when English people at large were told where they had to be buried'.[57] This timescale for churchyard burial is based largely on documentary sources, such as a law code of Æthelstan of *c.*930 that refers to burial within 'a hallowed graveyard', although it receives some support from archaeological evidence. At well-known sites such as Wharram Percy in Yorkshire and Raunds Furnells in Northamptonshire, excavations have shown that churchyard burial did indeed begin around the tenth century, but at Yarnton in Oxfordshire it appears that people started burying their dead in small family groups near to their homes in the 'Middle Saxon' period before the creation of centralized, communal churchyards.[58] If we return to East Anglia, the evidence from field-walking shows that some of the new 'Middle Saxon' settlements were abandoned quite quickly, for they lack 'Late Saxon' pottery, as occupation drifted towards the large greens and commons that were so characteristic of the East Anglian landscape. This left the churches in splendid isolation and suggests that widespread church foundation was contemporary with the 'Middle Saxon' settlement: if a church was founded in the tenth century it would surely have been located within what was the currently occupied settlement, not the abandoned 'Middle Saxon' site.[59] It would appear, therefore, that in East Anglia around the eighth century a dispersed settlement pattern was replaced by a more nucleated one, and that this nucleation may have occurred around early churches.

In the East Midlands early field-walking surveys consistently produced evidence for a dispersed settlement pattern associated with 'Early and Middle Saxon' pottery, but nothing later.[60] This implies that the replacement of these scattered farmsteads with nucleated villages occurred slightly later in the East

56 John Blair, *The Church in Anglo-Saxon Society* (Oxford, 2005), pp. 228–9.

57 Blair, *The Church in Anglo-Saxon Society*, p. 463; and see John Blair, *Anglo-Saxon Oxfordshire* (Stroud, 1994), 72–3; Dawn Hadley, 'Burial practices in the Northern Danelaw, *c.*650–1100', *Northern History*, 35.ii (1994), 199–216; Dawn Hadley, 'Burial Practices in Northern England in the Later Anglo-Saxon Period', in *Burial in Early Medieval England and Wales*, eds Sam Lucy and Andrew Reynolds (Leeds, 2002), pp. 209–28; Hamerow, *Early Medieval Settlements: the Archaeology of Rural Communities in North-West Europe 400–900*, p. 123.

58 R. D. Bell and M. Beresford, *Wharram Percy: the Church of St Martin* (London, 1987); A. Boddington, *Raunds Furnells: The Anglo-Saxon Church and Churchyard* (London, 1996); Hey, *Yarnton: Saxon and Medieval Settlement and Landscape*.

59 e.g. Mileham: see Hoggett in this volume, chapter 11.

60 Glenn Foard, 'Systematic fieldwalking and the investigation of Saxon settlement in Northamptonshire', *World Archaeology*, 9 (1978), 357–74; Christopher Taylor, *Village and Farmstead* (London, 1983).

Midlands, and sometime during the period in which 'Middle Saxon' pottery was in use, and so it is curious that the prevailing view of many is that village formation dates to sometime after the mid ninth century.[61] Dyer, for example, suggests that 'the first phase of occupation in many villages came no earlier than the eleventh century', but that 'some of the main elements of the common-field system were functioning in the tenth century'.[62] Part of the problem here is that different scholars have been examining different datasets. The field-walking evidence points to the abandonment of dispersed settlement patterns in the East Midlands before 'Late Saxon' (*c.*850–1150) pottery was in use, giving a *terminus ante quem* of *c.*850 for nucleation. Yet material from within medieval villages – and mostly deserted medieval villages at that – only dates from the 'Late Saxon' period onwards, giving a *terminus post quem* of *c.*850 for these village origins. The tenth-century date for open fields is based on a different dataset again – the features described in the boundary clauses of Anglo-Saxon charters – but this body of evidence also only shows that open fields existed by that date, another *terminus ante quem*: they may well have existed earlier but were simply not documented.[63]

Fortunately, new strands of evidence are starting to reconcile the apparent difference in the dates when the dispersed settlement patterns were abandoned, and villages appear to have formed. More recent field-walking has confirmed that the scattered farmsteads that were once spread across the East Midlands landscape were indeed occupied into the 'Middle Saxon' period but no later.[64] There is also growing evidence that, in some areas at least, medieval villages were first occupied in the 'Middle Saxon' period, such as Sempringham and Sleaford on the Lincolnshire fen-edge, and many of the Fenland villages.[65] The colonization of the Norfolk Marshland is particularly instructive as a line of

61 e.g. Lewis, Mitchell-Fox and Dyer, *Village, Hamlet and Field*, p. 198.

62 Dyer, *Making a Living in the Middle Ages*, pp. 21, 23; also see C. C. Taylor, 'Nucleated settlement: a view from the frontier', *Landscape History*, 24 (2002), 53–72, and Oosthuizen, 'The Anglo-Saxon kingdom of Mercia and the origins and distribution of common fields', 153–80.

63 H. S. A. Fox, 'Approaches to the adoption of the Midland system', in *The Origins of Open Field Agriculture*, ed. Trevor Rowley (London, 1981), pp. 64–111; Hooke, *The Landscape of Anglo-Saxon England*, pp. 121–7.

64 Peter Liddle, 'The archaeology of Anglo-Saxon Leicestershire', in *Anglo-Saxon Landscapes in the East Midlands*, ed. J. Bourne (Leicester, 1996), pp. 1–10; N. Cooper, *The Archaeology of Rutland Water: Excavations at Empingham in the Gwash Valley, Rutland, 1967–73 and 1990* (Leicester, 2000); N. Cooper and V. Priest, 'Sampling a medieval village in a day: the "Big Dig" investigation at Great Easton, Leicestershire', *Medieval Settlement Research Group Annual Report*, 18 (2000), 53–56; P. Bowman, 'Villages and their territories: Parts I and II', in *Leicestershire Landscapes*, eds P. Bowman and P. Liddle (Leicester, 2004), pp. 105–36; Richard Knox, 'The Anglo-Saxons in Leicestershire and Rutland', in *Leicestershire Landscapes,* eds Bowman and Liddle, pp. 95–104.

65 Peter Hayes, 'Roman to Saxon in the South Lincolnshire fens', *Antiquity*, 62 (1988), 321–6; Peter Hayes and Tom Lane, *The Fenland Survey, Number 6: Lincolnshire Survey, The South West Fens*, *East Anglian Archaeology*, 55 (1992); Tom Lane and Peter Hayes, 'Moving boundaries in the fens of South Lincolnshire', in *Flatlands and Wetlands*, ed. Julie Gardiner, *East Anglian Archaeology*, 50 (1993), 58–70.

settlements associated with 'Middle Saxon' pottery was established close to the contemporary coast as part of what appears to have been a planned sub-division of this previously largely unsettled landscape: clearly, in this region, and at this time, new settlements were created in a nucleated as opposed to a dispersed form.[66]

This evidence from Fenland and the Lincolnshire fen-edge is largely from the field-walking of deserted or shrunken settlements and chance finds from small-scale observations within still-occupied sites. However, this pattern of 'Middle Saxon' occupation beneath villages is increasingly being supported by larger-scale development-led excavations, carried out in accordance with PPG16 (government's Planning Policy Guidance Note 16), within vacant plots in still-occupied villages. A review of recently published work in Cambridgeshire provides an example. Field-walking confirms that in the fifth to eighth centuries there was a dispersed settlement pattern, but that this scatter of farmsteads was then swept away and replaced with open fields.[67] One example is Gamlingay where excavations have shown that a settlement associated with 'Early to Middle Saxon' pottery (including Maxey and Ipswich wares) was abandoned by the mid ninth century as 'Late Saxon' pottery was absent.[68] At West Fen Road in Ely large-scale excavations have shown that a village-like settlement was laid out in the early eighth century, and even if this was a somewhat atypical settlement – associated with the nearby monastery founded in *c.*673 – it still shows that the concept of planned, nucleated settlements surrounded by open fields existed in this region at the time.[69] Excavations within still-occupied Cambridgeshire villages are also pointing to their originating as substantial nucleated settlements during the eighth century – for example, Cottenham, Hinxton, Cherry Hinton and Chesterton.[70] 'Middle Saxon' pottery has also been recovered from the vil-

66 R. J. Silvester, *The Fenland Survey, Number 3: Norfolk Survey, Marshland and the Nar Valley*, *East Anglian Archaeology*, 45 (1988); Stephen Rippon, *The Transformation of Coastal Wetlands* (London, 2000), p. 174.

67 e.g. Caxton: Susan Oosthuizen, 'New light on the origins of open-field farming', 165–95; Cardinal Distribution Park, in Godmanchester: C. Gibson and J. Murray, 'An Anglo-Saxon settlement at Godmanchester, Cambridgeshire', *Anglo-Saxon Studies in Archaeology and History*, 12 (2003), 136–217; Haslingfield: Susan Oosthuizen, 'Medieval greens and moats in the central province', 73–88; Whittlesford: C. C. Taylor, 'Whittlesford: the study of a river-edge village', in *The Rural Settlements of Medieval England*, ed. M. Aston, D. Austin and C. Dyer (Oxford, 1989), pp. 207–30.

68 J. Murray and T. McDonald, 'Excavations at Station Road, Gamlingay, Cambridgeshire', *Anglo-Saxon Studies in Archaeology and History*, 13 (2005), 173–330.

69 R. Mortimer, R. Regan and S. Lucy, *The Saxon and Medieval Settlement at West Fen Road, Ely: The Ashwell Site*, *East Anglian Archaeology*, 110 (2005).

70 R. Mortimer, 'Village development and ceramic sequence: the Middle to Late Saxon village at Lordship Lane, Cottenham, Cambridgeshire', *Proceedings of the Cambridge Antiquarian Society*, 39 (2000), 5–33; A. Taylor, 'Field-work in Cambridgeshire: October 1993–September 1994', *Proceedings of the Cambridgeshire Antiquarian Society*, 83 (1994), 167–76; Taylor, 'Nucleated settlement: a view from the frontier', 53–72; C. Cessford, 'The manor of Hintona: the origins and development of Church End, Cherry Hinton', *Proceedings of the Cambridgeshire Antiquarian Society*, 94 (2005), 51–72; C. Cessford,

lages at Fordham, Whaddon and Willingham.[71] This gradually accumulating body of evidence from Cambridgeshire and the Fenland is therefore starting to show that the abandonment of dispersed settlement patterns and the earliest occupation within medieval villages both date to around the eighth century, as Brown and Foard have argued was also the case in Northamptonshire, where excavations are confirming evidence from field-walking that this 'coalescence' settlement did indeed occur within the 'Middle Saxon' period.[72] The same is seen at Catholme, in the Trent Valley just north of Tamworth, where a relatively stable – unlike sites such as Mucking – settlement was structured around a series of trackways and enclosures that had a distinctly village-like feel.[73] Based on a series of radiocarbon dates, occupation appears to have begun around the seventh century and ended around the ninth century, afterwards the site at some stage becoming part of an open field.

This 'Middle Saxon' date for the initial nucleation of settlement is appreciably earlier than Lewis *et al.* and Dyer have recently argued, although in one sense their view that our medieval villages were creations of the tenth to twelfth centuries may be right.[74] The archaeological evidence from Cambridgeshire summarized above shows that an increasing number of villages are being found to have 'Middle Saxon' occupation within them, and that these settlements appear to have replaced an earlier dispersed scatter of isolated farmsteads spread across the surrounding landscape. It seems, however, that the plans of these 'Middle Saxon' settlements were far from stable, and that it was only several centuries later that the present form of the villages developed. In Cottenham, for example, the cluster of settlement enclosures that developed during the eighth century was then abandoned as the focus of occupation shifted to the south where a radially arranged series of tenement plots developed that formed the basis of the modern village plan. At Hinxton, the group of 'Middle Saxon' farmsteads was replaced in the eleventh century by the present planned settlement, while at Cherry Hinton, the 'Middle Saxon' occupation was replaced in the late ninth or early tenth century by a large, possibly manorial, enclosure associated with a church and cemetery containing 670 east-to-west-oriented inhumations. As Brown and Foard have also argued for Northamptonshire, villages in their later

'The origins and early development of Chesterton', *Proceedings of the Cambridgeshire Antiquarian Society*, 93 (2004), 125–42.

71 Oosthuizen, 'Saxon commons in South Cambridgeshire', 93–100; Mortimer, 'Village development and ceramic sequence', 5–33; Taylor, 'Nucleated settlement: a view from the frontier', 53–72.

72 Tony Brown and Glenn Foard, 'The Saxon landscape: a regional perspective', in *The Archaeology of Landscape*, eds Paul Everson and Tom Williamson (Manchester, 1998), pp. 67–94; Hardy, Charles and Williams, *Death and Taxes*; for an example see S. Ford, 'The excavation of a Saxon settlement and a mesolithic flint scatter at Northampton Road, Brixworth, Northamptonshire', *Northamptonshire Archaeology*, 26 (1996), 79–108; for an overview see Rippon, *Beyond the Medieval Village*.

73 Stuart Losco-Bradley and Gavin Kinsley, *Catholme: An Anglo-Saxon Settlement on the Trent Gravels in Staffordshire* (Nottingham, 2002).

74 Lewis, Mitchell-Fox and Dyer, *Village, Hamlet and Field*; Dyer, *Making a Living in the Middle Ages*.

medieval form may indeed have originated in the 'Late Saxon' period, a process that appears to have occurred several centuries after the initial nucleation of settlement.[75]

Agricultural Intensification in the East and South Midlands and East Anglia

A range of evidence suggests that the physical restructuring of the landscape in parts of southern England was part of a far wider intensification of how it was being exploited, and the crucial evidence for this comes from a range of palaeoenvironmental data that has been all too often neglected by early medieval scholars who are generally more comfortable with historical and linguistic evidence. In Oxfordshire, for example, extensive survey and excavations within the former common fields of Cassington and Yarnton have revealed an unstructured 'Early Saxon' landscape of dispersed settlement that was joined in the 'Middle Saxon' period by a more compact and structured settlement – one that starts to have the characteristics of a village – immediately to the south of what became the church/manor complex. This period also saw significant agricultural intensification with increased arable production, the introduction of new crops, the more intensive use of the floodplain for pasture and meadow, and the manuring of common fields that certainly existed by the tenth century when all the earlier dispersed settlements had already been abandoned.[76] In the Thames Valley generally there was an increase in alluviation from around the eighth and ninth centuries, and the pollen sequence at Snelsmore on the nearby Berkshire Downs shows an increase in cereal cultivation around the ninth century.[77] In the Brue Valley, south of Glastonbury, the formation of freshwater peat was replaced by alluvial sedimentation around the seventh to ninth centuries, suggesting increased cultivation and/or autumn ploughing within the river's catchment of central Somerset.[78] There also appears to have been in increase in alluviation in the nearby Yeo valley at around the same time,[79] while at Aller Farm on the Blackdown Hills in southern Somerset there was an increase in cereal cultiva-

[75] Brown and Foard, 'The Saxon landscape: a regional perspective', pp. 67–94.

[76] Hey, *Yarnton: Saxon and Medieval Settlement and Landscape*.

[77] Mark Robinson, 'Environment, archaeology and alluvium on the river gravels of the South Midlands', in *Alluvial Archaeology in Britain*, eds S. Needham and M. G. Macklin (Oxford, 1992), pp. 197–208; P. V. Waton, 'Man's impact on the chalklands: some new pollen evidence', in *Archaeological Aspects of Woodland Ecology*, eds M. Bell and S. Limbrey (Oxford, 1982), pp. 75–91.

[78] Based on a radiocarbon date of 1247±34 BP (cal AD 679–872): Gerrard Aalbersberg, 'The Alluvial Fringes of the Somerset Levels' (unpublished PhD thesis, University of Exeter, 1999).

[79] N. Thew, 'Geology and geoarchaeology in the Yeo Valley at Ilchester', in *Ilchester Volume 2: Archaeology, Excavations and Fieldwork to 1984*, ed. Peter Leach (Sheffield, 1994), pp. 169–70.

tion from around the early ninth century.[80] In Northamptonshire, the palaeoeconomic evidence from Raunds and West Cotton suggests broad continuity in agriculture during the 'Early and Middle Saxon' periods, with an increase in alluviation on the floodplain around the eighth or ninth centuries, while preserved cereal remains suggest that open field farming had been introduced by the 'Late Saxon' period.[81]

In East Anglia, the well-dated pollen sequence from the Oakley palaeochannel at Scole suggests that around the eighth century (based on a radiocarbon date calibrated to AD 670–820) there was a period of agricultural intensification with an increase in cereal pollen, the emergence of viticulture and the cultivation of hemp, the latter also being seen at Diss and Old Buckenham (see below).[82] At Micklemere there was also a marked increase in cereal pollen (associated with a calibrated radiocarbon date of AD 588–972) at the same time as a high influx of minerogenic sediment, implying increased soil erosion in the catchment.[83] It is possible that other pollen sequences from northern East Anglia show a period of agricultural intensification around the 'Middle Saxon' period, although the dating evidence is not as good: at Old Buckenham Mere there is a decline in oak woodland dated '*c.*800AD', while at Diss Mere, Old Buckenham Mere and Sea Mere there is a marked increase in cereal at around the sixth century.[84] At Hockham Mere a similar expansion in cultivation is dated to around the ninth century.[85] Great care should be taken with such poor dating, but along with the well-dated sequences at Scole and Micklemere, it does appear that there was

80 J. Hatton and C. Caseldine, 'Vegetation change and land-use history during the first millennium AD at Aller Farm, East Devon as indicated by pollen analysis', *Proceedings of the Devon Archaeological Society*, 49 (1991), 115–21.

81 G. D. Keevill, 'Life on the edge: archaeology and alluvium at Redlands Farm, Stanwick, Raunds', in *Alluvial Archaeology in Britain*, eds Needham and Macklin, pp. 177–85; G. Campbell, 'The preliminary archaeobotanical results from Anglo-Saxon West Cotton and Raunds', in *Environment and Economy in Anglo-Saxon England*, ed. J. Rackham (York, 1994), pp. 65–82; A. G. Brown, 'The environment of the Raunds area', in *Raunds Area Survey*, ed. S. Parry (Oxford, 2006), pp. 19–30; A. G. Brown, 'Colluvial and alluvial response to land use change in Midland England: an integrated geoarchaeological approach', *Geomorphology*, 108 (1–2), 92–106.

82 P. E. J. Wiltshire, 'Palynological Assessment of a Mire Peat Sequence in the Eriswell Valley, Suffolk' (unpublished report for the Ministry of Defence, 1999).

83 Peter Murphy, 'The Anglo-Saxon landscape and rural economy: some results from sites in East Anglia and Essex', in *Environment and Economy in Anglo-Saxon England*, ed. Rackham, pp. 23–39.

84 H. Godwin, 'Studies in the post-glacial history of British vegetation, 15: organic deposits at Old Buckenham Mere, Norfolk', *New Phytologist*, 67 (1968), 95–107; S. M. Peglar, S. C. Fitz and H. J. B. Birks, 'Vegetation and land-use history at Diss, Norfolk, UK', *Journal of Ecology*, 77 (1989), 203–22; R. E. Simms, 'Man and vegetation in Norfolk', in *The Effect of Man on the Landscape: The Lowland Zone*, eds S. Limbrey and J. Evans (London, 1978), pp. 57–62.

85 Simms, 'Man and vegetation in Norfolk', pp. 57–62; K. Bennett, 'Devensian Late-Glacial and Flandrian vegetational history at Hockham Mere, Norfolk, England, I: pollen percentages and concentrations', *New Phytologist*, 95 (1983), 457–87; K. Bennett, 'Devensian Late-Glacial and Flandrian vegetational history at Hockham Mere, Norfolk, England, II: pollen accumulation rates', *New Phytologist*, 95 (1983), 489–504.

an intensification in landscape use at about the same time as the field-walking evidence suggests that dispersed settlement patterns were being abandoned in favour of nucleated settlements.

Agricultural Intensification in South-West England

So far discussion of the landscape of southern England has focused on the East Midlands and East Anglia, where it is argued that there was a nucleation of settlement around the eighth century. Unfortunately, similar archaeological techniques cannot be used in some other regions as the early medieval period is aceramic (i.e. pottery was not in widespread use), and in such areas radiocarbon-dated palaeoenvironmental sequences are therefore all the more important. In Devon, a series of pollen sequences from around Rackenford (Middle North Combe, Hares Down, Lobbs Bog and Windmill Rough) and the Clyst Valley (Broadclyst Moor, Hellings Park and Mosshayne) in mid Devon, the Blackdown Hills to the east (Bywood, Greenway, Middleton and Mosshayne) and the southern fringes of Exmoor to the north (Ansteys Combe, Gourte Mires and Long Breach) straddle the whole period from late prehistory through to the present day, and what follows is a summary of the detailed reports published elsewhere.[86]

Between the fourth and sixth centuries AD there is very little significant change in any of these pollen records, suggesting continuity at the end of the Roman period in an essentially pastoral landscape, with no evidence of woodland regeneration. Around the seventh to eighth centuries, however, many of these sequences do show significant changes in the local land use. At this time in the central lowlands of Devon, for example, a small peat bog at Hellings Park in the Loxbrook Valley, in Broadclyst north-east of Exeter, first saw the appearance of cereals and the weeds of disturbed ground, alongside an increase in grass and herbaceous species, and although this change in land use does not feature at nearby Mosshayne, or Bywood on the Blackdown Hills, this is because those peat sequences show the continuous presence of cereal cultivation in close prox-

86 For Rackenford and the southern fringes of Exmoor see: Fyfe, Brown and Rippon, 'Mid to Late-Holocene vegetation history of Greater Exmoor, UK: estimating the spatial extent of human-induced vegetation change', 215–32; Fyfe, Brown and Rippon, 'Characterising the Late Prehistoric, "Romano-British" and medieval landscape, and dating the emergence of a regionally distinct agricultural system in South West Britain', 1699–714; Fyfe and Rippon, 'A landscape in transition? Palaeoenvironmental evidence for the end of the "Romano-British" period in South-West England', pp. 33–42; Rippon, Fyfe and Brown, 'Beyond villages and open fields', 31–70. For the Clyst Valley and the Blackdown Hills see S. Hawkins, 'Vegetation History and Land-Use Change in the Blackdown Hills, Devon, UK' (unpublished report, Community Landscapes Project, University of Exeter, 2005); S. Hawkins, 'Vegetation History and Land-Use Change in the Clyst Valley, Devon, UK' (unpublished report, Community Landscapes Project, University of Exeter, 2005). All this palaeoenvironmental evidence is discussed further in Rippon, *Beyond the Medieval Village*, chapter 4.

imity to the pollen sites ever since the Roman period. Other sites in the Blackdown Hills, however, do show significant changes in land use. At Middleton, the stratigraphy within this valley-side mire changed from an organic clay to herbaceous peat. This may have been the result of erosion caused by local woodland clearance, reflected in the pollen sequence by a marked decline in trees and an influx of pine, which led to waterlogging of the site and the consequent growth of sedges and mosses; wheat/oats appear soon after. An increase in cereals and a decline in woodland at nearby Greenway may also have occurred at this time. Around Rackenford, in mid Devon, the evidence for a change in agricultural practice is especially clear around the eighth century with an increase in cereals, herbaceous taxa associated with arable cultivation and improved pasture. At Middle North Combe, Lobbs Bog and Windmill Rough the change is characterized by the appearance of significant amounts of cereal pollen, while at nearby Hares Down there is also an increase in heather alongside a further decline in *Alnus* (alder), suggesting the removal of streamside wet woodland.

Due to the aceramic nature of the early medieval period in South-West England, and the predominantly pastoral land use today, we will never be able to study the development of settlement using the techniques of field-walking and excavation that have been deployed so successfully in East Anglia and the East Midlands. What these palaeoenvironmental studies do show, however, is that around the eighth century there was a significant, and widespread, intensification in land use, which it has been argued elsewhere was related to the development of a new form of rotational agriculture known as convertible husbandry.[87] An analysis of the historic landscape suggests that the medieval countryside in this region was characterized by a dispersed settlement pattern of small hamlets and isolated farmsteads, associated with complex field systems that, while containing some small-scale open fields, also had large areas of closes held in severalty and unenclosed common land.[88] There is no evidence that this region ever saw the transformation of the landscape seen in England's central zone – where villages and open fields were created – yet there was still a significant change in how the landscape was exploited.

[87] Rippon, Fyfe and Brown, 'Beyond villages and open fields', 31–70.

[88] Martin Gillard, 'The Medieval Landscape of the Exmoor Region: Enclosure and Settlement in an Upland Fringe' (unpublished thesis, University of Exeter, 2002); Peter Herring, 'Cornish strip fields', in *Medieval Devon and Cornwall: Shaping an Ancient Countryside*, ed. Sam Turner (Macclesfield, 2006), pp. 44–77; Peter Herring, 'Cornish medieval fields, a case-study: Brown Willy', in *Medieval Devon and Cornwall: Shaping an Ancient Countryside*, ed. Sam Turner (Macclesfield, 2006), pp. 78–103; Lucy Ryder, 'Change and Continuity: A Study in the Historic Landscape of Devon' (unpublished thesis, University of Exeter, 2006); Rippon, *Beyond the Medieval Village*; Stephen Rippon, Peter Claughton and Chris Smart, *Mining in a Medieval Landscape: The Royal Silver Mines of the Tamar Valley* (Exeter, 2009).

The Wider Landscape in the 'Long Eighth Century'

The increasing intensity with which the landscape was being exploited from the late seventh century onwards manifests itself in a range of ways in addition to agriculture (Fig. 3.3). From the late seventh century there is documentary evidence for landed estates including fish weirs, such as Ombersley in Worcestershire.[89] Although there is no physical evidence for fishtraps of this date in the Severn, structures of eighth- to ninth-century date have been recorded elsewhere around the coastline of southern Britain, and in major rivers such as the Trent and the Thames.[90] An arrangement of timbers in a stream channel at Anslow's Cottage, near Burghfield in Berkshire, may also represent a seventh- or eighth-century fishtrap.[91] The increased intensity with which this new food source was being exploited suggests that either a growing population was placing increasing pressure on landed resources, or that dietary tastes were changing, while the ability to construct and maintain what were substantial timber structures is another example of the resources commanded by 'Middle Saxon' estate owners. One concentration of fishtraps lies in the Blackwater Estuary in Essex, including two off Mersea Island that are very similar to well-dated examples at Collins Creek, the Nass in Tollesbury and Sales Point off Bradwell (*Othona*).[92] In the late seventh century there was another significant feat of engineering when an artificial causeway known as the The Strood was built, connecting Mersea Island to the mainland (see above). A monastery is recorded on Mersea in the early eleventh century, and such is the scarcity of pre-Conquest charters for the East Saxon kingdom that there is no reason this church should not date back to the eighth century[93] and be responsible for the fishery as well.

Relatively stable estates are another important aspect of the control over resources that was emerging around the eighth century. There has been much debate about the potential survival of Romano-British estates into the medieval period, and while a case can be made for certain locations within the landscape maintaining an importance – such as the reoccupied hillfort at Cadbury

89 H. P. R. Finberg, *The Early Charters of the West Midlands* (Leicester, 1972); S. Godbold and R. C. Turner, 'Medieval fishtraps in the Severn Estuary', *Medieval Archaeology*, 38 (1994), 19–54.

90 P. M. Losco-Bradley and C. R. Salisbury, 'A Saxon and a Norman fish weir at Colwick, Nottinghamshire', in *Medieval Fish, Fisheries and Fishponds in England*, ed. M. Aston (Oxford, 1988), pp. 329–54; N. Cohen, 'Boundaries and settlement: the role of the River Thames', *Anglo-Saxon Studies in Archaeology and History*, 12 (2003), 9–20; see Peter Murphy in this volume, chapter 12.

91 C. A. Butterworth and S. J. Lobb, *Excavations in the Burghfield Area, Berkshire: Developments in the Bronze Age and Saxon Landscapes* (Salisbury, 1992).

92 R. L Hall and C. P. Clarke, 'A Saxon inter-tidal timber fish weir at Collins Creek in the Blackwater Estuary', *Essex Archaeology and History*, 31 (2000), 125–46; see Peter Murphy in this volume, chapter 12.

93 Nina Crummy, 'Mersea Island: the 11th-century boundaries', *Essex Archaeology and History*, 14 (1982), 87–93; P. Crummy, J. Hillam and C. Crossan, 'Mersea Island: the Anglo-Saxon causeway', *Essex Archaeology and History*, 14 (1982), 77–86.

Congresbury that lies adjacent to a substantial Romano-British settlement, a possible villa[94] – there is no unequivocal evidence that the boundaries of fourth-century estates have survived in anything more than very localized cases. In the fifth to seventh centuries southern Britain was probably divided between a series of large autonomous or semi-autonomous tribal areas or folk-groups that Latin authors dubbed *regiones*.[95] As more stratified societies evolved from around the seventh century, these territories developed into what Dyer calls 'great estates' that were the property of the king, who initially granted some of them to the church or his major followers for the duration of an individual life.[96] These 'great estates' were commonly assessed as fifty to a hundred hides, and covered hundreds of square kilometres. They were based in fertile agricultural areas (the *inland*), often in river valleys, and extended out into adjacent environments that may have supported specialist settlements, for example in areas of wetland, woodland and upland summer pasture (the *warland*). Their boundaries were often natural features such as rivers or streams, or ran through areas of unenclosed 'waste' in higher areas (i.e. along watersheds). These territories have also been variously described as 'river estates',[97] 'multiple estates',[98] 'federal estates',[99] 'federative estates'[100] and 'large terrains'.[101] These early estates may have been coterminous with the territories (*parochiae*) of seventh- or eighth-century minster churches which some have argued were founded on royal vills, although Blair has recently questioned this on the basis that there were no stable royal centres during the seventh and eighth centuries.[102]

From the late seventh century these great estates started to fragment as kings granted land in perpetuity to the church (from the 670s) and noble families (from the 770s) as *bookland*. The stability afforded by the perpetual ownership of estates would have created a new security that would have made investment in improving the productivity of the landscape far more worthwhile. Some of

94 Philip Rahtz, Ann Woodward, Ian Burrow, Anne Everton, Lorna Watts, Peter Leach, Susan Hirst, Peter Fowler and Keith Gardner, *Cadbury Congresbury 1968–73: A Late/Post-Roman Hilltop Settlement in Somerset* (Oxford, 1992).

95 S. Bassett, 'In search of the origins of the Anglo-Saxon kingdoms', in *The Origins of Anglo-Saxon Kingdoms*, ed. S. Bassett (Leicester, 1989), pp. 3–27; Hooke, *The Landscape of Anglo-Saxon England*, pp. 46–54.

96 Dyer, *Making a Living in the Middle Ages*, p. 27.

97 W. G. Hoskins, 'The making of the agrarian landscape', in *Devonshire Studies*, ed. W. G. Hoskins and H. P. R. Finberg (London, 1952), pp. 289–334; Alan Everitt, *Continuity and Colonization: The Evolution of Kentish Settlement* (Leicester, 1986); Tom Williamson, *The Origins of Norfolk* (Manchester, 1993).

98 G. R. J. Jones, 'Multiple estates and early settlement', in *English Medieval Settlement*, ed. P. H. Sawyer (London, 1979), pp. 9–34; G. R. J. Jones, 'Multiple estates perceived', *Journal of Historical Geography*, 11.iv (1985), 339–51.

99 Lewis, Mitchell-Fox and Dyer, *Village, Hamlet and Field*, pp. 9, 20.

100 John Blair, *Early Medieval Surrey* (Stroud, 1991), 24.

101 Andrew Fleming, 'Prehistoric landscapes and the quest for territorial pattern', in *The Archaeology of Landscape*, eds Everson and Williamson, pp. 42–66.

102 Richard Morris, *Churches in the Landscape* (London, 1989); Hooke, *The Landscape of Anglo-Saxon England*, p. 70; Blair, *The Church in Anglo-Saxon Society*, pp. 266–90.

those estates received by the church survived intact, forming vast territories of fifty hides or more in the Domesday Survey, although others appear to have been sub-divided into smaller holdings typically of five or six hides. Secular estates were particularly prone to continued fragmentation through partible inheritance, and together this sub-division led to the formation of the multiplicity of manors that came to form the tenurial framework of post-Conquest England.[103] What is crucial here, however, is the emergence of stable ownership through *bookland*, being yet another feature of the 'long eighth century' that encouraged investment and innovation, which in turn were essential if the growing burdens placed on landowners to provide for obligations such as borough-work and bridge-work were to be met. In another indication of the territorial stability that started to emerge around the eighth century, Reynolds has demonstrated that from this time there is increasing evidence for 'execution cemeteries' which show a very strong relationship to hundred boundaries.[104] Pantos has shown a similar correlation between early medieval assembly places and parish/township, hundred/wapentake and county boundaries:[105] both the meeting places and boundaries tend to occur in 'neutral territory', and taken together they contribute to the impression that the landscape was starting to be divided up into relatively stable territories.

Conclusions

This paper has sought to explore the context for the emergence of marked regional variation in landscape character that developed across England over the course of the medieval period. That champion countryside of villages and open fields emerged across England's central zone is well known, but the origins of these aberrant forms of landscape management have dominated research into the medieval countryside at the expense of the regions to the east and west. Oosthuizen's recent paper (2007) attributing both village formation and the laying out of open fields to the emergence of the kingdom of Mercia is yet another example of the highly Midland-centric perspective that has dominated recent scholarship, and this needs to be challenged. Firstly, and as Oosthuizen's (2007, fig. 2) own maps show, common fields occur far more widely than Mercia, and around half of Mercia never saw the development of common fields. Secondly, we must see the bigger picture: there was life in 'Middle Saxon' England outside the Midlands. The nucleation of settlement in the 'Middle Saxon' period is clearly

103 R. Faith, *The English Peasantry and the Growth of Lordship* (London, 1997); Ryan Lavelle, *Royal Estates in Anglo-Saxon Wessex: Land, Politics and Family Strategies* (Oxford, 2007).

104 Andrew Reynolds, *Anglo-Saxon Deviant Burial Customs* (Oxford, 2009); and see Simon Draper, 'Roman estates to English parishes', in *Debating Late Antiquity in Britain AD 300–700*, eds R. Collins and J. Gerrard (Oxford, 2004), pp. 55–64.

105 Aliki Pantos, '"On the edge of things": the boundary location of Anglo-Saxon assembly sites', *Anglo-Saxon Studies in Archaeology and History*, 12 (2003), 38–49.

demonstrable outside Mercia, for example in East Anglia, while palaeoenvironmental sequences from the South-West and East Anglia – both areas beyond the champion countryside – show an intensification of agriculture at this time. Indeed, by the post-Conquest period, when we have good documentary sources for the first time, we see forms of rotational husbandry in both areas and it is possible that this developed around the eighth century across large parts of southern England, including the East Midlands. We then appear to see a divergence in how landscapes across southern Britain developed: in areas such as the South-West farming practices and the structure of the landscape remained stable for many centuries, while in East Anglia settlements started to drift away from their early nucleations around churches towards nearby greens and commons. The central zone, in contrast, saw the development of champion countryside with its nucleated and sometimes planned villages and regularly arranged two- and three-field system around the tenth century.

Major investment of labour and resources in infrastructure developments is seen in places as far afield as Hereford in the Welsh Marshes, Mersea Island in Essex and Ebbsfleet in Kent, although other examples are also to be found within England's 'central province', such as Tamworth and Oxford. The emergence of international trade at the *wics* at Southampton, London and Ipswich, along with the many smaller coastal sites in the South-East, looks like a feature of the region outside the 'central province', and the inland centres of exchange represented by recently recognized 'productive sites' occur right across southern and eastern England from East Anglia to the East Midlands. If York turns out to be another *wic*, then it reinforces this picture of a growing economy around the eighth century that shows no correspondence to areas that had villages and open fields, or a correlation to any one kingdom. The widespread use of coinage, seen so clearly on 'productive sites', appears both in the champion countryside and elsewhere, and the early flickerings of urban life are seen in places as far afield as Canterbury, Norwich and the Mercian strongholds such as Northampton that lay within the champion countryside and Hereford that was without. It is time, therefore, to take a broader view of the early medieval landscape. Yes, there was change, innovation and economic expansion in the East Midlands, but there were equally important developments in areas both to the east and west that taken together make the 'long eighth century' one of the key formative periods of the landscape in southern England.

4

Population Ecology and Multiple Estate Formation: The Evidence from Eastern Kent

STUART BROOKES

Multiple Estates in Early England

One of the more widely encountered narratives of territorial development in early medieval England focuses on the existence of large multi-vill estates in the Early to Middle Anglo-Saxon period (*c.*400–850) and their subsequent fragmentation into the smaller manorial units recorded by Domesday Book. The details of these *multiple* or *federate* estates are not entirely clear, nor is the theory itself uncontroversial.[1] However, there remains a consensus that the early medieval productive landscape was organized into large territories from which tribute was extracted through important central places. The essential features of these territories were the links created between functionally differentiated settlements and the core, and the range of resources over which they lay claim, commonly combining arable areas of lowland with pastoral uplands. In some instances these linked settlements came to be fossilized in place-name or boundary evidence recorded in charters, suggesting that multiple estates were well-defined functional units incorporating economic and administrative roles.

A number of recent studies have shown the complex evolution of such estates and have highlighted the dangers of assuming greater uniformity than may have existed in the organization of landscape. By conflating administrative, economic

1 The idea of the 'multiple estate' was developed particularly in the works of Glanville Jones, who applied it to Anglo-Saxon England in: 'Basic patterns of settlement distribution in northern England', *Advancement of Science*, 18 (1961), 191–200; 'Early territorial organization in England and Wales', *Geografiska Annaler*, 43 (1961), 174–81; 'Settlement patterns in Anglo-Saxon England', *Antiquity*, 36 (1962), 54–5; 'The multiple estate as a model framework for tracing early stages in the evolution of rural settlement', in *L'habitat et les paysages ruraux d'Europe*, ed. Frans Dussart, Les Congrès et Colloques de l'Université de Liège, 58 (Liège, 1971), 251–67; 'Multiple estates and early settlement', in *Medieval Settlement: Continuity and Change*, ed. Peter H. Sawyer (London, 1976), 15–40; 'Multiple estates perceived', *Journal of Historical Geography*, 11.4 (1985), 352–63. Criticism of this model was expressed particularly by Nicky Gregson, 'The multiple estate model: some critical questions', *Journal of Historical Geography*, 11.4 (1985), 339–51; Stephen R. Bassett, 'In search of the origins of Anglo-Saxon kingdoms', in *The Origins of the Anglo-Saxon Kingdoms*, ed. Stephen R. Bassett (Leicester, 1989), 3–27.

and social links underlying estate structure, these studies have argued that the model as a concept conceals rather than reveals variations in territorial organization and the dynamics by which these have come about.[2] In contrast to Jones' original thesis, which argued that the multiple estate was a relict feature of Celtic organization, these studies have stressed the need to see it as part of a process in the evolution of lordship over the course of the early medieval period.[3] Tim Unwin, for example, suggested that multiple estates may have been created in areas outside those initially settled by Anglo-Saxons as a way of recolonizing peripheral regions that had been depopulated during the fifth and sixth centuries.[4] John Blair, by contrast, saw them very much as a secondary stage in the evolution of kingdoms in which large and complex estates were created through the internal division of larger tribal *regiones*.[5]

In keeping with the emphasis in recent writings on the multiple estate, this paper seeks to explore the dynamism underlying landscape evolution during the fourth to ninth centuries. Using theories derived from behavioural ecology, it is argued that the economic and demographic structure of multiple estates take its appearance from the processes by which they were first created. Furthermore, it is argued that they are the products of particular sets of ecological conditions, and represent adaptive responses aimed at improving group fitness in these particular circumstances. With the aim of exploring this theory, this paper considers the formation of multiple estates in eastern Kent during the early medieval period. Moreover, by emphasizing population and ecology as significant determinants in the formation of these landscape structures, it is suggested that the concept of multiple estates might be applicable to a wide variety of other contexts, even if it has until recently mostly been applied to explain Anglo-Saxon landscape organization.

Demography and Habitat in Anglo-Saxon Kent

Two premises lie at the heart of this argument and it is important to establish these conditions before expanding on the theory. These are firstly, that population growth and dispersal are evident in the archaeological record for Early to Middle Anglo-Saxon Kent; and secondly, that the Kentish landscape represents a heterogeneous – or patchy – resource territory of the sort identified by evolutionary biologists.

The second of these premises is fairly uncontroversial. In a series of works, Alan Everitt has presented a convincing picture of the many unique contrasting

2 Cf. Dawn Hadley, 'Multiple estates and the origins of the manorial structure of the Northern Danelaw', *Journal of Historical Geography*, 22.1 (1996), 3–15.

3 Roz Faith, *The English Peasantry and the Growth of Lordship* (Leicester, 1997), 12.

4 Tim Unwin, 'Towards a model of Anglo-Scandinavian rural settlement in England', in *Anglo-Saxon Settlements*, ed. Della Hooke (Oxford, 1988), 77–98, at 97.

5 John Blair, 'Frithuwold's kingdom and the origins of Surrey', in *The Origins of the Anglo-Saxon Kingdoms*, ed. Bassett, 97–107, at 105.

countrysides of Kent.[6] These separate, sharply contrasted regions, *pays* or habitats, are defined by environment (topography, geology, geography, flora), but are also the *loci* of specific localized practices and customs, as evidenced in agrarian history, settlement patterns, and place names. In Everitt's definition *pays* are areas in which physical setting and human activities coalesced to create distinctive landscape characters, and were in this way both the product of divergent settlement histories and a way of describing landscape.

Largely, the *pays* of Kent are related to the geological boundaries comprising the worn-down Wealden dome in the south and outcrops of successive strips of east–west strata that rim it to the north. Eastern Kent is dominated by the wide eastern extension of North Downs Chalk, an area of moderately fertile hills and scattered settlement stretching from Chatham to Dover. On either side of this belt exist bands of more fertile, easily worked soils, underlying the Foothill plains of the Lower Stour and Wantsum Channel to the north of the Downs, and along a thin, continuous vale of Gault Clay, known as the Holmesdale, to the south. Finally, separating the Holmesdale from heavy Wealden Clays in the extreme south of the region is a narrow syncline of Chart Hills of Lower Greensand, broadly comparable with the Downland *pays*.

In Everitt's view, this highly varied landscape was an important factor influencing multiple estate formation. By exploring the complex webs of relationships that existed between settlements he has identified a number of estate centres which he suggests lay at the heart of large land units of dispersed resource patches comprising woodland, common upland and marsh pasture, agricultural soils, and so on. Initially, these outlying patches were utilized seasonally from the centre (i.e. as classic site exploitation territories[7]), but they slowly became settled more permanently as dependent appurtenances of heartland estates. Although the boundaries of these land units are not clear, unweighted Thiessen polygons imposed on Everitt's list of estate centres support the view that they were deliberately organized to lay claim to a suite of resources across *pays* (Fig. 4.1). Through central vills, elites, such as the king and his family but also secular and ecclesiastical lords, could exploit a range of resources (and populations) spread unevenly across the kingdom. To facilitate this, the pattern of estate centres is characterized by linear chains of parent settlements laid out around the main Roman roads and the Pilgrim's Way, that is to say the principal routes of itineration, with sites regularly 4–6km apart.[8] Exceptions to

6 Alan Everitt, 'The making of the agrarian landscape of Kent', *Archaeologia Cantiana*, 92 (1976), 1–31; Alan Everitt, 'River and wold: reflections on the historical origin of regions and pays', *Journal of Historical Geography*, 3 (1977), 1–20; 'Place-names and pays: the Kentish evidence', *Nomina*, 3 (1979), 95–112; *Continuity and Colonization: the Evolution of Kentish Settlement* (Leicester, 1986).

7 Eric S. Higgs and Claudio Vita-Finzi, 'Prehistoric economies: a territorial approach', in *Papers in Economic Prehistory*, ed. Eric S. Higgs (London, 1972), 27–36.

8 Stuart Brookes, 'Walking with Anglo-Saxons: landscapes of the living and landscapes of the dead in Early Anglo-Saxon Kent', *Anglo-Saxon Studies in Archaeology and History*, 14 (2007), 143–53; *Economics and Social Change in Anglo-Saxon Kent AD 400–900: Landscapes, Communities and Exchange* (Oxford, 2007), 76–101.

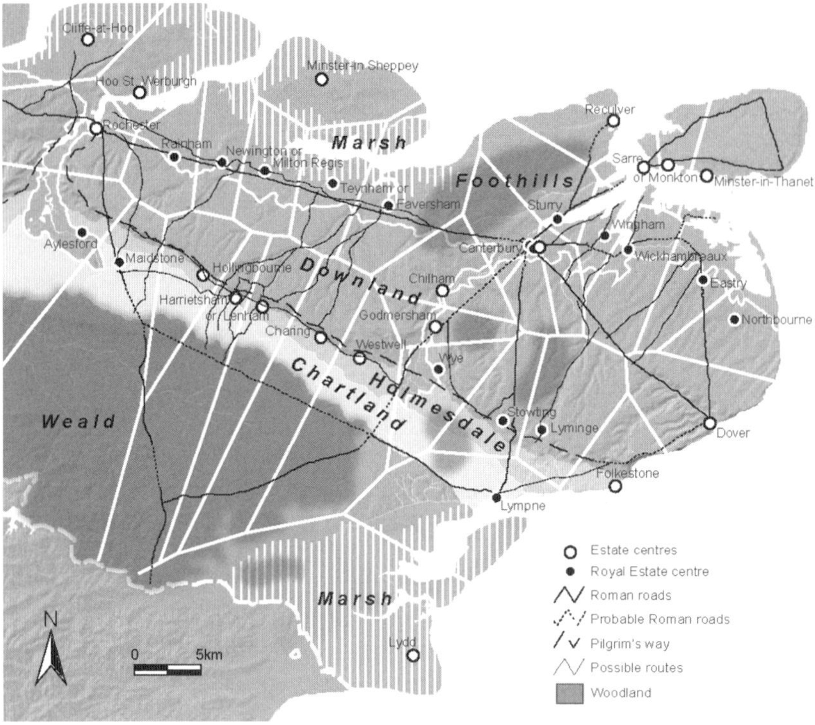

Figure 4.1. The Anglo-Saxon estate centres and *pays* of eastern Kent.

this spacing occur around Minster-in-Sheppey and Reculver,[9] two early minster sites of the coastal marshes, which have greater than average distance from their neighbours, perhaps reflecting certain ascetic ideals. Despite the apparent 'isolation' of these two centres the schematic hinterlands of all estate centres are similarly sized, and commonly lay claim to a range of patched resources including marshland, river valley, downland, and wood.[10] Demonstrating the functional links that existed between appurtenant settlements occupying these patches and the central vill, large numbers of small secondary routeways such as droveways and denn-routes cut across the spine of the *pays*.[11]

Unfortunately there is little excavated settlement evidence from eastern Kent by which to analyse the origins of this system. In many cases it is simply assumed

[9] As well as the possible eighth-century minster of Lydd on Romney Marsh.

[10] Thiessen polygons have also been used to suggest contrasting economic systems in operation in Kent. Whereas western estates usually have hinterlands of four or more *pays*, i.e. classic multiple estates, a minority in the east have only one or two. Significantly these economically dependent estate centres are those that emerged as specialized inter-regional trading settlements, or emporia, during the Middle Anglo-Saxon period. Brookes, *Economics*, 144–81.

[11] Kenneth P. Witney, *The Jutish Forest: A Study of the Weald of Kent from 450 to 1380 AD* (London, 1976).

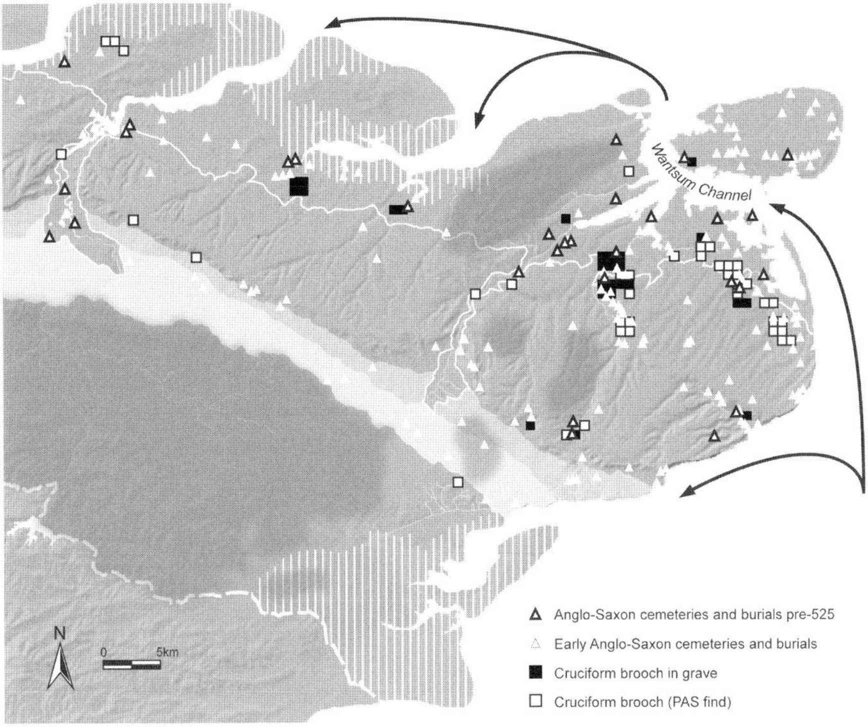

Figure 4.2. A comparison of burial and find-spot data, showing the location of pre-525 cemeteries and burials and late-fifth/early-sixth-century cruciform brooch finds relative to the Kentish *pays*. (PAS data courtesy of Andrew F. Richardson, Kent Finds Liaison Officer)

that these sites represent continuously occupied settlements because there is a topographical relationship between estate centres and the same soils and landscapes favoured by pre-existent settlement.[12] However, archaeological evidence from excavated cemeteries and find-spots produced by the Portable Antiquities Scheme (PAS) challenge this view. These data appear to indicate a chronological model of settlement, moving from specific core areas into others – a pattern that finds correlation also with the fragmentary evidence from estate centres themselves. From cemetery evidence, the driving dynamic for this process of colonization is argued to be population dispersal – the second premise.

Although a large number of sites and finds of the period 400–800 are known from eastern Kent, these generally fall into a limited spectrum of site types. Compared with some 176 burial sites only *c.*20 settlements have been identified for the same period.[13] To this may be added a large number of finds recorded by the PAS. Importantly, metal-detectoring has produced an over-representation of certain

[12] Everitt, *Continuity and Colonization*, 69–92.

[13] Brookes, *Economics*, 78, 102.

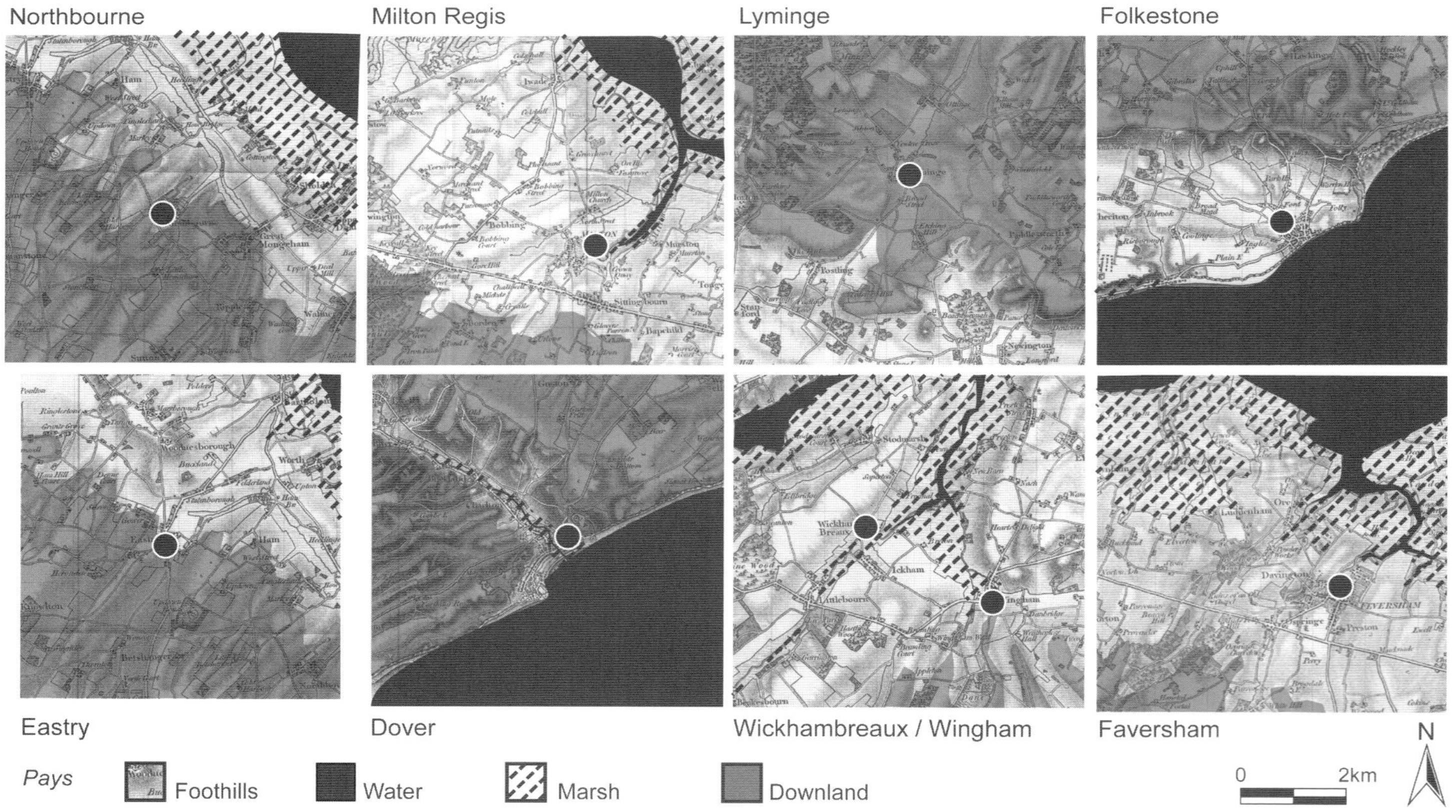

Figure 4.3. Prime-choice settlement, showing the relationship between early estate centres and resource patches within their site exploitation territories. With the exception of Lyminge, all sites occupy nodal positions between patches.

brooch types compared with finds from burials, indicating potentially different depositionary processes, such as casual losses rather than deliberate burial,[14] yet appears to confirm the overall distribution pattern identified from burials.

When plotted against the *pays* of eastern Kent, the archaeological corpus appears to support a clear pattern (Fig. 4.2). Earliest, pre-525, burials are almost wholly confined to lower courses of main rivers and the sheltered landing places of Dover and Folkestone, i.e. Everitt's Foothill *pays*.[15] In the later sixth century Early Anglo-Saxon finds are found more widely throughout those areas first settled with an expansion along the narrow, fertile strip of the Holmesdale. Finally in the seventh century there was an infilling of the Downs; a pattern which is paralleled by the distribution of chronologically 'later' place names containing the elements *-inga-*, *-ingas*, and *-hamm*.[16]

Close examination of this distribution suggests that the earliest Anglo-Saxon settlements are the result of very strategic land-use decisions. Generally settlement was close to navigable rivers and the coast, often with access to marshland resources within 2km (Fig. 4.3). Sites are located within a few hundred metres of spurs of chalk upland as well as routeways.[17] Early settlement *foci* in the Holmesdale (and to the west in the Darenth valley) occupied the best agricultural soils (rank 5: good) of the entire south-east, as defined by Soilscape's (National Soil Resources Institute copyright) soil fertility survey.[18] As a rule they inhabit, in other words, the optimum resource patches within easy access to roads and the coast. Whatever other social cues may have helped to determine site locations,[19] there appears to be an overarching economic rationale governing primary settlement.

This same burial evidence can be used to chart general population trends over the Early Anglo-Saxon period. Table 4.1 compares total numbers of excavated individuals from the 150 years before 600 with the 150 after. Overall there is an

14 Andrew Richardson, 'Identity and Material Culture in the 5th Century South East', forthcoming.

15 Andrew Richardson, *The Anglo-Saxon Cemeteries of Kent* (Oxford, 2005), 65–9; for the assignation of graves to particular chronological phases see Brookes, *Economics*, 122–4.

16 Brookes, *Economics*, 68–9; John McN. Dodgson, 'The significance of the distribution of the English place-name in -ingas, -inga- in South-East England', *Medieval Archaeology*, 10 (1966), 1–29; Sarah Kirk, 'A distribution pattern: -ingas in Kent', *Journal of the English Place-Name Society*, 4 (1972), 37–59; Barrie Cox, 'Place-names of the earliest English records', *Journal of the English Place-Name Society*, 8 (1976), 12–66; John McN. Dodgson, 'Place-names from *hām*, distinguished from *hamm* names, in relation to the settlement of Kent, Surrey and Sussex', *Anglo-Saxon England*, 2 (1973), 1–50. A similar chronological pattern in the distribution of these place-name elements has recently also been suggested by John Baker, *Cultural Transition in the Chiltern and Essex Region, 350 AD to 650 AD* (Hatfield, 2006), at 187–243.

17 Brookes, 'Walking'.

18 I am grateful to Dr Sue Harrington for letting me see data from her forthcoming book *Beyond the Tribal Hidage.*

19 For e.g. visibility from the sea, Stuart Brookes, 'The view from the sea: maritime migration and the colonised landscapes of Early Anglo-Saxon Kent', in *The Archaeology of Water*, eds Fay Stevens and Ruth Whitehouse (London, forthcoming).

Table 4.1 Distribution of burials in eastern Kent with respect to *pays* by period.

Area	burials pre-AD 600	% individuals	burials post-AD 600	% individuals	% Δ
East Kent	1810.35	100.0	3093.65	100.0	70.88
Downs	800.26	44.2	1983.74	64.1	147.88
Foothills	894.78	49.4	1097.22	35.5	22.62
Holmesdale	99.50	5.5	1.50	0.0	-98.49
Marsh	2.17	0.1	2.83	0.1	30.41
Weald	0.50	0.0	1.50	0.0	200
Chart	13.15	0.7	6.85	0.2	-47.91

increase in the eastern Kent population of 171% across these phases; however, significantly this figure also shows that the Downland *pays* saw an expansion of nearly 248% during the seventh and eighth centuries, whilst the Foothills witnessed only a modest increase.

A similar pattern of colonization is apparent in the evidence for Anglo-Saxon settlement.[20] Amongst the list of seminal estate centres identified by Everitt some sites appear to demonstrate considerable settlement continuity from the Roman through to later medieval periods. At Eastry, Milton Regis or even Teynham, archaeological complexes of Roman to medieval date are all seen to lie within a radius of *c*.500m of one another. However, at settlements such as Charing, Hollingbourne, Harrietsham or Lenham earlier remains are often scattered over a wide landscape, if they are present at all. Comparison of these data suggests four groups, potentially indicative of separate phases of settlement (Fig. 4.4):

1. Settlements with both Romano-British and Early Anglo-Saxon archaeological evidence; an early minster/nunnery or church foundation. These are all located within the Foothill *pays*, or with close proximity (i.e. 5km) to the sea. Stowting is an anomaly as it never had a minster but fits the other criteria. The only other exceptions to this pattern are Maidstone and Aylesford, which although situated within the Foothill *pays*, are located over 5km inland. As the River Medway is still navigable at these reaches it is argued that their location may indicate the furthest inland settlement penetration of a 'primary' phase.
2. Settlements with no visible Romano-British precedent, but clear Early Anglo-Saxon evidence. These are always located within the Foothill *pays*, but not necessarily associated with an early church foundation, i.e. areas of either 'primary' *de novo* settlement or 'secondary' infilling.
3. Settlements without consistent Romano-British or Early Anglo-Saxon archaeological evidence; possible evidence of an early ecclesiastical presence or some tentative Middle Anglo-Saxon finds. These tend to be located in the

20 Brookes, *Economics*, 95–6.

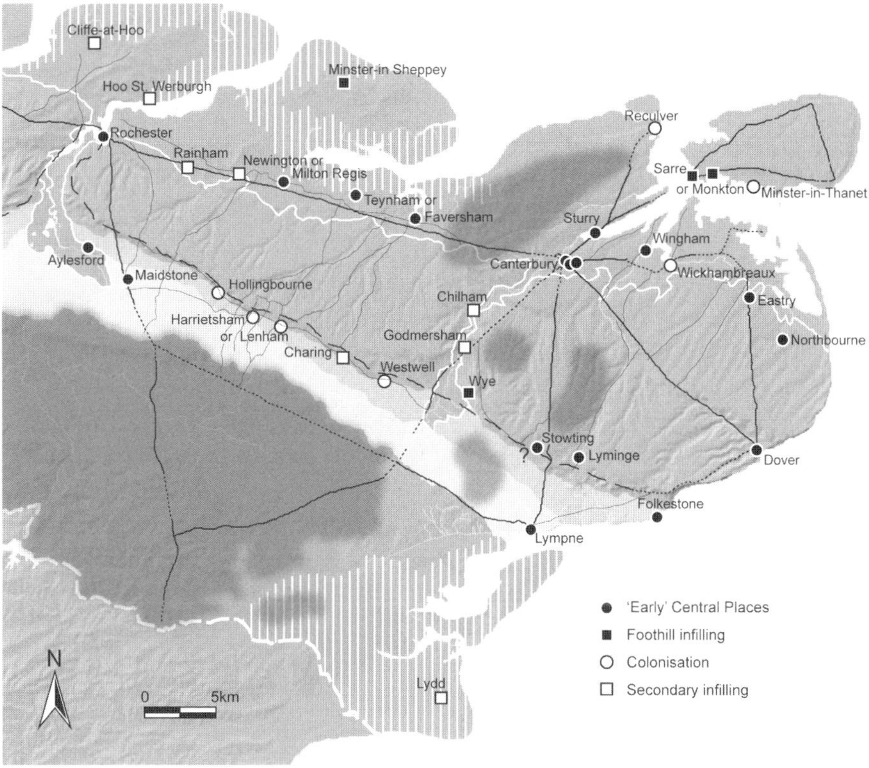

Figure 4.4. Phases of estate centre development.

Holmesdale or on the margins of the Downland, but generally over 10km from the coast, i.e. areas of possible 'secondary' colonization.

4. Settlements with and without a Romano-British precedent, but no Early Anglo-Saxon archaeological evidence; possible evidence of an early ecclesiastical presence or some tentative Middle Anglo-Saxon finds. These are located either within the Foothill or Marsh *pays*, i.e. areas of possible 'secondary' infilling.

This spatial model of colonization fits closely with that of the burial evidence, and is provided with temporal fixed points by both archaeological evidence and the *terminus post quem* of the foundation of individual churches. With excavated settlement features from Canterbury and Dover dating to the later fifth century, Group 1 settlements are likely to originate in the late fifth/early sixth century. Graves such as Sarre 63, 85 and 148 and Monkton 7 and 26 provide evidence for settlement of Group 2 sites from the first half of the sixth century. Occasional Early Anglo-Saxon material from sites in Group 3 tentatively places 'secondary' colonization in the seventh and early eighth centuries,[21] whilst the

[21] The distinction between Groups 1 and 3 may become blurred with future archaeological

lack of similar material from Group 4 settlements suggests a later seventh- and early eighth-century date for the start of 'secondary' infilling.[22]

Habitat Selection and Resource Dispersion in Evolutionary Ecology

In the preceding analysis a comparison of burial and settlement data was argued to support a model of territorial colonization characterized by a movement from primary coastal areas into more marginal habitats. Archaeological evidence for the earliest 'Germanic' material culture of the late fifth century was exclusively restricted to those areas where there was easy access to good, easily worked agricultural soils, meadow pasture in both winter and summer, and major route-ways. These sites appear to have utilized pre-existing settlement, and generally it seems that later on they also developed into major centres of large economic estates. Through the sixth and seventh centuries similar settlements emerged further inland, although drawing less clearly on Roman precedents, whilst at the same time there was a major expansion in the occupation of more marginal landscapes.

This model finds good parallels with human dispersals at other times and places,[23] as well as in those of animal species.[24] These cases support the hypotheses of behavioural ecology that argue there is an inherent relationship between forms of social organization and the habitat in which we live. It also supports the contention of a number of archaeologists who have regarded habitat variation as an important determinant of the settlement patterns of the medieval period.[25] These studies suggest that forms of social behaviour can be linked to the distribution and predictability of resources, such as food, water, and shelter – those things which determine our reproductive success in evolutionary terms.[26] There

research. Currently, there are few well-excavated cemeteries from within the Holmesdale that allow refined dating of the phase of settlement. However, increasing numbers of sixth-century metalwork objects are being recorded in the Holmesdale through the Portable Antiquities Scheme: pers. comm., Andrew Richardson.

22 An eighth-century date for the existence of Group 4 settlements could possibly also be suggested on the basis of charter evidence. The monastery of Hoo St Werburgh was in existence by the early ninth century at the latest (S22), and possibly already in the later seventh century (depending on how much authentic material was retained in the fabricated S233), cf. Heather Edwards, *The Charters of the Early West Saxon Kingdom*, British Archaeological Reports, British Series (Oxford, 1988), at 300–5; Nicholas Brooks, *The Early History of the Church of Canterbury* (Leicester, 1984), at 191–7.

23 For e.g. the Viking *landnám* of Iceland and Greenland or Paleoindian dispersal into North America, cf. e.g. Orri Vésteinsson, Thomas H. McGovern and Christian Keller, 'Enduring impacts: social and environmental aspects of Viking Age settlement in Iceland and Greenland', *Archaeologia Islandicai*, 2 (2002), 98–36; James Steele, Jonathan Adams and Tim Sluckin, 'Modelling Palaeoindian dispersal', *World Archaeology*, 30.2 (1998), 286–305.

24 Charles J. Krebs, *Ecology* (New York, 1994), 61–74.

25 For e.g. Cyril Fox, *The Personality of Britain: Its Influence on Inhabitants and Invader in Prehistoric and Early Historic Times* (Cardiff 1932); Henry C. Darby, *Domesday England* (Cambridge, 1977); Tom Williamson, *Shaping Medieval Landscapes* (Bollington, 2003).

26 Dominic D. P. Johnson, Roland Kays, Paul G. Blackwell and David W. Macdonald, 'Does

are several ways in which to consider the exploitation of habitats, and a number of models have been proposed that appear to have direct relevance to the results discussed here.

The 'theory of habitat selection' states that when individuals disperse into areas, they choose to live in those habitats which provide best fitness.[27] The suitability of a habitat will depend on a variety of factors: food supply, the availability of shelter, but also the density of other individuals.[28] Thus it argues that over time populations will distribute themselves in response to the value of these resources. There are several different factors that need to be considered. Firstly, habitat selection assumes that depletion will affect the choices available to agents within each habitat. Overcrowding within a particular habitat will reduce the availability of resources and its suitability drops for everyone. There exists therefore an inverse relationship between population size, the amount of resources, and the rate at which they are harvested (Fig. 4.5). The model assumes that initial settlers will occupy the best habitat, but with further growth or immigration individuals may choose to seek out better habitat opportunities elsewhere. As population density increases, individuals are more likely to occupy poorer quality territories. This rank order can be modelled functionally, with human densities apportioned between different grades of habitat such that their marginal value to residents is equalized.

A second factor influencing habitat selection is time and effort; it is a feature of habitat selection that individual movements are an essential component.[29] There is a relationship between the effort that is required to move to a new habitat and the rate of return. This time dimension determines when an agent should abandon his/her efforts and switch to a fresh opportunity. Of course the longer the travel-time, the longer the residence time to maximize returns, but this is going to be offset by the rate of diminishing returns within each new habitat.

This habitat selection model has further implications regarding the group structure populations adopt as a formation strategy. For each habitat there is an optimal group size, which means that if there are new joiners to the group, conflict can arise between members.[30] In rich habitats with abundant resources,

the Resource Dispersion Hypothesis explain group living?', *Trends in Ecology and Evolution*, 17.12 (2002), 563–70, at 563.

27 Krebs, *Ecology*, 61; John D. Goss-Custard and William J. Sutherland, 'Individual behaviour, populations and conservation', in *Behavioural Ecology* [4th edn], eds John R. Krebs and Nicholas B. Davies (London, 1997), 373–95.

28 Goss-Custard and Sutherland, 'Individual behaviour', 70.

29 John A. Wiens, 'The landscape context of dispersal', in *Dispersal*, eds Jean Clobert, Etienne Danchin, Andre A. Dhondt and James D. Nichols (Oxford 2001), 96–109; Hillard Kaplan and Kim Hill, 'The evolutionary ecology of food acquisition', in *Evolutionary Ecology and Human Behavior*, eds Eric A. Smith and Bruce Winterhalder (New York, 1992), 167–201; David W. Stephens and John R. Krebs, *Foraging Theory* (Princeton, 1986).

30 James L. Boone, 'Competition, conflict, and the development of social hierarchies', in *Evolutionary Ecology and Human Behavior*, eds Eric A. Smith and Bruce Winterhalder (New York, 1992), 301–17.

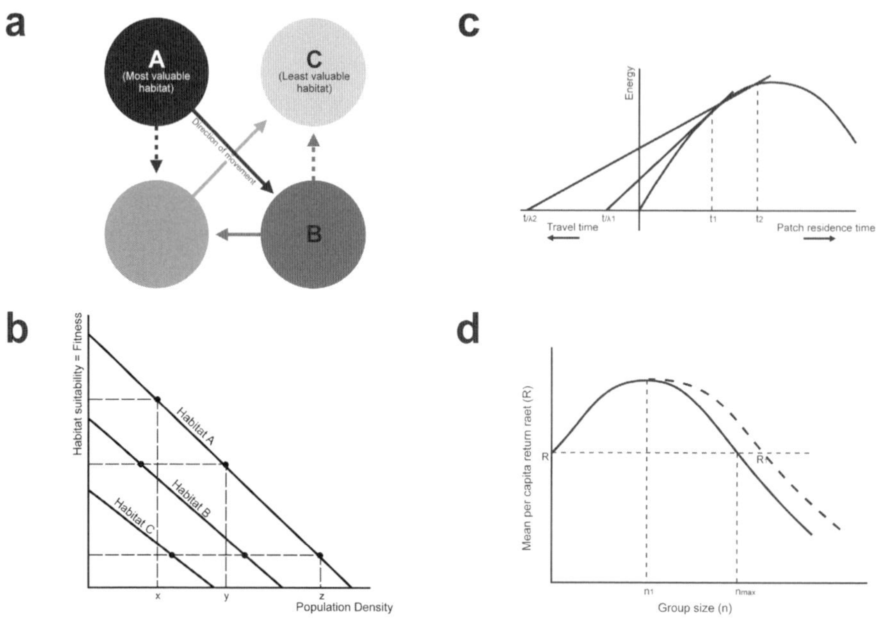

Figure 4.5. Models of habitat selection: a) Individuals choose to live in habitats that provide best fitness, however, habitat suitability is affected by population density; b) The model assumes that in all habitats fitness declines as population density goes up and crowding occurs. At low density x, an individual can achieve the highest fitness by living in habitat A, and habitats B and C will be empty. At high density z, an individual can choose to live in habitat A under crowded conditions, in habitat B under less crowded conditions, or in the poorest habitat C, with the least crowding. If individuals choose their habitat as in this simple model, fitness of individuals will be equal in all three habitats at high density (after Krebs, *Ecology*, fig. 5.6). Ways of mitigating the effect of population growth include: c) exploiting patches further afield, although this is constrained by travel time and the relative value of patches. In this graph travel time increases from the origin to the left, and patch residence time increases to the right. The optimum residence time can be found by constructing a line tangent to the gain function that begins at the point $1/\lambda$ on the travel time axis. The slope of this line provides the long-term average of energy intake. When the travel time is long ($1/\lambda_2$) then the rate-maximising residence time (t_2) is long. When the travel time is short ($1/\lambda_1$) so is the rate-maximising residence time (t_1) (after David W. Stephens and John R. Krebs, *Foraging Theory* (Princeton, 1986), fig. 2.2. d). Alternatively group size may grow beyond the optimal because of conflict between members and joiners. In this graphical model of group formation the mean *per capita* return rate first increases, then decreases with group size. Optimal group size is at n; maximum group size is at nmax. Increases beyond nmax require a proportionate increase in returns R1. (after Eric A. Smith, 'Optimization theory in anthropology: application and critiques', in *The Latest on the Best: Essays on Evolution and Optimality*, ed. John Dupré (Cambridge, Mass, 1987), pp. 201–49, at p. 212.

groups tend to split into small territories of more or less equal size such that each retains its former *per capita* intake. Archaeological examples of this process are the arrangement of linear river-valley territories that run from river to watershed, or the 'concave landscapes' discussed by Bryony and John Coles,[31] and the same process appears relevant to the multiple estates of the Holmesdale. Here, the linear arrangement of *pays* means that long territories centred on parent-estates can be subdivided, yet still retain equal access to the varied resource patches.

However, if resources are spread heterogeneously across territories such that splitting would result in uneven access to them, additional strategies are adopted to maintain the integrity of resource territories. There are two choices: either implement a member's rule and exclude newcomers, or allow the group to grow beyond optimum size, thereby decreasing the benefits for the existing members.[32] The result is the hierarchical social organization of groups in which there is an unequal access to resources. In this scenario a strategy which groups can adopt in order to mitigate conflict is to share extra-resources, thereby raising the net returns for the group. This is what is known as the 'Resource Dispersion Hypothesis'.[33] It argues that the economics of exploiting patched resources enable a larger population to share resources over a common area. Groups have to forage further afield, or develop other co-operative production systems in order to have more resources to pool. The important point here is that where resources within a territory are heterogeneous (in time and space) the net produce of the territory can exceed what is needed by the primary exploiter.[34] By utilizing a range of resources, greater excess can be produced. This means territories can accommodate secondary exploiters at no extra cost to the original settlers until a higher threshold is reached. This form of resource exploitation therefore potentially satisfies larger populations and can be seen as a causal mechanism for group living.[35] In these circumstances individuals behave co-operatively because it is in their own direct self interest. A common form this co-operation takes is what has been termed 'central-place sharing', which is the principle behind the multiple estate.

Whilst the conditions in which communal sharing of this kind might arise are fairly common, it is a prediction of this model that the increasing size of sharing groups inevitably moves towards inequality.[36] As the group increases in

31 Bryony Coles and John Coles, *Sweet Track to Glastonbury* (London, 1986).

32 Boone, 'Competition'.

33 Graham M. Carr and David W. Macdonald, 'The sociality of solitary foragers: a model based on resource dispersion', *Animal Behaviour*, 34 (1986), 1540–9; P. J. Bacon, Frank Ball and Paul Blackwell, 'A model for territory and group formation in a heterogeneous habitat', *Journal of Theoretical Biology*, 148.4 (1991), 445–68.

34 David W. Macdonald, 'The ecology of carnivore social behaviour', *Nature*, 301 (1983), 379–84.

35 Johnson *et al.*, 'Resource Dispersion Hypothesis'.

36 Boone, 'Competition', 305, in which the primary motivation of central-place sharing is to reduce risk. For a fuller treatment of how this may be applicable to multiple estate formation and the development of social bonding in Kent, see Brookes, *Economics*, 174–81.

size, the problem develops whether subordinates can do better either solitarily or by becoming members of other groups. For dominant groups, on the other hand, the optimum group size as a whole is always larger than is in the interests of subordinates. Consequently, a number of strategies can be adopted to allow for greater co-operation in larger groups, including: the punishment of defectors; increased hierarchical group structure, including the development of privileged groups charged with maintaining some public good unilaterally; and social exclusion.[37]

Multiple Estate Formation in Anglo-Saxon Kent

The models developed by behavioural ecology provide important insights into the formation of landscape territories in Early to Middle Anglo-Saxon Kent. In the first instance, the archaeological sequence can be used to support a model of habitat selection, witnessing the strategic dispersal of populations into a territory on the basis of ranked resources. Given the ongoing re-examination of the genetic evidence for Germanic migration during the fifth and sixth centuries, a reassessment of the dynamics of settlement appears warranted.[38] This research has suggested that the best-fit model to explain Y-chromosome variation in the modern English gene pool is to consider a significant 'immigrant' population (*c*.20%) in combination with apartheid-like social engineering taking place during the early Anglo-Saxon period.[39] In this regard population estimates based on burial evidence from Kent are equivocal. These suggest exponential growth of around 0.26% per annum over the course of the period 475–750, which is roughly equitable with that suggested for early modern societies.[40] However, most of the excavated burials probably date to *c*.500–700 and it is to this more contracted period that the population increase most likely dates, with effects of 'incoming' populations on gross numbers more pronounced.

37 Brookes, *Economics*, 308–9.

38 Michael E. Weale, Deborah A. Weiss, Rolf F. Jager, Neil Bradman and Mark G. Thomas, 'Y chromosome evidence for Anglo-Saxon mass migration', *Molecular Biology and Evolution*, 19.7 (2002), 1008–21; Mark G. Thomas, Michael P. H. Stumpf and Heinrich Härke, 'Evidence for an apartheid-like social structure in Early Anglo-Saxon England', *Proceedings of the Royal Society B*, 273 (2006), 2651–7.

39 More conservative estimates for the scale of the Anglo-Saxon settlement have been suggested by Stephen Oppenheimer, *The Origins of the British: A Genetic Detective Story* (London, 2006), who nevertheless suggests an up to 15% increase in genetic markers in parts of eastern England attributable to Germanic migration of the early medieval period. If, as Thomas *et al*., 'Evidence', argue, this increase must be modelled within a time-frame of only one or two generations, it certainly represents a significant genetic input. By way of comparison, the mass-migration following the Rwandan crisis of 1994 altered the overall population of neighbouring Zaire by only 3.06%, and Tanzania by 2.03%, albeit over a very short time-frame (numbers as recorded by the United Nations Refugee Agency, www.unhcr.org/publ/PUBL/3ebf9bb60.pdf).

40 e.g. 0.3% suggested by Goran Ohlin, 'Mortality, marriage and growth in pre-industrial populations', *Population Studies*, 14.3 (1961), 190–7, at 197.

It is significant that during the first phase of colonization considerable freedom appears to have been exercised in the choice of settlement location (i.e. Group 1 sites), with prime suitable habitats selected on the boundary between Downland, Foothill and Marsh, where patched resources are typically contracted within small territories. In this regard the Kentish example is not an isolated case; Wendy Davies and Hayo Vierck's survey of East Anglian cemetery distributions recognized a similar correlation between settlement, soils, and topography.[41] How much this settlement pattern rested on earlier land-use systems remains, however, conjectural.

Clearly post-Roman Kent was no pristine landscape; the name of the county itself derives from the Iron Age place name *Cantii* or *Cantiaci* as *Cantware* ('the dwellers of Kent'), hinting at a level of sub-Roman continuity. Unlike other, later, settlements, those of Group 1 consistently display a Romano-British association, suggesting that in the Foothills 'primary' settlement may have related to pre-existing patterns of land use. Perhaps significantly, the north Kent Foothill *pays* consists of land of far poorer soil fertility (rank 2–3) than that of the Holmesdale. Nevertheless, within the Foothills the clear and repeated pattern of Early Anglo-Saxon material indicates a strategic dispersal in which specific locales were chosen again and again. On this basis patch-resource modelling explains the principal dynamic underlying the pattern of Early Anglo-Saxon colonization, but agricultural productivity tells only part of the story. Patches comprise the most fertile areas of Kent, but, perhaps critically, also include those areas, particularly in the Foothill *pays*, where important nodal positions on the network of Roman roads and coastal inlets provided access to the full range of productive resources.[42] By whatever mechanism this was achieved it is clear the visible – elite, Germanic – material culture dominated the territory from prime-choice locations. If Thomas *et al.* are correct in their identification of apartheid-like social structures during this period, this process may also have included the allocation of land to native populations. It is noticeable that the few place-names referring perhaps to surviving Romano-British communities, such as Walton or Eccles, are all located in the primary area of Foothill settlement, possibly reflecting a level of socio-economic dependence on nascent estate centres.

Both Everitt's model of *pays* colonization and the 'habitat selection model' assume population growth as contributing dynamics to the formation of the territorial patterns of Anglo-Saxon Kent. The evidence from both settlement and burial indicates that this expansion originated in the Foothill area, dispersing through the Holmesdale into the poorer patch environments of the Downs, Chart and Weald, over the course of the sixth to eighth centuries. This same phenomenon may well explain the continuity of the place name *Cantii* in the Anglo-Saxon period. As the core of the Roman *civitas* was translated to new leadership, it came also to be applied to all regions under the control of the

41 Wendy Davies and Hayo Vierck, 'The contexts of the tribal hidage: social aggregates and settlement patterns', *Frühmittelalterliche Studien*, 8 (1974), 223–93.

42 Brookes, *Economics*, 72–4

Kentish kings as these expanded in the sixth and seventh centuries. Barbara Yorke has demonstrated how the name *Cant* may have come to include west Kent as part of territorial expansion during the sixth century, and a similar process might underline Bede's assertion that the people of Kent and the inhabitants of the Isle of Wight were of Jutish origin.[43]

Whether Foothill settlements claimed access to large territories of thinly settled marginal land from the outset is difficult to assess. Certainly a handful of denn-roads linking coastal settlement and inland patches were already being utilized by the sixth century, but the majority of these routes are likely to date to later periods of transhumance.[44] The available evidence suggests that the sixth century also witnessed the infilling of prime-patches as well as the first settlement of less accessible and poorer quality land in the coastal zone (Group 2), with the latter most likely economic dependants of groups based in 'prime' locations. Behavioural ecological models suggest that this process was in order to acquire extra-resources, thereby raising the net returns for the core group around the principle of central-place sharing.[45]

The pattern of Holmesdale, Downs and Marsh colonization has mirrored that predicted by models of population growth and dispersal.[46] According to these theories it is reasonable to expect that the settlement of territories matched the rank-order quality of resource patches. As part of this process the settlement of the good quality Holmesdale in the seventh century seems to have been critical to the evolution of multiple estates. It seems highly significant that both secondary colonization and infilling, as represented by Group 3 and 4 settlements, do not find consistent correlation with known landscape structures. Although a partial explanation for this phenomenon may lie in the operation of different Romano-British agricultural practices between the inland and the coast, the lack of Early Anglo-Saxon finds in their proximity is nevertheless significant. The Holmesdale vills are generally not royal centres but give the impression of being settlements planned to exploit regular compact territories of dispersed resources. Perhaps accompanying this careful organization of the landscape, a number of other economic indicators tentatively suggest a parallel concern with increased

43 Barbara Yorke, 'Joint kingship in Kent *c.*560 to 785', *Archaeologia Cantiana*, 99 (1983), 1–19; *Kings and Kingdoms of Early Anglo-Saxon England* (London, 1990), 27; *HE*, I, 15.

44 Brookes, 'Walking'.

45 Of course this discussion has restricted itself only to the estate-centres themselves; small-scale colonization further afield follows along the same principles. Early place names relating to named communities, the various -ingas people, are likely to be related to this movement into more marginal landscapes outside the core.

46 Given the nature of the archaeological evidence, another possibility is that the habitat selection model as it has been outlined here is in fact charting a process of acculturation as opposed to colonization, by which a dominant Germanic material culture slowly spread beyond the core areas of original settlement. Whilst this process probably does account for some of the changes outlined in this chapter, there are grounds for discounting this as a major dynamic. We would expect greater correlation with Late Roman structures of the Downs and the Weald if this were the case, whereas the impression from archaeological and place-name evidence of Anglo-Saxon settlement in these areas is of something fundamentally different by the early eighth century at the latest.

productivity. During the seventh century there was a significant re-emergence of cloth production, primarily of the so-called *pallium fresonicum*,[47] as well as greater restrictions on iron consumption.[48] These western and southern estates are also the location of high densities of Domesday slaves, perhaps reflecting long-standing surplus production in this region.[49]

In these patterns of settlement there is some indication that the value of patches can be equated with status, with low quality patches occupied by lower status communities. There are noticeable distinctions in the consumption profiles of Early Anglo-Saxon burials occupying different *pays*.[50] A marked fall-off in the amount of both imported and locally provenanced material further away from the primary communities of the Wantsum and Dover coasts has been discussed elsewhere.[51] Accompanying this pattern there are potentially significant clusters of curated Romano-British material in the Foothills area of Wickhambreaux (as might be expected by the place name) but also in the Holmesdale area of Stowting–Lyminge.[52] Perhaps these patterns reveal tantalizing traces of indigenous populations occupying either patches on the spatial margins of society or directly managed close to its centre.

Using this same line of argument it may also be possible that middle value patches were the location of greatest social conflict. The habitat selection model predicts that in-group competition will result from the creation of ever larger groups organized on central-place sharing, particularly if some habitats are consistently better than others. There develops an asymmetric relationship between less risk prone and more risk prone areas, resulting in a greater net flow in one direction. During the final phases of pagan burial, Downland communities in particular appear to have been investing greater effort in displaying status in the form of visible grave structures, possibly an indication of tensions in the links established with primary centres.[53]

Similar tensions may be visible at a regional scale. The establishment of compact territories in the Holmesdale during the seventh and eighth centuries meant that Foothill vills needed to stipulate more explicitly rights to common

47 Sue Harrington, 'Aspects of Gender and Craft Production in Early Anglo-Saxon England, with reference to the Kingdom of Kent' (unpublished PhD thesis, London, 2002), 57; Lise Bender Jørgensen, *North European Textiles until AD 1000* (Aarhus, 1992), 78.

48 Brookes, *Economics*, 119, 138–42, 150.

49 Alexandra Sanmark and Frode Iverson, 'Social landscape and royal organisation in Anglo-Saxon England' (forthcoming).

50 Brookes, *Economics*, 144–81.

51 Brookes, *Economics*; 'The Early Anglo-Saxon framework for Middle Anglo-Saxon economics: the case of East Kent', in *Markets in Early Medieval Europe: Trading and 'Productive' Sites, 650–850*, eds Tim Pestell and Katarina Ulmschneider (Macclesfield, 2003), 84–96.

52 Brookes, *Economics*, Fig. 73.

53 John Shephard, 'Anglo-Saxon Barrows of the Later 6th and 7th Centuries AD' (unpublished PhD thesis, Cambridge, 1979); 'The social identity of the individual in isolated barrows and barrow cemeteries in Anglo-Saxon England', in *Space, Hierarchy and Society: Interdisciplinary Studies in Social Area Analysis*, eds Barry C. Burnham and John Kingsbury (Oxford, 1979), 47–80.

beyond these *de novo* estates, in effect leapfrogging them. It is conceivable that, as part of these two dynamics of *de novo* estate formation and contest over resources, areas of planned common came about.[54] Significantly, documents specifically mentioning common-land holdings belong mostly to the eighth century, just when scrambles over resources might be predicted by population ecology. The same processes may have promoted the development of the lathe: large provinces of civil organization recorded in Domesday Book.[55] In the outlined scenario these may be the result of further attempts to hold together the contrasting economic basis of agrarian wealth, by binding together cross-*pays* communities through tighter jurisdictional bonds.

Conclusions

In this paper I have attempted to suggest that there exist sound behavioural ecological bases for the formation and use of multiple estates. It is acknowledged that this analysis has by necessity involved a broad-brush approach that merits more detailed archaeological investigation. Nevertheless it is argued that only through such analysis can the study of cemeteries begin to be reconciled with that of landscape archaeology. Rather than simply seeing cemeteries as landscape features, this approach uses burial evidence to inform rural settlement studies, and *vice versa*. Furthermore, as burial can provide high quality chronological resolution it must be seen as a fundamental source for the interpretation of landscape evidence which is both highly fragmentary and poorly datable.

This call for inter-disciplinarity is not mere pragmatism. In the preceding analysis population dynamics have been demonstrably important to understanding territorial organization. By using the strong theoretical foundations that underpin behavioural ecology, empirical archaeological data can be used to extrapolate population-level phenomena so as to explain social and economic change in the past. The Resource Dispersion Hypothesis will potentially play a role wherever resources are heterogeneous at a relevant scale. However, it is clear that patch resource exploitation and central-place sharing are particularly relevant in the specific circumstances of population growth and dispersal. It is for these reasons – population growth and ecology – that multiple estates may characterize settlement at other times and places, and also why they are absent from other parts of Anglo-Saxon England.

[54] Witney, *Jutish Forest*, 78–103; Diana Chatwin and Mark Gardiner, 'Rethinking the early medieval settlement of woodlands: evidence from the Western Sussex Weald', *Landscape History*, 27 (2005), 31–49.

[55] Johannes K. Wallenberg, *Kentish Place-Names: a Topographical and Etymological Study of the Place-Name Material in Kentish Charters dated before the Conquest* (Uppsala, 1931); *The Place-Names of Kent* (Uppsala, 1934).

5

Exploring Black Holes: Recent Investigations in Currently Occupied Rural Settlements in Eastern England*

CARENZA LEWIS

This paper reviews the results to date of an ongoing archaeological research project at the University of Cambridge into the historic development of currently occupied rural settlements (CORS), and considers their implications for our understanding of the development of the Anglo-Saxon rural settlement pattern. Until recently, most excavation of Anglo-Saxon and medieval rural settlement has focused on sites which are now deserted,[1] with much less attention given to

* In a project such as this, the help of hundreds of people, too numerous to name here individually but without whom the project could not have proceeded, is vital, and this has been very gratefully received. First and foremost, the pupils and teachers who carried out the excavations are all to be thanked for their hard work and enthusiasm for a task to which nearly all of them were new. Thanks are also due to the owners of each and every plot of land on which a test pit was excavated, many of whom provided support and hospitality well beyond the call of duty, and special thanks go to the coordinators who arranged access to these sites. Thanks are also due to the McDonald Institute for Archaeological Research, the Higher Education Subject Centre for Archaeology, Aimhigher, HEFCE, the European Social Fund, English Heritage and the Society for Medieval Archaeology for the financial support they have given the HEFA project. Catherine Ranson is the site supervisor for the project, Paul Blinkhorn the pottery consultant and Jessica Rippengal the faunal remains analyst: their knowledge, support and enthusiasm have been invaluable. Ruth Shaw carried out the phosphate analysis in 2007 and Chris Morris assessed the 2005 faunal remains. Special thanks are also due to Dan Aukett, Tom Birch, Mary Chester-Kadwell, Jon Clynch, David Crawford-White, Rob Hedge, David Page, Natalie White and Victoria Wooldridge for the support they have given the project. Staff in archaeological units, HERS and record offices have provided much invaluable support and advice. While this paper has benefited hugely from discussions with all these, named and unnamed, any errors remain entirely my responsibility.

1 Carenza Lewis, 'New avenues for the investigation of currently occupied medieval rural settlement: preliminary observations from the Higher Education Field Academy', *Medieval Archaeology*, 51 (2007), 133–6; James Rackham (ed.), *Environment and Economy in Anglo-Saxon England* (York, 1994); Andrew Reynolds, *Later Anglo-Saxon England: Life and Landscape* (Stroud, 1999); Stephen Rippon, *Beyond the Medieval Village* (Oxford, 2008). The history of the study of medieval archaeology has most recently been reviewed in Chris Gerrard, *Medieval Archaeology: Understanding Traditions and Contemporary Approaches* (London, 2003), which includes discussion of the development of rural set-

sites which are lived in today. This is largely due to the apparent invisibility of the evidence, lack of opportunities for developer-funded excavation and difficulties (both real and perceived) of gaining access to land within currently occupied settlements for research-driven excavation. It is ironic that existing villages, which are lived in and visited by so many people today, can constitute one of the most inaccessible parts of the English landscape for the archaeologist. With the aim of addressing this problem, since 2005 the University of Cambridge CORS project, working with members of the public including hundreds of teenagers participating in the university's Higher Education Field Academy (HEFA), has investigated eighteen occupied rural settlements across six counties in eastern England by carrying out large numbers of test-pit excavations in an attempt to establish the extent, distribution and date of human activity within, across and around these sites. This paper will review the early results of this project, which have not only demonstrated the wealth of primary evidence that can be retrieved using this approach, but have also shown the extent to which such evidence can challenge existing ideas about settlement development, character and plan, and point to new patterns of occupation and change within settlements.

Landscape and settlement are inextricably linked in the search for knowledge and understanding: settlements were focal points in a rural landscape occupied by more than 90% of the population in the Anglo-Saxon period. Crucial to an understanding of the landscapes that people in the past worked, traversed, observed and experienced is knowledge of the settlements where they lived; similarly the development and character of settlements cannot be fully investigated independent of their landscape context. In the past, the scope of archaeological investigations into Anglo-Saxon settlements in eastern England, as elsewhere, ranged widely from detailed excavations of single sites such as West Stow and Mucking;[2] to field-walking often covering whole parishes such as Brixworth in Northamptonshire, Loddon, Hales and Heckingham in Norfolk and the Fenland Survey in Cambridgeshire;[3] to top-down reviews of entire counties (or even larger areas) such as the East Midlands.[4] This work has informed, underpinned

tlement studies in each chapter. For a shorter summary of the development of medieval rural settlement studies, see Carenza Lewis, Patrick Mitchell Fox and Christopher Dyer, *Village, Hamlet and Field* (Manchester, 1997), pp. 5–21.

2 Helena Hamerow, *Excavations at Mucking. Volume 2: the Anglo-Saxon Settlement* (London, 1993); Stanley West, *West Stow, The Anglo-Saxon Village. Volumes 1 and 2* (Ipswich, 1985).

3 Glenn Foard, 'Systematic fieldwalking and the investigation of Saxon settlement in Northamptonshire', *World Archaeology*, 9 (1978), 357–74; A. Davison, *The Evolution of Settlement in Three Parishes in South-East Norfolk*, *East Anglian Archaeology*, 49 (1990); David Hall and John Coles, *Fenland Survey. An Essay in Landscape and Persistence*, English Heritage Archaeological Report 1 (London, 1994).

4 Royal Commission on the Historical Monuments of England, *Archaeological Sites in Northamptonshire*, 6 volumes (London, 1975–85) and *Archaeological Sites in North-West Lincolnshire* (London, 1991): R. F. Hartley, *The Medieval Earthworks of North-West Leicestershire* (Leicester, 1981–89); R. F. Hartley, *The Medieval Earthworks of Central Leicestershire* (Leicester, 1981–89); B. Cushion, and A. Davison, *Earthworks of Norfolk*, *East Anglian Archaeology*, 104 (2003).

and advanced academic debate about the origins and development of the Anglo-Saxon settlement, particularly with regard to the development of the nucleated village from the eighth century AD onwards.[5] Field-walking and excavation in the arable fields of Northamptonshire, for example, identified a tier of previously unknown pre-ninth-century, small dispersed rural settlements, which appear to have been abandoned sometime before the advent of hard-fired later Anglo-Saxon pottery.[6] However, those parts of that same rural landscape which are the sites of today's villages have seen much less archaeological investigation, even though they are in many cases presumed (although less frequently proven) to have been the direct successors of the dispersed settlements. Furthermore, much of the archaeological investigation which has occurred has been reactive rather than research orientated, mostly limited to observations or minor explorations carried out in advance of small-scale development,[7] which in most cases fail to record any evidence for activity of Anglo-Saxon date.[8]

However, the few research-driven archaeological investigations which have been carried out within CORS, most notably in Shapwick (Somerset, 1989–99)[9] and Whittlewood Forest (Buckinghamshire/Northamptonshire border, 2000–05),[10] have produced evidence which has questioned established theories about the development of rural settlement in the historic period. These projects have developed strategies for carrying out research-driven excavation within CORS, including the excavation of small 'test pits'. These can be carried out in even the smallest open spaces, including private gardens, and enable material culture and other indicators of past activity to be recovered whose date and distribution can be analysed in order to help reconstruct the development of the settlement. This is the strategy that has been employed in the HEFA project, under which since 2005 more than 400 test pits have been dug in twenty-one occupied rural settlements, including eighteen in East Anglia (Fig. 5.1). This paper reviews the evidence from the East Anglian sites and considers its implications for the investigation and understanding of the Anglo-Saxon landscape.

5 e.g. Christopher C. Taylor, *Village and Farmstead* (London, 1983); Della Hooke (ed.), *Medieval Villages* (Oxford, 1985); Mick Aston, David Austin and Christopher C. Dyer (eds), *The Rural Settlements of Medieval England* (Oxford, 1989); Lewis et al., *Village, Hamlet and Field*; Brian Roberts and Stuart Wrathmell, *Region and Place* (London 2002); Tom Williamson, *Shaping Medieval Landscapes* (Macclesfield, 2003); R. Jones and M. Page, *Medieval Villages in an English Landscape* (Macclesfield, 2004); Rippon, *Beyond the Medieval Village*.

6 Foard, 'Systematic fieldwalking', 357–74.

7 These are now reported every year in large numbers in the 'Discovery and Excavation' section of the *Annual Report* of the Medieval Settlement Research Group, the 'Medieval Britain and Ireland' section of this journal, and in many county archaeological journals.

8 e.g. the significant number of submissions for inclusion in the 'Discovery and Excavation' section of the *Medieval Settlement Research Group Annual Report* which report on watching briefs within CORS during which no evidence of Anglo-Saxon date was observed, noted by this author while editor.

9 Christopher Gerrard with Mick Aston, *The Shapwick Project, Somerset. A Rural Landscape Explored* (Leeds, 2007).

10 See Jones and Page, *Medieval Villages*.

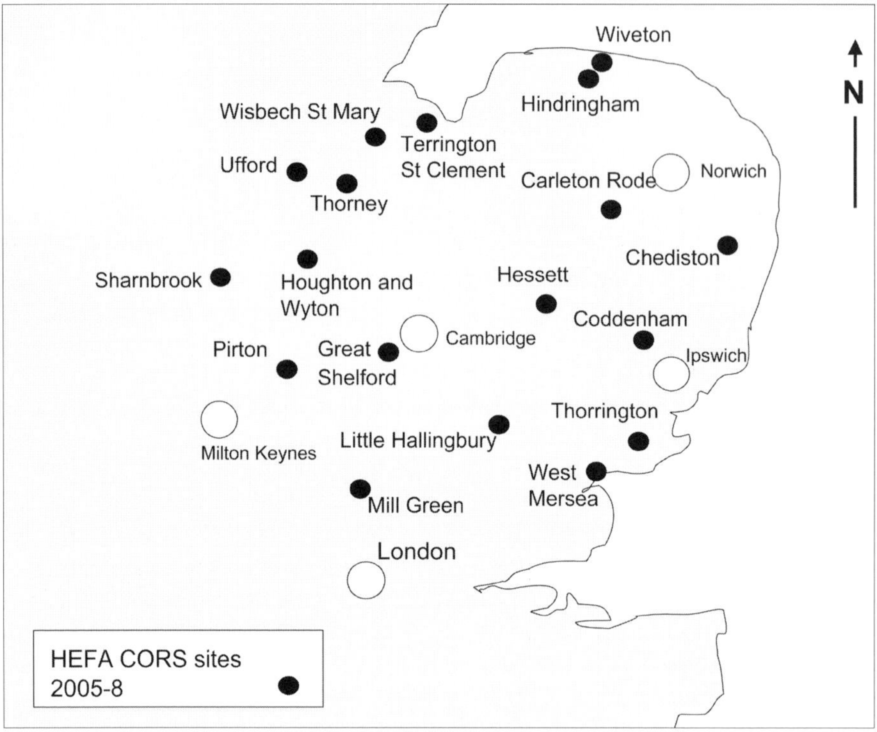

Figure 5.1. Location map of southern England showing the locations of the CORS sites investigated by the HEFA project in East Anglia in 2005–08.

Aims

The Higher Education Field Academy CORS project is notable in that it has at its core two quite distinct aims which have achieved a high level of synergy in the investigation of CORS. The first aim, as discussed above, is to advance knowledge and understanding of the development of the rural settlement pattern in the Anglo-Saxon and medieval periods by expanding the number and geographical distribution of CORS which have seen detailed research-driven archaeological investigation. The second aim of the HEFA project is to provide high quality, structured, aspiration-raising educational activities for school-age learners. Since 2005 the University of Cambridge has met both these aims by giving learners the chance to carry out a systematic test-pit excavation to the standards required for academic enquiry in one of eighteen East Anglian rural settlements.[11]

11 Lewis 'New avenues', 136–9, details the aims and methods of the HEFA project and a summary of these can be viewed at www.arch.cam.ac.uk/aca/cors.html.

Methods

CORS included in the HEFA project are distributed widely across East Anglia, selected primarily on the basis of educational and social requirements and the availability of local coordinators able to arrange access to sites to excavate. Within selected CORS, test pits are sited wherever access can be arranged, mostly within private gardens or small plots of unoccupied land. There is thus very little site selection based on prior assumptions as to the likelihood of finding archaeological evidence of Anglo-Saxon or medieval date in the HEFA CORS project, which effectively introduces a necessary element of randomness to the process of site selection and excavation.

Excavation of the HEFA CORS test pits follows a standardised protocol based on normal procedures for small-scale excavation, with the work here carried out by volunteer learners from local schools and communities. Following an initial instruction session, small teams use an instruction pack and pro-forma recording system, with on-site support from professional archaeologists to ensure all aspects of the process are carried out and recorded correctly. Each team measures out a 1m square, records its location, removes any turf and then excavates to a maximum depth of 1.2 m in a series of 10cm spits or contexts. All spoil is sieved or hand-searched for finds, which are retained, cleaned and analysed. Once each test pit is completed, the team draws sections, takes soil samples from each spit/context for phosphate analysis, then backfills and replaces the removed turf to restore the site. Most test pits are completed when they reach natural or the maximum safe depth of 1.2m. A minority will stop on encountering a feature (ancient or modern) which is deemed inadvisable or impossible to remove, or will have to finish at a level above natural due to time constraints.

Results[12]

Fifteen CORS investigated by the HEFA project within the six East Anglian counties of Bedfordshire, Cambridgeshire, Essex, Hertfordshire, Norfolk and Suffolk have revealed evidence for activity of Anglo-Saxon date. The results from these are summarised below, followed by a discussion accompanied by a map showing the distribution of early, middle and later Anglo-Saxon material by settlement.[13] Three other settlements in the East Anglian region which have

[12] This paper includes data from excavations which took place before December 2008. Data from the HEFA CORS excavations including maps and summaries of the ceramic finds from all the test pits excavated to date can be found at www.arch.cam.ac.uk/aca/excavationreports.html.

[13] For the purposes of the discussion below, early Anglo-Saxon refers to the period *c*.450–650 AD, middle Anglo-Saxon to *c*.650–850 AD and later Anglo-Saxon to *c*.850 AD until the Norman Conquest. 'High medieval' refers to the period between the Norman Conquest

to date revealed no evidence that can firmly be dated to the Anglo-Saxon period (Mill Green, Thorrington and Wisbech St Mary), and a further three settlements which have been investigated by HEFA but lie outside the East Anglian region, will not be discussed here.

Carleton Rode, Norfolk (NGR TM 115925)

Carleton Rode is today a small rural village situated less than 26km south-west of Norwich in Norfolk. The settlement now falls into two distinct parts: a small cluster to the south-east around the church which includes a primary school, Church Farm and the old and new rectories, and a more attenuated arrangement of housing to the north-west which extends for more than 0.5km along two sinuous roads (Flaxlands and King Street) intersecting at a crossroads on the western margin of the settlement. The area to the west of the approximately north–south oriented King Street is shown on the tithe map as a large common, and this part of Carleton Rode thus appears to be a common-edge settlement, which would be considered, on the basis of field-work in other parts of this region, most likely to be of twelfth- to fourteenth-century date.[14] The earliest fabric of the church dates to *c.*1300,[15] and one farm along the edge of the common is of medieval origin,[16] otherwise the earliest standing buildings date to the seventeenth century AD.[17]

Thirteen test pits have been dug by HEFA participants in Carleton Rode to date. In common with most of the HEFA sites, no material of fifth- to eighth-century AD date was recovered from any of them. However, five of the test pits produced ceramics dating to 850–1100 AD. Interestingly, these were all located in the Flaxlands/King Street part of the settlement, near to the common. Two separate sites produced sufficient numbers of sherds to indicate with some confidence the likely presence of Anglo-Saxon settlement in the vicinity, with two other sites each producing a single sherd of Thetford Ware which may indicate other areas of settlement or, possibly, less intensive activity in these areas.[18] Notably, the Flaxlands 'common-edge' area of Carleton Rode also produced large amounts of eleventh- to fourteenth-century material, which was recovered from nearly all the excavated pits. A very different pattern, however, was noted in the area around the church where none of the eight excavated pits produced any material of Anglo-Saxon date. Indeed, the whole of this area only produced two sherds of eleventh- to fourteenth-century pottery, indicating that, despite the presence of the church by *c.*1300 at the latest, this area is likely to have remained unoccupied until the post-medieval period (when two pits produced

and the late fourteenth century, generally expressed in ceramic terms by wares dating to *c.*1100–1400 AD. Where dates of pottery types used in discussion diverge significantly from these parameters (e.g. Ipswich Ware), these are indicated in the text.

14 Davison, *The Evolution of Settlement in Three Parishes in South-East Norfolk*.

15 www.heritage.norfolk.gov.uk, NHER 10039.

16 www.heritage.norfolk.gov.uk.

17 www.heritage.norfolk.gov.uk.

18 see Lewis, 'New avenues', 139–40, for a discussion of the interpretation of pottery assemblages recovered from test-pit excavations.

modest quantities of glazed red earthenwares). It is interesting to note that a similar absence of archaeological evidence was noted during the construction of new buildings at the school.[19] No material of Romano-British date has been recovered from any of the pits at Carleton Rode, although one site between the two parts of the present village revealed a cut feature of Iron Age date. In conclusion, it seems at present that the earliest Anglo-Saxon settlement at Carleton Rode was in the area immediately east of the later common land (although the character of this area in the late Anglo-Saxon period is obviously unknown). At this time the settlement, however, constituted at least two (possibly more) separate foci of occupation, probably taking the form of farmsteads or small hamlet clusters. Occupation in this area expanded, with separate elements coalescing to become an interrupted row along the edge of the common during the eleventh to fourteenth centuries, during which time the church would have stood in isolation, apparently surrounded by arable fields manured from the Flaxlands/common-edge settlement.

Chediston, Suffolk (NGR TM 358778)

Chediston is located approximately 2km west of Halesworth in eastern Suffolk, and lies on clay and alluvial deposits between 19m and 46m OD. The settlement today comprises two quite separate elements. One small cluster of around a dozen properties surrounds the church which lies on the north side of the valley of a small tributary of the River Blyth. Half a kilometre to the north-west on higher ground away from the stream valley, Chediston Green consists of a string of properties on the edge of a former green. Here, settlement presently favours the north side of the green, with residences set well back from the road along the presumed former edge of the green. In addition, several farms are located within 500m of these two main settlement foci, with others further away within the parish. A Roman settlement site has been excavated immediately beyond the eastern limits of the present settlement around the church, and numerous finds of prehistoric and Roman date have been recovered by field-walking and metal detecting in the parish.[20] A late fifteenth-century AD kiln site was excavated in Chediston Green near the site of The Duke.[21]

Twenty-eight test pits have been excavated by the HEFA project in Chediston to date. Material of later Anglo-Saxon date has been recovered from four pits around the church, with one of these revealing a floor surface cut by a post hole sealed by a layer containing four sherds of Thetford Ware and fragments of burnt daub (tentatively interpreted as part of an oven or possibly a burnt building), with no later material. This was interpreted as the site of a late Anglo-Saxon structure, probably domestic. Nearby, and just a few metres west of the present churchyard boundary, the skull of an east–west oriented inhumation

19 www.heritage.norfolk.gov.uk, NHER 41993.

20 SHER CHD017. Report compiled for HEFA from the Suffolk Historic Environment Record by John Newman.

21 SHER CHD052. Report compiled for HEFA from the Suffolk Historic Environment Record by John Newman.

burial was found in 2007. Supine, facing east and lacking grave goods within the (limited) area exposed, it appears likely to be Christian, but it was not excavated and thus no further information or firm dating evidence has yet been recovered: it may or may not be contemporary with the late Saxon structure. Elsewhere, no material pre-dating the eleventh century was found in any of the pits excavated in Chediston Green; however, three outlying farms (Bridge Farm, Packhouse Farm and Chediston Grange) have all produced material of later Anglo-Saxon date. This is particularly interesting as it raises the possibility that the dispersed farms which are characteristic of the more recent settlement pattern in this area may have been in existence in the later Anglo-Saxon period, at the same time as a small cluster of settlement existed around the church.

Coddenham, Suffolk (NGR TM 133542)

Coddenham is a small village 10km north of Ipswich, mostly lying on the east side of a small stream valley between 25m and 45m OD. The settlement today is arranged along School Road and Church Road (both running along the stream valley) and a third route (High Street) which leads east and steeply upwards out of the valley and the present village. Coddenham church lies *c.*100m south-west of the point where these three roads meet, on the southern edge of the present settlement. Coddenham Green is a separate settlement around 2km to the north-west while the small Roman town of *Combretovium* lies a similar distance to the west. Nearer to the present village, at Coddenham House, a smaller Romano-British site has been excavated by a local group and has produced substantial evidence for Iron Age and Roman activity nearby.[22] Middle Saxon settlement and a cemetery have been discovered along the small valley south-west of the present village. Records of six or seven churches or parts of churches in Domesday Book suggest the site may have been an Anglo-Saxon minster. Little, however, is known about the development of the village itself.

Thirty test pits have been dug in Coddenham to date. Surprisingly, perhaps, given the known intensity of Romano-British activity in the area, very little material of Roman date has been found – just a single 6g sherd from the southern extremity of the present village. However, unusually within the HEFA project sites, Coddenham has produced pottery of both early and middle Anglo-Saxon date. This material has all come from test pits immediately west of the present church, suggesting the presence of a small settlement in the area later chosen as the site of the church, at the southern edge of the present village (significantly further north than the previously known settlement/cemetery). This area has also produced pottery of late Anglo-Saxon date, but ceramic material from this period was also found further to the north, suggesting that in the ninth to eleventh centuries the settlement grew and expanded northwards up the valley. This appears to represent a significant settlement 'shuffle', as the settlement/cemetery to the south-west seems to have been abandoned by this time. As in

22 Report compiled for HEFA from the Suffolk Historic Environment Record by John Newman.

Chediston, an outlying farm (Choppins Hall, located more than 1km north of the church) produced pottery of late Saxon date, hinting at the possibility of an additional, probably new, locus of activity at this time.

Great Shelford, Cambridgeshire (NGR TL 458518)

This large village lies immediately south-west of Cambridge at *c.*88m OD on the east side of the River Cam. It has seen much growth over the last 150 years with the advent of the railway and now extends for more than a mile along a road linking adjacent city satellite settlements around the periphery of Cambridge. Several Roman and prehistoric sites and extensive remains of field systems have been recorded around the village (SCDC 2003, 4–5). The church and many of the older houses are located on the western edge of the present settlement near the river, while the tithe map provides evidence for a large green occupying the triangular area between Woollards Lane, the High Street and Tunwells Lane, and extending north to encompass High Green.[23] Prior to HEFA, the earliest areas of settlement at Great Shelford were thought to lie west of the church and around Granham's manor, beyond the north-east limits of the present village, with late medieval expansion colonising the margins of High Green.[24]

Twenty-eight test pits were excavated in Great Shelford by HEFA volunteers and university students. These indicate that activity in the early Roman period was focused in the area near the later church. Although no material of early or middle Anglo-Saxon date has been recovered (from anywhere in Great Shelford), the same area also produced pottery of late Anglo-Saxon date. By this period, however, activity seems also to have focused on another area, 200m to the north-east, extending either side of the present High Street. It is notable that the test pit which produced the largest quantity of late Anglo-Saxon pottery in the entire settlement is located in this area, which is suggested in the village design statement to lie within the green.[25] This pit produced eleven sherds of Anglo-Saxon pottery (including Thetford Ware, St Neots Ware and Stamford Ware), all found in undisturbed levels containing no later material and including two large conjoining sherds of Thetford Ware found 90cm below the surface. It seems that Anglo-Saxon settlement at Great Shelford may have existed in two separate locations, one of which was near the site of the church, with the other, along High Street, developing either contemporaneously or as an almost immediate addition. It is interesting to note that a single small sherd of St Neots Ware found in undisturbed levels in the north of the village came from an area which appears to have been much more intensively occupied from the eleventh century, and thus that the Anglo-Saxon material here (possibly deposited during manuring of arable land) may immediately anticipate later settlement expansion. At Great Shelford, therefore, settlement in the later Anglo-Saxon period seems to have extended north from the area around the church to occupy the

23 Christopher Taylor, *From Domesday to Dormitory* (Cambridge (SCDC), 2003), p. 4.

24 Taylor, *Domesday to Dormitory.*

25 Taylor, *Domesday to Dormitory.*

southern part of the later green (if this is indeed what this area was), and then expanded north in the post-Conquest period.

Hessett, Suffolk (NGR TL 936618)

Hessett today is a small village located around 8km south-east of Bury St Edmunds, between 64m and 69m OD. The northern, lower lying, end of the present village takes the form of a linear settlement aligned either side of a single north–south-oriented street with a church on the east side, approximately in the centre of this part of the settlement. The southern end of the village lies around 5m higher than the north and is arranged around a former small rectangular green (now bisected by the road) whose boundaries are clearly visible on the first edition Ordnance Survey 6-inch map, and survive today as sharply cut ditches. There are several farms of a pre-Victorian date in or near (within 500m) the village, some of which are associated with moats. Two other deserted moated sites also lie within 500m of the main village street.[26]

Twenty-seven test pits were dug in Hessett during 2006–08. Ceramic material of pre-ninth-century date is limited to two small sherds of Romano-British wares, which are unlikely to indicate settlement in the near vicinity, but do hint at some sort of presence in the Roman period. However, for the later Anglo-Saxon period several test pits near the church have produced evidence indicative of intensive settlement in this area. This is the same area which produced the only Romano-British material to come from an undisturbed context. Interestingly, no late Anglo-Saxon material has been recovered from any other locations excavated to date, suggesting that it was not until the twelfth to fourteenth centuries that more intensive use was made of the sites of the three outlying farms which have been investigated so far (Maltings Farm, Elm's Farm and the moated site 600m west of Hessett Green). Around Hessett Green itself, only one site, *c.*300m south-east of Maltings Farm, produced pottery of twelfth- to fourteenth-century date. If, as seems plausible, these sites are evidence of a pattern of dispersed farmsteads around Hessett in the high medieval period, then there is currently no indication that these sites were in existence in the Anglo-Saxon period. Settlement at Hessett in the late Anglo-Saxon period appears to have taken the form of a small nucleated settlement tightly clustered around the church, with expansion in the post-Conquest period leading to the foundation of at least four new foci of settlement, probably dispersed in the form of farmsteads or common-edge settlement.

Hindringham, Norfolk (NGR TF 985365)

Hindringham is a small village situated 11km north-east of Fakenham in north Norfolk. Settlement in the parish today is dispersed in character with the village itself comprising an intermittent scatter of farms with intermediate infilling mostly appearing to be the result of development within the last 150 years. The

26 Report compiled for HEFA from the Suffolk Historic Environment Record by John Newman.

church lies on rising ground just on the northerly side of the most concentrated area of present settlement, *c.*600m south-east of Hall Farm, a building dating mostly to the Tudor period but associated with a moat and fishponds which may be earlier. Metal detecting in the parish has revealed evidence for all periods, including metalwork of pagan Anglo-Saxon date from an area south-east of the church.[27]

Eleven test pits were dug in Hindringham in 2007, sited widely over more than a kilometre within the present settlement. Four of these produced Thetford Ware dating to *c.*850–1100AD, in three of which this material was derived from undisturbed contexts and in sufficient quantity to be considered likely to indicate contemporary settlement in the immediate vicinity. One of these lay immediately south of the church. The fourth produced just one sherd from a disturbed level, but of a reasonable size (10g), and is more difficult to interpret: it may be evidence of settlement nearby, but could also be the product of less intensive use of the area, such as manuring for arable cultivation. Notwithstanding this uncertainty, these four sites were separated from one another by at least 400m, so appear likely to represent at least three discrete nodes of late Anglo-Saxon settlement, probably of limited extent, rather than a large nucleated settlement at this period. Further test pitting in the intervening areas will be needed to test this hypothesis. Notably, the four pits which produced late Anglo-Saxon material also produced larger quantities of high medieval ceramics, suggesting a process of continued expansion of the areas occupied in the late Saxon period in the eleventh to fourteenth centuries, a pattern noted in several HEFA settlements.

Houghton and Wyton (NGR TL 281721)

Houghton and Wyton are two small villages, each recorded separately in Domesday Book and each with its own medieval church, but now conjoined to form a single, polyfocal nucleated settlement sited on alluvial gravel between 5m and 10m OD close to the northern banks of the River Ouse 4km east of Huntingdon in Cambridgeshire. Prior to HEFA, the area had received no significant archaeological attention, although a Romano-British cemetery lies a little to the north of the village on Houghton Hill,[28] while the history of the villages was reviewed some time ago by the Victoria County History.

Several of the pits contained material of Roman date, all either in or around Houghton, and all derived from test pits between the edge of the flood plain and the present NW–SE road linking the villages (Huntingdon Road). These extend along the flood plain in a zone at least 300m long. A single sherd (6g in weight) of early/middle Anglo-Saxon pottery, recovered from the western edge of this area, close to the river and within 100m of Houghton church, provides a rare example of evidence of ceramic material for this period. Found 0.4m below the surface, this level contained no material later than 1200 AD, and is therefore

27 www.heritage.norfolk.gov.uk, NHER.

28 W. Page, G. Proby and S. Ladds, *The Victoria History of the County of Huntingdon*, II (London, 1932), p. 179.

unlikely to have been disturbed recently, thus is more likely to indicate early/middle Anglo-Saxon activity in the vicinity, and thus hints at a degree of continuity of use of this zone from the Roman period onwards. The same zone also produced material of later Anglo-Saxon date, but in this period ceramic material in significant quantities also appears in Wyton, for the first time. Here, however, there is less evidence for intensive activity around the church, with a site 200m to the north-west revealing pottery of 1100–1400 date and also two small sherds of Stamford Ware, one from the lowest levels which contained no material post-dating 1100 AD. Finds of single sherds of late Anglo-Saxon pottery between the two villages and to the east of Houghton may indicate manuring in these areas. Examination of the sections of test pits north of Huntingdon Road, neither of which produced any pre-nineteenth-century pottery, indicated the presence of arable soils immediately beneath the topsoil, suggesting this area was not settled until the early modern period. It seems that early settlement in Houghton and Wyton extended along the edge of the flood plain focused primarily on the Houghton area. This seems likely to have been occupied fairly continuously from the Roman period onwards, with settlement at Wyton perhaps originating in the later Anglo-Saxon period.

Little Hallingbury, Essex (NGR TL 503175)

Little Hallingbury is situated around 10km north-east of Harlow in Essex immediately west of the M11 motorway. It is today a sprawling but still very rural settlement, much of which appears to be the result of twentieth-century expansion and infilling. The medieval church has a Norman doorway and contains Roman brick and tile in its walls,[29] and is surrounded by a small cluster of houses including Monksbury Farm. Nearly 1km to the south-east lies a medieval moated site containing a sixteenth-/seventeenth-century timber-framed farmhouse, named 'Romans House' following the discovery of a Roman site nearby during excavations along the line of the M11.[30] The dispersed nature of the pre-modern settlement of Little Hallingbury is hinted at by the presence of several place names containing the element 'green' within the semi-continuous spread of settlement, which are presumed formerly to have been separate hamlets. Ribbon development extending for more than a kilometre lies either side of the main modern road which leads north to the nearby market town of Bishop's Stortford. No archaeological investigation had previously been carried out within the village.

Thirty test pits were dug in 2007–08 in and around the present village. Test pits in two separate sites produced middle Anglo-Saxon Ipswich Ware (*c*.720–850 AD). The first of these lies on the eastern side of the present hamlet of Gaston Common, where a single sherd was found *c*.30cm below the surface in a disturbed layer. This was a large sherd (25g) and is therefore considered more likely to indicate activity of some sort in the vicinity in the middle Saxon period. The second site lies more than a kilometre to the west, within the moated site of

29 unlockingessex.essexcc.gov.uk, EHER 4432, 4433.
30 unlockingessex.essexcc.gov.uk, EHER 4318.

Romans House. The test pit here contained four sherds of Ipswich Ware, three from undisturbed levels of which one was sealed within a cut feature interpreted as a beam slot. This clearly indicates the presence of a substantial timber-framed building on this site in the middle Saxon period. This same test pit also produced seven small (all less than 5g) sherds of Romano-British greyware, derived from the same lower, undisturbed levels as the Ipswich Ware, including three in the fill of the beam slot: these were interpreted as residual within the cut feature, but are likely to indicate activity of some sort in the vicinity in the Roman period. This may or may not be associated with the nearby Roman site discovered during construction of the M11 motorway.

In view of the unusually large quantity of evidence for the middle Anglo-Saxon period, it is interesting to note that no material at all of later Anglo-Saxon date has been found in any of the test pits excavated to date in Little Hallingbury. Consequently, the development of settlement in this area at this time remains something of a mystery. The distribution of material from the eleventh to fourteenth centuries, found in test pits in six separate locations, suggests the thinly spread settlement pattern of the post-Conquest period took the form of small dispersed hamlets or farmsteads, some of which may have been arranged around small commons or greens.

Pirton, Hertfordshire (NGR TL 145315)

Pirton is situated just over 5km north-west of Hitchin in Hertfordshire. It is today a nucleated village located centrally within the parish of Pirton, clustered around an eleventh-century parish church and the adjacent earthwork remains of Toot Hill, an imposing motte and bailey castle of probable eleventh- or twelfth-century date.[31] Extensive earthworks south and east of the motte known as 'The Bury' are variously considered to represent the remains of either manorial or village settlement. A number of early post-medieval buildings survive within the village: several of these lie on the edge of or just outside the present village, including Burge End Farm, a sixteenth-century building associated with the remains of a possible moat, which lies *c.*300 m to the north of the present village, and a second, better preserved moat 500m to the south-west at Rectory Farm. Hammonds Farm and Docwra Manor are also considered likely to be the sites of former manors.[32]

Twenty-nine test pits have been dug in Pirton to date and an interesting pattern has emerged. Five pits have produced Romano-British material, all from deeply buried, undisturbed contexts. Single sherds have been recovered from the south-west margin of the present settlement and from Burge End, but larger numbers have been recovered from three pits clustered on the east of the present village. It is possible tentatively to suggest that this area may have been the site of a small Romano-British settlement, surrounded by its arable fields as hinted at by the single sherds, possibly from manuring, recovered to the north and

31 *Pirton Village Design Statement* (Pirton Parish Council, 2003); H. Hofton, *Pirton Motte and Bailey*, Local History Society Report (2007); www.pirtonhistory.org.uk.

32 *Pirton Village Design Statement*, p. 4.

west. Twelve of the excavated pits have produced material of later Anglo-Saxon date, all from the north-eastern half of the present village. One focus of late Anglo-Saxon activity is indicated south of Burge End, a second in the centre of the north-eastern part of the present village, and a third to the east of the earthworks south-east of the church. None of the six pits excavated to date west of the church/Toot Hill area have produced any pre-Norman Conquest material, but they have produced considerable quantities of ceramics dating to the three centuries immediately following the Conquest. It appears likely that the later Anglo-Saxon settlement may have comprised at least three main nodes of settlement, possibly constituted as separate elements rather than one large village, occupying the same area as the Roman settlement. In the eleventh or twelfth centuries, it seems likely that the construction of the castle prompted a westward expansion of activity onto land which may have previously been occupied by fields, although the absence of even a single sherd of Anglo-Saxon pottery from this area might argue against this interpretation.

Sharnbrook, Bedfordshire (NGR SP 995595)

Sharnbrook today is a large village less than 15km north of Bedford, with a range of shops, primary and secondary schools and large areas of relatively recent housing. It lies between 50m and 60m OD on Oxford Clay. The village is a nucleated settlement mainly arranged as a double row along the NW–SE oriented High Street which runs parallel with the Sharn Brook to the north. The Norman parish church of St Peter's lies *c.*200m south of the High Street within a large churchyard, while *c.*0.5km west of the church lies Castle Close which contains the oval banked and ditched remains of a probable medieval moated site.[33] Tofte Manor and Manor Farm both lie outside the village, north of the Sharn Brook, and Barleycroft is a separate hamlet 0.5km to the north-east of the village.

Sixteen test pits have been excavated in Sharnbrook so far, focused mainly on the High Street. No Roman material has been found in the village to date, but two test pits have produced material of later Anglo-Saxon date. These are both located on the High Street, close together in an area *c.*300m north of the church. This area is also the focus of relatively intensive activity between the eleventh and mid fourteenth centuries. The areas around the church and along the southern stretch of the High Street have produced no material of later Anglo-Saxon date, suggesting that occupation in Sharnbrook at this time may have been of limited extent, restricted to the northern end of the present High Street. This area continued in occupation in the post-Norman Conquest period, when the settlement expanded north and south along the High Street. The site of Manor Farm was clearly occupied at this time, but has so far produced no evidence of Anglo-Saxon date.

33 Beds HER 994.

Terrington St Clement, Norfolk (NGR TF 551204)

Terrington St Clement was the first settlement to be investigated by the HEFA CORS project. Today it is an irregular, sprawling village located around 8km west of King's Lynn in the Fenland region of west Norfolk, lying on peat and alluvial and marine deposits. It sits at around 3m OD and is now protected from inundation by a sea bank known as Roman Bank, 1km north of the church. Previously it has been subject to some historical research by local historians resident in the village,[34] while archaeological investigation has most notably included field-walking during the Fenland Survey,[35] although this largely excluded the area around the present settlement.

Over two seasons, a total of sixteen test pits have been excavated as part of the HEFA project. Late Anglo-Saxon pottery has been found in pits in four different locations. The first of these lies north of the church where three test pits were sited on the advice of a resident who had farmed the land for several decades. All three of these contained late Anglo-Saxon wares, which in two of the test pits were derived from levels more than 40cm below the surface containing no material of post-medieval date and which were deemed to be undisturbed since that time. Archaeologically sterile deposits were encountered below these levels. It can reasonably be inferred that this area of Terrington St Clement was intensively exploited for the first time in the ninth or tenth century, which coincides with the earliest references to the church. This would only have been possible after the construction of Roman Bank, which extends in an east–west line north of the present village, along the line of the present road south of Bellmount and acts as a defence against inundation from the nearby Wash. The evidence from the test pits suggests that this bank is likely in fact to date to the ninth or tenth century AD. This period of activity appears to have been most intensive in the southern part of the field nearest the church, and lasted until the later fifteenth century, after which increased flooding may have caused this area to be abandoned.

Other areas of Anglo-Saxon activity include a site immediately west of the church where a test pit revealed undisturbed early deposits including a floor surface dating to *c.*1080–1400 AD which was overlain by deposits which included a large (25g) sherd of Thetford Ware. The floor was not removed, and it is possible that earlier deposits may lie underneath. Some 250m south of the church, a third site, now a small ditched field set well back from the road, produced a significant assemblage (10 sherds totalling 74g) of late Anglo-Saxon pottery accompanied by early medieval sandy wares and a considerable quantity of faunal remains, mostly concentrated in a 30cm deep deposit lying 40–70cm below the surface. This may represent accumulated material built up between

34 B. Howling, 'Terrington St Clement – a History' (short unpublished paper obtainable through King's Lynn Museum); Terrington St Clement History Group, *A History of Terrington St Clement* (King's Lynn, 2005).

35 R. J. Silvester, *The Fenland Project No. 3: Marshland and the Nar Valley, Norfolk*, *East Anglian Archaeology*, 45 (1988).

850 and 1400 AD, but could equally well represent a much shorter period of intensive occupation between *c*.1100 and *c*.1150. The area between this site and the church has to date revealed no material of pre-nineteenth-century date.

A third site, on the western side of the presently most intensively occupied part of the village, produced two small sherds of Thetford Ware, also accompanied by later medieval material, suggesting that this location, a saltern mound, may have been in use in the later Anglo-Saxon and high medieval period, possibly for dairying, before being abandoned *c*.1400 AD until a bungalow was constructed in the mid twentieth century. Further south, one of two test pits at Lovell's Hall produced a single sherd of Stamford Ware which may relate to manuring rather than more intensive occupation. It is interesting to note that this area is close to the early and middle Anglo-Saxon settlement previously identified at Hay Green.[36]

Overall, the evidence from the test pits to date suggests that several discrete locations within the area occupied by the present village of Terrington St Clement were in active use in the late Anglo-Saxon period, possibly as part of a highly dispersed settlement. Areas of settlement north and south of the church, for example, may not have represented a continuous spread of settlement, but instead two separate elements with the church itself surrounded by open space. The later Anglo-Saxon period appears to have been one of energetic expansion at Terrington St Clement, which saw land reclaimed by the construction of the sea bank, the founding of the church, the appearance of new foci of settlement and the use of the surrounding landscape for dairying and possibly agriculture.

Thorney, Cambridgeshire (NGR TF 283042)

Thorney today is a small fenland village dominated by its great abbey church, located on a small island in the fens which rises to a maximum height of *c*.7.1m OD. South of the church the land falls away to *c*.4.2m OD at a crossroads, with most post-medieval development arranged along Wisbech Road which runs to the east where the land surface continues to drop gently onto the fen. Much of this housing comprises uniform rows of south-facing terraced cottages constructed as a model village for the Duke of Bedford in the eighteenth century. Larger houses, mostly recent, are sited south of the Wisbech Road, while a densely packed cluster of buildings occupies the area immediately north of the abbey church, which was retained after the Dissolution for use as the parish church. The area south of the abbey church is today occupied by a small close of large post-medieval houses arranged around a small green, with other buildings associated with the Duke of Bedford's post-Reformation estate to the west. Archaeological excavation by the University of Leicester immediately north of the abbey church revealed medieval and other activity probably associated with

[36] A. Crowson, T. Lane, K. Penn and D. Trimble, *Anglo-Saxon Settlement on the Silt-land of Eastern England*, Lincolnshire Archaeological and Heritage Series Report 7 (Lincoln, 2005), pp. 147–70.

the Dissolution,[37] while a community excavation in the pasture land of Abbey Fields west of the abbey church revealed a thirteenth-century stone-footed, aisled building.[38]

Twenty-two test pits were dug by HEFA in Thorney in 2006 and 2007. Those in the low lying eastern part of the present village were all devoid of any pre-modern finds. Although excavation was only able to proceed to a depth of 20cm in the northernmost of these as the water table was reached at this point, this in itself indicated the likely reason for the rejection of this low lying part of the present village for occupation in the Anglo-Saxon and medieval period. Three test pits in Thorney produced material of later Anglo-Saxon date. Although none has yielded more than a single sherd, the two largest were found in pits located in the same area, north of the abbey church and south-east of the present road crossing. Although inferences based on such a small amount of data must inevitably be regarded as somewhat tentative, it seems reasonable to infer that some sort of secular occupation was present immediately north of the abbey precinct in the late Anglo-Saxon period, but that this was of very limited extent and intensity. Not until the post-Norman Conquest period does any activity seem to have taken place north of the crossroads.

Ufford (NGR TF 094040)

Ufford today is a small linear village lying on limestone at between 21m and 46m OD, approximately 10km north-west of Peterborough. Prior to HEFA, the only known archaeological finds comprised a concentration of Roman material, including a silver spoon, discovered casually by the landowner in an arable field south-west of the church (recorded in the SMR for Peterborough Unitary Authority). The history of Ufford was reviewed in an early volume of the Victoria County History,[39] and, more recently, in a less academic format, by a local resident.[40]

Twenty-three test pits have been excavated in Ufford. Roman and late Anglo-Saxon material has been recovered from pits in two discrete areas of the village: in the south in the area around the church, and in the north in the garden of Ufford Farm. In the latter case, this was found in several places including the fill of a small gully underlying a fourteenth-century stone wall.[41] No finds predating *c.*1700 AD have been found from the area between these two locations, suggesting that settlement at Ufford was arranged as two separate nodes during the Roman period and the later Anglo-Saxon/early Norman period.

37 J. Thomas, 'Evidence for the dissolution of Thorney Abbey: recent excavations and landscape analysis at Thorney, Cambridgeshire', *Medieval Archaeology*, 50 (2006), 179–241.

38 R. Mortimer (OA East), pers. comm., report in preparation.

39 R. M. Serjeanston and W. Adkins, *The Victoria History of the County of Northampton*, II (London, 1906), 533–7.

40 F. Gosling, *Our Ufford Heritage* (Stamford, 2000).

41 C. Ranson, 'Excavation of an Anglo-Saxon and medieval site at Ufford, 2007' (in preparation).

West Mersea, Essex (NGR TM 009125)

West Mersea today occupies more than 2.5 sq km of the south-western part of Mersea Island, just off the Essex coast around 8km south of Colchester, at 3–12m OD. However, the first edition Ordnance Survey map shows most of the area of the present village to be devoid of settlement, with occupation limited to the areas around the church and a scatter of outlying farms. A Roman tessellated pavement was revealed during recent garden landscaping,[42] and Roman tile has been noted in the walls of the church,[43] otherwise little archaeological investigation has been carried out within the village.

Thirty-eight test pits have been excavated in West Mersea to date. Romano-British material has been found in five of these, clustered in two separate locations: one (as might have been expected) due west of the church near the tessellated pavement, and the second a new site *c.*300m to the north of this. Two test pits in this latter area have also produced a total of three sherds of Ipswich Ware, all located in undisturbed levels. A single 10cm spit in the easternmost of these produced two large sherds (totalling 47g), along with six sherds of Roman date. The latter were interpreted as evidence of nearby Romano-British activity surviving as residual material within a likely middle Saxon occupation layer. It is perhaps noteworthy that this area lies some 300m from the church. No material dating to the later Anglo-Saxon period has been recovered from any of the excavated test pits, leaving the development of the area at this time unclear. Pottery of eleventh- to fourteenth-century date, by contrast, has been found in test pits around the church, up the High Street to its north, and in the west of the present village, along Coast Road, the first period for which this latter area has produced archaeological evidence.

Wiveton, Norfolk (NGR TG 043428)

Wiveton lies little more than 1.6 km from the north Norfolk coast near Blakeney, on boulder clay and fluvial deposits at between 5m and 10m OD, and is today a small, quiet, rather extenuated nucleated village of brick-and-beach-cobble houses extending north from the church along two winding lanes which intersect to form an elongated figure of eight. These lanes run parallel with the nearby River Glaven whose floodplain, previously a tidal inlet, the village mostly overlooks. Wiveton Hall lies barely a kilometre to the north of the present village, on the seaward side of the east–west oriented road between Blakeney and Cley-next-the-Sea. Previous archaeological investigation, including metal detecting, has revealed finds of all periods in the parish of Wiveton, but little from within the village itself.

Twenty-five test pits were excavated in Wiveton in 2006 and 2008. Roman material was found in four discrete areas within the village, but pottery of later Anglo-Saxon date was mostly restricted to the area west of the church. This suggests a small area of moderately intensive activity in the ninth to eleventh

42 unlockingessex.essexcc.gov.uk, EHER 2191; 2214.

43 unlockingessex.essexcc.gov.uk, EHER 2274.

centuries in this area. Single sherds of Anglo-Saxon pottery from two separate locations further to the north may be interpreted as evidence for non-intensive activity, possibly manuring, which might indicate agricultural or horticultural activity in these areas in this period. It is notable that a considerable expansion of activity at Wiveton north from the area around the church in the immediate post-Anglo-Saxon period is clearly indicated by the wide distribution of eleventh- to fourteenth-century pottery, which was found in all bar two of the test pits, and may in part relate to a trade in Grimston Ware to Norway from wharfs at Wiveton.[44]

Discussion

The data from the HEFA CORS test-pitting programme in East Anglia prompts a number of observations with respect to our understanding of settlement in the Anglo-Saxon period. The test-pitting strategy has clearly demonstrated its capacity to produce data which can be used to reconstruct the development of occupied sites and landscapes in much more detail than is otherwise possible, based on archaeological evidence rather than morphologically based inference. Furthermore, during the HEFA programme in East Anglia a *modus operandi* has been developed for involving volunteer labour in large-scale archaeological data-collection programmes within and around CORS which can retrieve data useful for academic research in the large quantities which are needed to truly advance knowledge and understanding: there is considerable potential to apply the HEFA approach in other sites and regions.

A number of general observations can be made from the evidence unearthed to date, many of which relate to issues currently the subject of active debate within the field of settlement studies and which are of relevance to the study of the Anglo-Saxon period.[45] Firstly, the HEFA CORS excavations have indicated that considerably greater amounts of archaeological evidence for the extent and nature of settlement and the development of the landscape in the past, including the Anglo-Saxon period, do survive underneath rural settlements which are inhabited today than has previously been acknowledged. The test-pitting technique is effective in recovering evidence for Anglo-Saxon activity in the form of ceramics and/or cut features dateable to the fifth to eleventh centuries AD. Evidence for this period has been recovered from all but three of the rural communities which have been investigated in East Anglia (Fig. 5.2), with more than one test pit in five (87 out of 420 pits, 21% of the total) producing pottery of fifth- to eleventh-century date. In most cases these have provided the first archaeological evidence for activity of Anglo-Saxon date from the site,

44 Carenza Lewis, 'Archaeological excavations in Wiveton village – preliminary results from the Higher Education Field Academy CORS test pits in 2006', *Glaven Historian*, 10 (2007), 57–70.

45 See Rippon, *Beyond the Medieval Village*, pp. 138–200 for a recent review of the evidence and discussion of the issues in East Anglia.

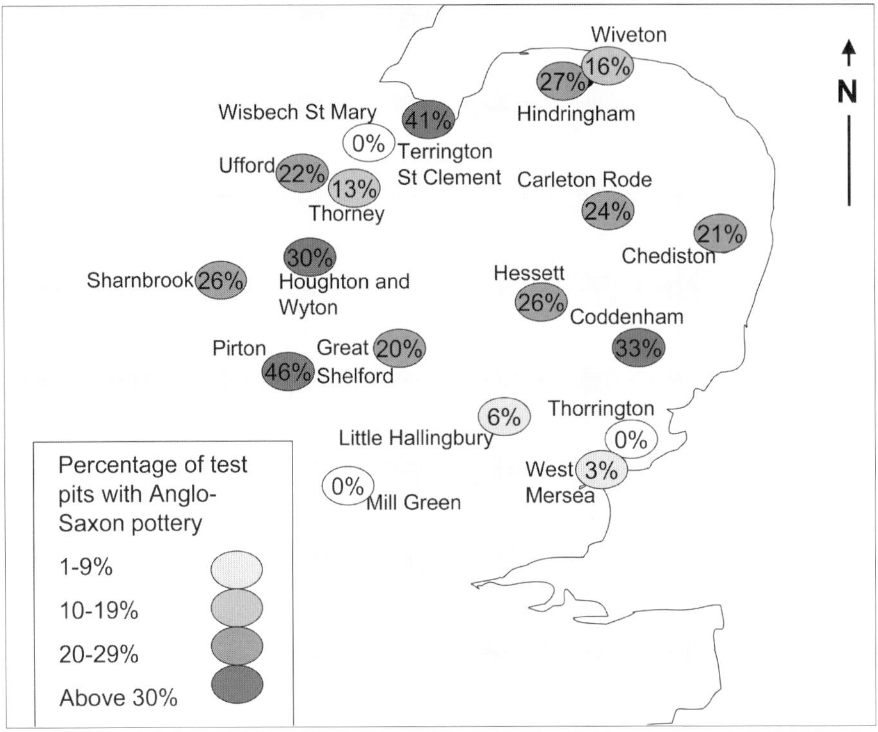

Figure 5.2. East Anglia, showing the percentage of excavated test pits which produced pottery of Anglo-Saxon (mid fifth to mid eleventh century AD) date.

whether in village centres or at outlying dispersed hamlets or farms. As a result, estimates of the antiquity of these sites can now based on archaeologically demonstrable fact: in effect, dozens of ‘new’ Anglo-Saxon sites have been identified. At least four late Anglo-Saxon sites have been discovered at Terrington St Clement, for example, at least two at Carleton Rode, four at Chediston, three at Hindringham, three at Pirton and two at Ufford, to mention just a few. Some observations can be made regarding the form these settlements are likely to have taken: in some cases, as at Hessett, Coddenham and Chediston, they appear to be nucleated settlements tightly clustered near the church; in other instances, they are small dispersed entities likely to be farmsteads or very small hamlets, as have been identified in or near Carleton Rode, Terrington St Clement and Chediston. At Pirton and Terrington St Clement, late Anglo-Saxon settlements may have taken the form of larger nucleated villages, possibly, in the case of Terrington, with open spaces within them. Interestingly, several are associated with moats of (presumed) later date.

For all of the investigated settlements, the data from the test pits has allowed their chronological and geographical development to be reconstructed in often considerable detail in a way that has simply not been possible before. These individual histories are important both for what they tell us about the sites individually (as has been reviewed above), and also for the contribution they can make when considered together to the broader understanding of the development of the rural settlement pattern in the Anglo-Saxon period (and, of course, for other periods, although consideration of this is beyond the scope of this paper). Although detailed consideration of this would be premature in a project which is still ongoing, a few points will be examined briefly below.

The relationship of Roman period activity to the later settlement pattern is one area for which interesting data has been recovered. It is evident that most of the HEFA settlements (thirteen out of eighteen) have produced pottery of Roman date, but notable that few have done so in large quantities. Two of those which have produced Romano-British material (Thorrington and Wisbech St Mary) have yielded none for Anglo-Saxon activity and of the remainder, three (Terrington St Clement, Hessett and Coddenham) have produced only one or two sherds – unlikely to indicate settlement in the vicinity. Of the eight settlements which have produced more than a couple of sherds of Roman pottery in association with Anglo-Saxon pottery (i.e. within 300m), two have produced pottery of early/middle but not later Anglo-Saxon date. Overall, 40% of sites producing late Anglo-Saxon pottery are associated with significant quantities of Roman material, whereas closer to 90% of early/middle Anglo-Saxon sites show the same association. Thus it appears that the correlation of Roman activity with settlement post-850 AD is generally low. In geographical terms, this lack of correlation is particularly evident in central Norfolk and Suffolk. On the other hand, there is some evidence here, although based on a very small number of sites, for a significant correlation between settlement of Roman and fifth- to eighth-century date, but only in the south of the region.

Developments in the early and middle Saxon period are generally difficult to assess, largely due to the small amount of recovered evidence: it is notable that few areas of current habitation investigated by HEFA have produced any archaeological evidence of early or middle Anglo-Saxon date (Fig. 5.3).[46] Notably, however, nearly all of those which have done so are located in the south of the region. Given that all the sites investigated in the HEFA CORS project are inhabited today, this suggests that there seems to be a regional distinction in the level of correspondence between sites used in the early/middle Anglo-Saxon and those occupied later: there is very little evidence for any co-location at all in most of the region, with the notable exception of Essex and south Suffolk where the incidence seems higher. It is perhaps worth noting, however, that only two of these five sites (Coddenham and Houghton) have also produced evidence nearby of later Anglo-Saxon date, thus the degree of 'continuity' (however that might be defined or identified) may be lower even in this area.

In respect of the later Anglo-Saxon period, most of the HEFA CORS sites have revealed archaeological evidence in one or more areas in sufficient quantities to appear likely to indicate settlement at that date in the vicinity, indicative of considerable expansion at this time. There are some important qualifica-

[46] n.b. two middle Anglo-Saxon sites have been discovered in Little Hallingbury.

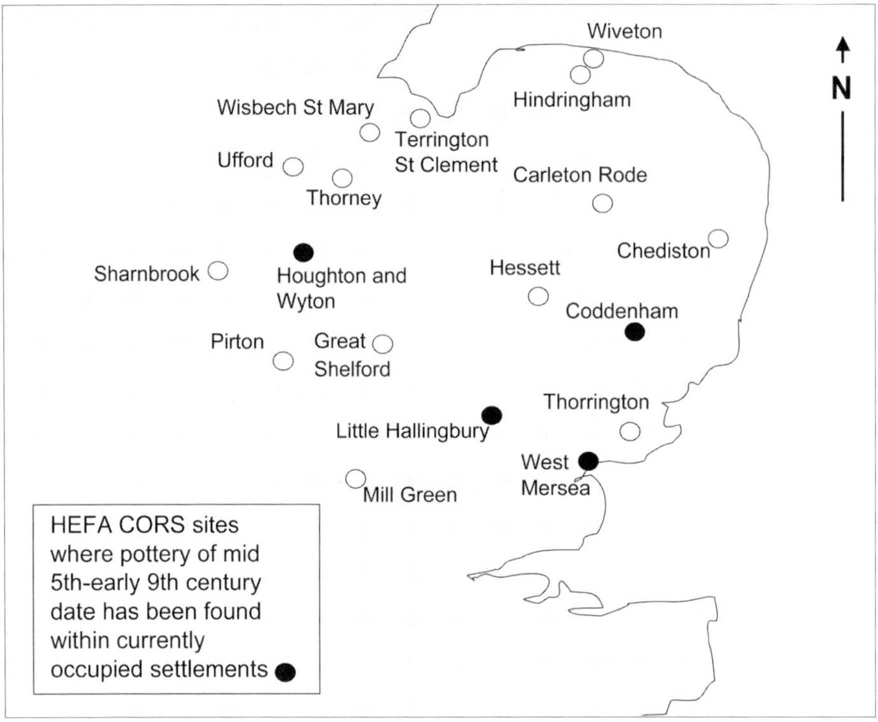

Figure 5.3. East Anglia, showing the location of HEFA sites where pottery of mid-fifth- to mid-ninth-century date has been recovered from test pits within currently occupied settlements.

tions to this statement, however. Nearly all of the sites from which late Anglo-Saxon pottery is entirely absent are located in the south of the study region (Fig. 5.4). Here, Mill Green may be disregarded as it appears to have been a minor secondary settlement of post-medieval foundation around a mill; otherwise, however, it is notable that none of the CORS in Essex have produced any evidence for late Anglo-Saxon occupation within post-Conquest and later settlements. This contrasts with the high level of correlation between late Anglo-Saxon and post-eleventh century occupation elsewhere in the region: in only two instances have areas which produced significant quantities of late Anglo-Saxon pottery failed to yield similarly significant volumes of material of post-Conquest date. It is interesting to note that the two exceptions here (Thorney and the northern settlement in Ufford) are located within a few miles of each other in or near the north Cambridgeshire Fens. In most cases, areas close to parish churches are occupied in the late Anglo-Saxon period, although there are notable exceptions to this rule in Essex and also at Carleton Rode in Norfolk. In some areas dispersed farms appear to come into existence at this time, although in others this seems to happen later. Generally, the late Anglo-Saxon period appears to be one when many new sites, ranging from nucleated village clusters to dispersed farms, arrived in the landscape, and these seem generally prone to

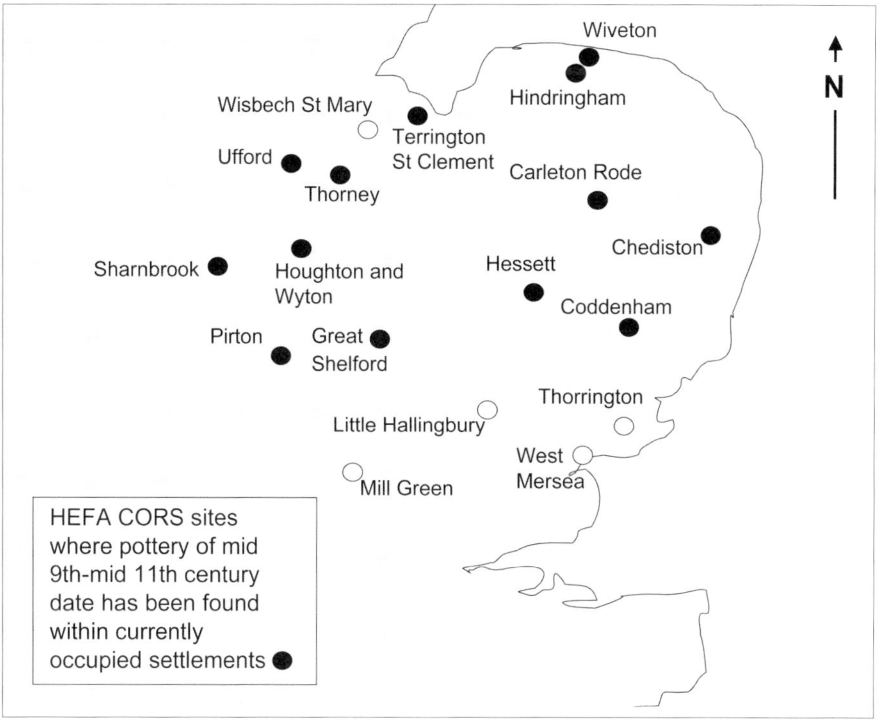

Figure 5.4. East Anglia, showing the location of HEFA sites where pottery of mid-ninth- to mid-eleventh-century date has been recovered from test pits within currently occupied settlements.

continue and expand in the post-Norman Conquest period. The arable base of some of these settlements is hinted at by the many test-pit sites which produced limited amounts of ninth- to eleventh-century pottery and may indicate the presence of Anglo-Saxon arable fertilized by manuring.

These and other observations are interesting, particularly in the context of current ideas regarding the pattern of settlement in the past and the regionally varying character and impact of its drivers. In many respects, however, it can be suggested that the most significant results of the HEFA CORS project do not at this stage relate to grand theorising regarding the development of the rural settlement pattern, not least because work is still ongoing on most sites and such pronouncements must still be premature. Of more importance, for now, is the promise the results hold for our ability in the future to be able to reconstruct the phased development of the settlement pattern, including in the areas which are inhabited today, in very much more detail and with more spatial precision than has hitherto been the case. Similar exercises, in many more places, would revolutionise our understanding of the character and development of the pattern of rural settlement.

6

Medieval Field Systems and Settlement Nucleation: Common or Separate Origins?

SUSAN OOSTHUIZEN

For more than a century, historians and archaeologists have explained the emergence in the Anglo-Saxon period of open and common fields and nucleated settlement as the contemporary products of a new, co-ordinated approach by Germanic migrants and/or their descendants to improving the efficiency of agricultural production. Protagonists have argued about whether the social relationships underpinning this change were proto-manorial or an expression of community decision-making, but have not disagreed that these features were linked or that they emerged in the post-Roman period.

'Nucleated' settlement is concentrated in just one place in a township, rather than dispersed in scattered farms and hamlets. Such settlements might originate in a single place, or be polyfocal; and they might contain planned elements or have informal origins and additions, or a combination of both. By the Middle Ages, nucleations tended to be concentrated in the 'central province', a distribution lying across England roughly along a line from the Isle of Wight in the south-west to Northumberland in the north-east (Fig. 6.1).[1] 'Open fields' – that is, sub-divided fields whose internal divisions were not sufficient to hamper access across them – were found throughout medieval England (Fig. 6.2).[2] Across central southern England, however, a specialised subset of open fields, often characterised as 'common' or 'Midland', had developed by about 1300, identified by a rigorous regularity of layout, tenure, and cropping (Fig. 6.3).[3]

1 Brian K. Roberts and Stuart Wrathmell, *Region and Place* (Swindon, 2002), pp. 124 and 144; see also Figure 1.

2 Mark Bailey, *Medieval Suffolk* (Woodbridge, 2007), pp. 102–15. Most were characterised by a good deal of irregularity in the total area of arable, the number of fields, the size and layout of fields, patterns of distribution of demesne and villein holdings, and the degree to which they were cultivated in common or in severalty. Patterns of cropping and fallowing might be organised in common or in severalty by field, furlong or even by strip holding.

3 'Common' or 'Midland' field systems tended to develop in predominantly arable vills, combining all the plough land in just two or three very large fields of roughly equivalent area. Demesne and villein holdings tended to be intermingled in regular sequences, and to be fairly equally distributed between each field; both cropping and fallowing were communally regulated. There is a lack of clarity within the scholarly literature about the distinction, and the importance of the distinction, between the more widespread, irregular,

While there have been attempts over the past forty years to narrow down the period in which both nucleation and field systems were introduced, what has not been at issue has been the conviction that both shared a common origin. This paper explores the contribution to this latter thesis of a growing body of archaeological evidence.

Historiography

The earliest known observations of differences between the 'planned' landscape of predominantly nucleated villages and regular common-field systems in 'Midland' England, and the 'ancient' landscapes of dispersed settlement and irregular open-field systems, were recorded in the sixteenth century.[4] Since the later nineteenth century, scholars have taken such descriptions a step further by arguing that both originated in the same period, and as part of the same historical processes, thus establishing a foundation for research that has provided the dominant discourse for explanations of the making of the Anglo-Saxon landscape for over a hundred years.

Frederick Seebohm, in his prescient *English Village Community* (heavily influenced by his experience of common-field landscapes in Hertfordshire and Cambridgeshire), simply assumed that the medieval village was nucleated and that it was integrated with open-field systems.[5] Frederic Maitland, who disagreed with Seebohm on most points, nonetheless concurred in this. He took Seebohm's view of the connectedness of villages and fields a step further by introducing a description of the process that underlay that association: 'The outlines of our nucleated villages may have been drawn for us by Germanic settlers, whereas in the land of hamlets and scattered steads old Celtic arrangements may never have been thoroughly effaced'.[6] Frank Stenton followed Maitland in his arguments that open fields and nucleated settlement were examples of the

open-field systems on the one hand and the more restricted, regular, common-field systems on the other, despite the publication of major papers by Thirsk and Fox which established the distinctive characteristics of each form. Both regarded the communal organisation of fallowing on arable land as *the* distinctive feature of common-field systems, arguing that this principle underpinned the division of the arable into just two or three large fields so that a half or a third could be set aside as fallow each year, compared with open fields in which the arable might be divided into any number of fields and in which fallowing could be undertaken communally and/or in severalty in any fields in the same vill. Harold S. A. Fox, 'Approaches to the adoption of the Midland System', in *The Origins of Open Field Agriculture*, ed. Trevor Rowley (London, 1981), 64–111; Joan Thirsk, 'The common fields', *Past and Present*, 29 (1964), 3–25; Fox, 'Approaches', pp. 66–8.

4 Roberts and Wrathmell, *Region*, p. 1.

5 Frederick Seebohm, *English Village Community* (London, 1883; 1915 edn), p. 76 (my additions).

6 Frederic M. Maitland, *Domesday Book and Beyond* (Cambridge, 1907), p. 15.

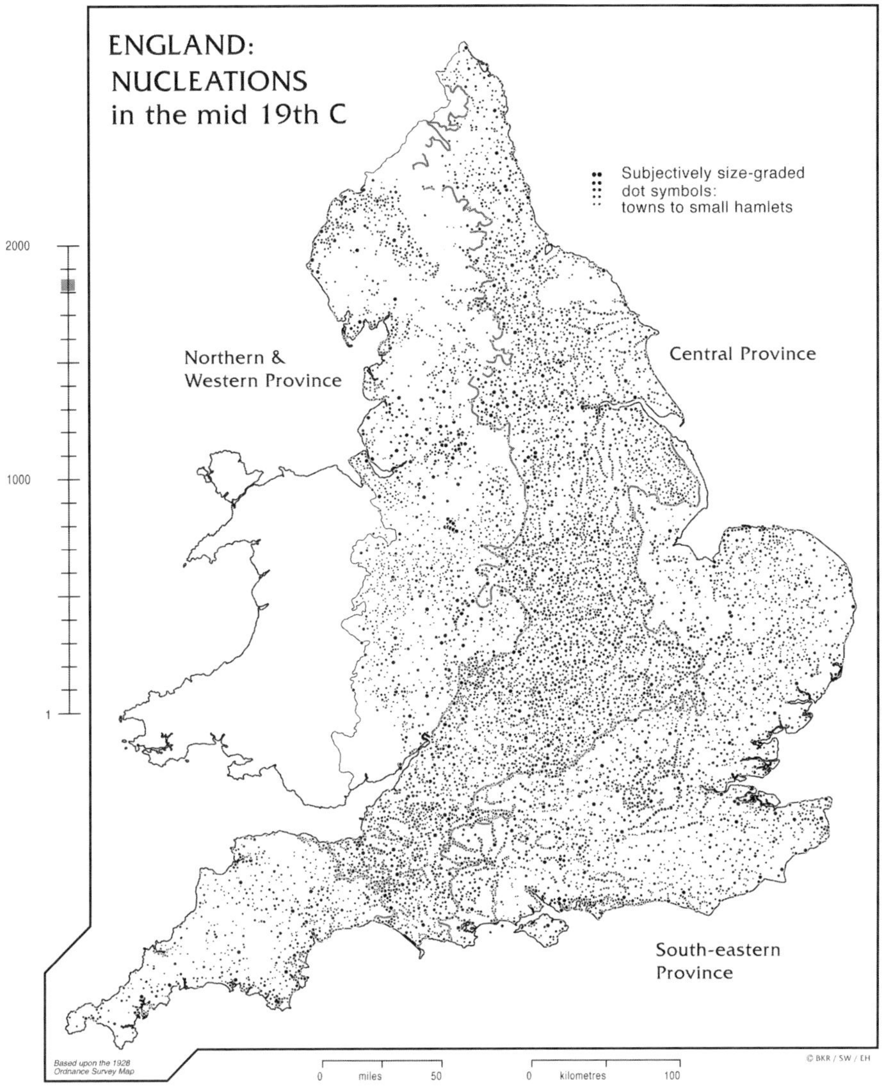

Figure 6.1. England: nucleations in the mid-nineteenth century. (Reproduced from B. K. Roberts and S. Wrathmell, *Region and Place* (Swindon, 2002), figure 1.1, by kind permission of Professor B. K. Roberts)

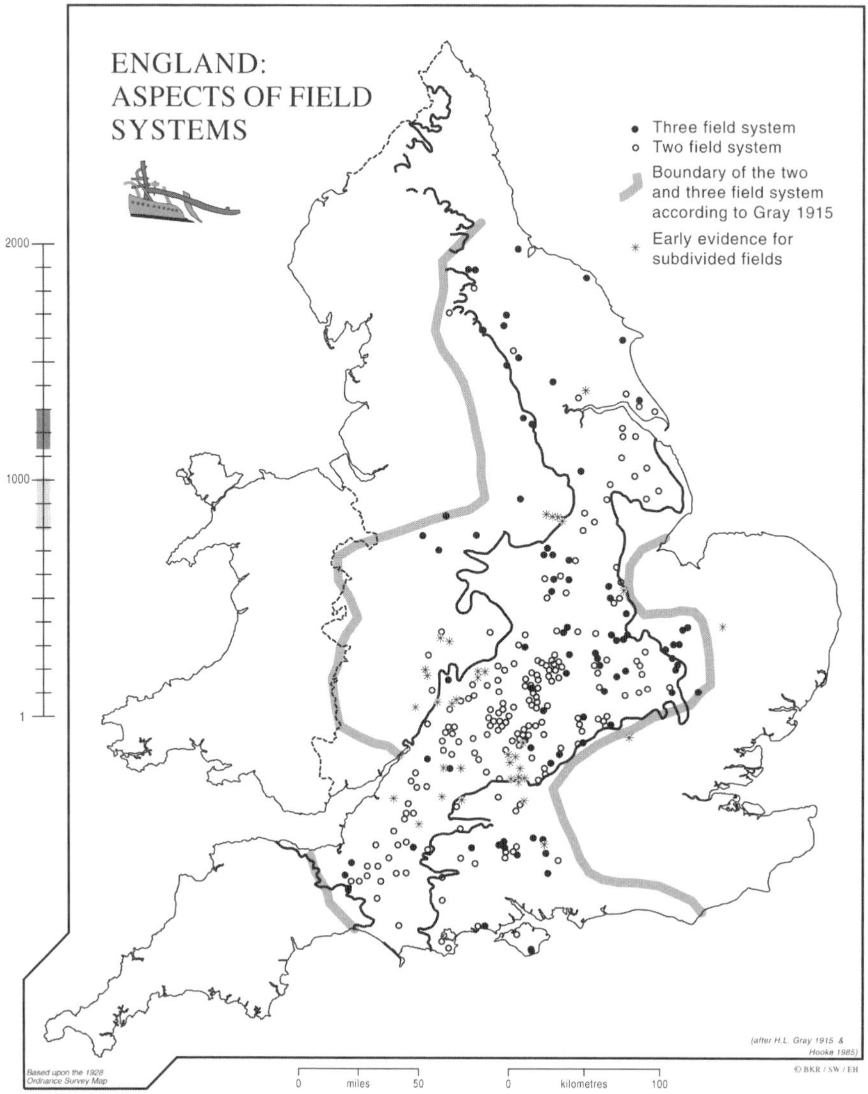

Figure 6.2. England: aspects of field systems. (Reproduced from Roberts and Wrathmell, *Region*, figure 5.4, by kind permission of Professor B. K. Roberts)

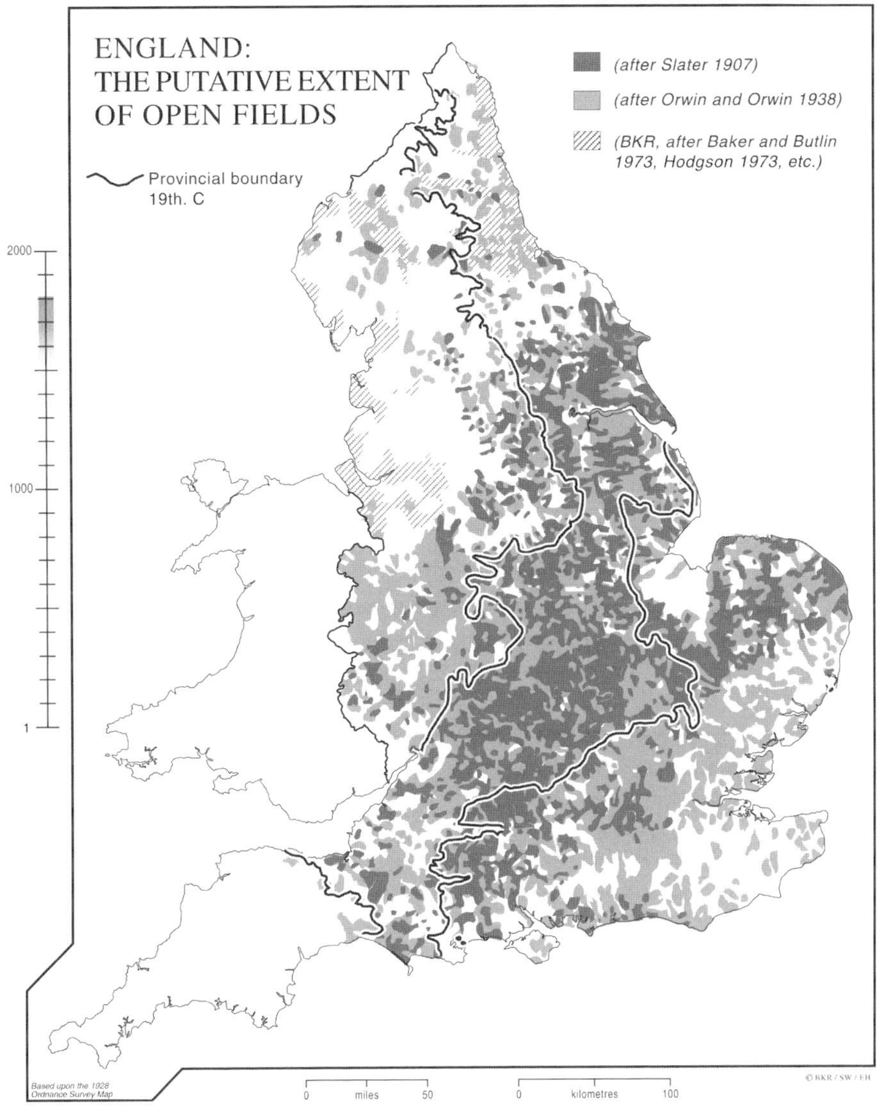

Figure 6.3. England: the putative extent of open fields. (Reproduced from Roberts and Wrathmell, *Region*, figure 5.10, by kind permission of Professor B. K. Roberts).

'ways in which the Anglo-Saxons in England adhered to their own native [i.e. Germanic] traditions'.[7]

The earliest landscape historians adopted the same framework. The Orwins, for example, described how, 'Under the open-field system, at the time that we first begin to see it clearly, those parts of England covered by it consisted of communities living in what, today, are termed nucleated villages.'[8] And, in his masterpiece, the *Making of the English Landscape*, Hoskins concluded that 'Compact villages, of varying size, are to be found in all counties, dating for the most part from Anglo-Saxon times. Everywhere they were accompanied originally by the open-field system.'[9]

Seminal large-scale archaeological field-walking undertaken by David Hall in Northamptonshire in the 1970s and 1980s appeared to confirm that a single period and process lay behind the introduction of nucleated settlements and open fields, especially in their common-field form. Early Anglo-Saxon dispersed settlements, deserted for nucleations by the ninth century, lay under strip fields which continued to be ploughed throughout the medieval period. He concluded that 'a late eighth-century date is suggested for both the desertion of the Saxon sites and the first formation of strip fields'.[10]

Hall's work has been a formative influence on landscape historians over the succeeding twenty-five years. A leading study of Midland England concluded that the likelihood that 'nucleated villages were a product of a development in agrarian methods … is strengthened by the likelihood that [fields and villages] came into existence at the same time', between about 850 and 1200.[11] Although it was acknowledged that the orderliness of planned settlements and the origins of common-field systems could be the result of later restructuring, the consistent degree of order in field systems compared with settlements suggested that 'it seems likely that the nucleated village was really a by-product of the agricultural changes that encouraged the formation of the fields'.[12] The view that 'by the late ninth and tenth centuries nucleated settlements at the core of several large open arable fields were gradually replacing earlier scattered farmsteads' continues to form the generally accepted explanation of medieval landscape origins and their development.[13]

7 Frank M. Stenton, *Anglo-Saxon England* (Oxford, 1946; 1971 edn), p. 15; see also pp. 280 and 286.

8 Charles S. Orwin and Christabel S. Orwin, *The Open Fields* (2nd edn, Oxford, 1954), p. 60.

9 William G. Hoskins, *The Making of the English Landscape* (London, 1955), p. 45.

10 David Hall, 'The origins of open-field agriculture – the archaeological fieldwork evidence', in *The Origins of Open Field Agriculture*, ed. Trevor Rowley (London, 1981), 22–38, at pp. 35–6.

11 Carenza Lewis, Patrick Mitchell-Fox and Christopher Dyer, *Village, Hamlet and Field* (Manchester, 1997), pp. 202–3, my additions.

12 Lewis *et al.*, *Village*, p. 204.

13 Della Hooke, *The Landscape of Anglo-Saxon England* (Leicester, 1998), p. 115; see also Tom Williamson, *Shaping Medieval Landscapes* (Macclesfield, 2003), p. 181.

Such conclusions appear to be strengthened by the growing formalisation of the overlapping distributions of nucleated settlement and common fields in particular (Figs. 6.1 and 6.3). Gray provided the first scholarly demonstration of the restricted occurrence of common fields in his map showing the 'Boundary of the Two- and Three-Field System'.[14] By the early 1980s the association between common fields and the English Midlands had led to the characterisation of the former as 'the Midland system'. Rackham categorised this area (and the nucleated settlements associated with it) as 'planned' England, contrasting it with the 'ancient' England of open fields and dispersed settlement.[15] More recently, the area in which both nucleations and common fields principally occur has been more tightly quantified, and defined as the 'central province'.[16]

A shared origin for common fields and nucleated settlement has not, however, been universally accepted. As long ago as 1983, Taylor observed that 'the open field could, and in some places certainly did, operate successfully without a nucleated village at its centre'.[17] Other chronologies for nucleation have emerged which are independent of those for the development of open and common fields. In Northamptonshire, 'the available evidence suggests in many villages an intermediate "polyfocal" stage, fully nucleated villages only developing later by coalescence'.[18] A further study agreed that 'whether the process of nucleation was associated with a fundamental reorganisation of the decayed late Roman landscape is unclear', as 'the creation of regular settlements was not the inevitable corollary of the laying out of planned field systems'.[19] Instead, the authors suggested, the formation of nucleated settlements might have occurred in the middle Anglo-Saxon period – predating the introduction of planned common-field systems which may have emerged from the tenth century onwards, when many settlements themselves were also replanned.[20] Instead, a two-phase period of landscape formation was proposed in which nucleation and field systems had separate origins: in the first phase, middle Anglo-Saxon nucleated settlements were established in association with royal vills, leading to the desertion of smaller hamlets and farmsteads; in the second phase, in the ninth and tenth centuries, a regular common-field landscape was imposed over 'whole townships' regardless of the degree of nucleation achieved within them.[21]

Taylor agreed that nucleation might have been a phased process which both post-dated the emergence of open fields, and followed a different developmental

14 Howard L. Gray, *English Field Systems* (Cambridge, 1915), frontispiece and p. 403.

15 Oliver Rackham, *The History of the Countryside* (London, 1986), p. 178.

16 Roberts and Wrathmell, *Region*, pp. 10 and 124.

17 Christopher Taylor, *Village and Farmstead* (London, 1983), p. 131, my addition extrapolated from context.

18 Glenn Foard, 'Systematic fieldwalking and the investigation of Saxon settlement in Northamptonshire', *World Archaeology*, 9, 3 (1978), 357–74, at p. 370.

19 Anthony E. Brown and Glenn Foard, 'The Saxon landscape: a regional perspective', in *The Archaeology of Landscape*, eds P. Everson and T. Williamson (Manchester, 1998), 67–94, at pp. 81 and 89.

20 Brown and Foard, 'Saxon landscape', pp. 75–9.

21 Brown and Foard, 'Saxon landscape', pp. 90–1.

trajectory. He suggested that middle and late Anglo-Saxon settlement gradually began to cluster in an irregular way around the edges of areas of roughly oval pasture at about the same time that the first open fields began to appear; he argued that, in the late eleventh or early twelfth centuries, such irregular nucleations were replaced by planned settlements at places like Whittlesford and Pampisford (both Cambs.).[22] Similar explanations have been offered for Great Doddington (Northants.) and the Bourn Valley (Cambs.), where it is proposed that loose, informal nucleations preceded the planned settlements of the eleventh century, both often co-existing with surviving or new dispersed farms and hamlets.[23]

The debate has recently been revivified by the Whittlewood Project, which concluded that 'What cannot be substantiated anywhere but in a few special cases, either because the evidence remains too vague or because it simply did not happen, is a link between nucleation and abandonment of outlying farmsteads, the freeing-up of the countryside, and the laying-out of open fields.'[24]

Methodology

The review that follows is hampered both by the focus of archaeological attention away from the temporal and physical relationships between Anglo-Saxon settlement and field systems, and by the paucity of published excavation results. As Hamerow has observed of early Anglo-Saxon settlements, 'Fewer than a dozen of the hundreds of [early] Anglo-Saxon settlements so far investigated have been excavated (and published) on a scale and under conditions which allow for a detailed analysis of their layout and development over time' or, it might be added, of their relationship with the wider fieldscape within which they stood.[25] There have been similarly few exhaustive excavations of middle Anglo-Saxon settlements, and only a handful where the relationship between settlement and field systems has been deliberately explored. The absence of the 'grey literature' (unpublished excavation preceding construction and other development) from open and peer-reviewed publication is a difficulty exacerbated by the rapid rate at which such literature has (until recently) been produced.

This paper takes an empirical approach within these constraints. It deals first with the few sites in which archaeological evidence has been found for the spatial and temporal relationship between nucleated settlements and open/common-field systems in the Anglo-Saxon period. It then approaches the ques-

22 Christopher Taylor, 'Nucleated settlement: a view from the frontier', *Landscape History*, 24 (2002), 53–71.

23 Foard, 'Systematic fieldwalking', p. 370; Susan Oosthuizen, *Landscapes Decoded: The Origins and Development of Cambridgeshire's Medieval Fields* (Hatfield, 2006), pp. 146–7.

24 Richard Jones and Mark Page, *Medieval Villages in an English Landscape* (Macclesfield, 2006), p. 104.

25 Helena Hamerow, *Early Medieval Settlements: The Archaeology of Rural Communities in North-West Europe, 400–900* (Oxford, 2002), p. 93.

tion from another direction, by reviewing archaeological research on the periods of origin of nucleated settlement on the one hand, and of open- and common-field systems on the other, and comparing the results to establish what, if any, the degree of overlap might be between the origins and development of the two.

The Relationship between Nucleated Settlements and Open- or Common-field Systems

There are just four places in which relationships between Anglo-Saxon settlements and field systems have been systematically investigated: Raunds (Northants.), Chalton (Hants.), Wharram Percy (Yorks.) and the Norfolk silt fens. The Raunds Survey represents the largest of only a handful of archaeological investigations of the relationship between open or common fields and nucleated settlement, and within the survey the best evidence comes from the polyfocal settlements that make up Raunds, and from its subsidiary settlement at West Cotton.[26]

In Raunds itself, the polyfocal medieval settlement was underlain by two small middle Anglo-Saxon settlements. In the tenth century, the area occupied by the first was formally replanned and enlarged, and a new planned settlement was laid out (North End). The second (Thorpe End) – a dense, middle Anglo-Saxon settlement – was deserted. In the fields, scatters of late Anglo-Saxon pottery resulting from manuring lie contained within the boundaries of medieval common-field furlongs, suggesting that these furlongs might also have been created in the tenth century. The strips within the furlongs overlie the sites of middle Anglo-Saxon settlements, and must therefore post-date their abandonment.[27] It might therefore be concluded that the case for contemporary layout of both common fields and nucleated settlement at Raunds has been decisively established.

At West Cotton, in the west of the parish, a formal nucleated settlement was laid out over about 6 acres in the tenth century, replacing a small middle Anglo-Saxon settlement. Intensive late Anglo-Saxon manuring of the nearby fields respected a (later) medieval furlong boundary, suggesting that there, too, the latter was probably at least contemporary with the planned village.[28]

Of the remaining settlements within the parish, that at Mill Cotton, which may have been planned, was probably not established before about 1100, while that at Mallows Cotton was laid out over existing ridge and furrow which it therefore post-dated.[29] In both these cases, settlement was later than the origins of medieval field layouts.

The results from Raunds may however be more ambiguous than they appear at first sight, in that they do not reveal the extent to which the middle Anglo-

26 Stephen Parry, *Raunds Area Survey* (Oxford, 2006).

27 Parry, *Raunds*, pp. 223–4 and 229, 236, 133, 275.

28 Parry, *Raunds*, pp. 173–6.

29 Parry, *Raunds*, pp. 192 and 183.

Saxon settlements underlying the later Anglo-Saxon nucleations at Raunds and West Cotton were also nucleated. There is also the tantalising coincidence that the late Anglo-Saxon infields broadly coincided in locality with those of the middle Anglo-Saxon period. An excavation of one of the medieval furlong boundaries which limited late Anglo-Saxon manuring did not, however, reveal any underlying boundaries, and the question of the relationship between the medieval field system and its predecessors therefore remains unexplained.[30]

The later Anglo-Saxon evidence from Raunds and West Cotton is therefore anomalous. It certainly shows evidence of tenth-century replanning, but it cannot yet be claimed as an example of initial nucleation in association with the earliest medieval fields, since there is no evidence of middle Anglo-Saxon nucleation and no firm evidence that new field layouts and patterns of management were introduced in the tenth century.

At Chalton Down (Hants.), a nucleated settlement was laid out in the seventh century, with houses set out 'in rows running across the ridge of the down'.[31] Its inhabitants continued to cultivate the prehistoric or Romano-British fields which predated the settlement. A major shift of settlement in the ninth century to the locations of the modern villages coincided with the abandonment of those earlier fields and the establishment of others which later evolved into the medieval open fields of the parish.[32] Here, nucleation and medieval open field creation were not contemporary, although they were both features of the later, ninth-century, landscape.

At Wharram Percy (Yorks.), probably in the seventh century, a nucleated settlement of unknown form was inserted into an existing Roman or Iron Age landscape layout. A system of broad ridge cultivation later developed in association with the settlement, but did not entirely respect the earlier land divisions (and was, itself, significantly remodelled in the medieval period). The eastern ends of these ridges were truncated in the tenth century by the encroachment of a new, informal row settlement, which was replaced by a formally planned settlement in the twelfth century. There is no evidence that Anglo-Saxon or medieval field systems and settlement, whether informal or planned, were contemporary developments.[33]

30 Parry, *Raunds*, pp. 93 and 134–5.

31 Peter Addyman and David Leigh, 'The Anglo-Saxon village at Chalton, Hampshire: second interim report', *Medieval Archaeology*, 16 (1972), 13–31, at p. 17.

32 Barry Cunliffe, 'The Saxon and medieval settlement-pattern in the region of Chalton, Hampshire', *Medieval Archaeology*, 16 (1972), 1–12, at p. 11; Barry Cunliffe, 'Chalton, Hants, The Evolution of a Landscape', *Antiquaries Journal*, 53, 2 (1973), 173–90, at p. 187.

33 Maurice Beresford and John G. Hurst, 'Wharram Percy: a case study in microtopography', in *English Medieval Settlement*, ed. Peter Sawyer (London, 1979), 52–85, at p. 68; John G. Hurst, 'The Wharram Research Project: results to 1983', *Medieval Archaeology*, 27 (1984), 77–111, at pp. 82–3; A. Oswald, *Wharram Percy Deserted Medieval Village, North Yorkshire: Archaeological Investigation and Survey* (Swindon, 2004), at pp. 39, 74–82 and 98–100.

Evidence from the Norfolk silt fens is particularly interesting, since the landscape there only became available for settlement in the middle Anglo-Saxon period, having been inundated by the sea in the immediate post-Roman centuries. The landscape that emerged was one of unplanned, irregular nucleated settlements, associated with relatively irregular field systems at places like Terrington St Clement and the Walpoles – St Andrew and St Peter. These early fields continued to be cultivated into the Middle Ages and long after, their area having been extended by the addition of further (more regular) furlongs in successive centuries. There is a little evidence that they may have been cultivated as open fields from their inception, since they appear to have been divided into strips from the outset.[34] Here, nucleation and open fields were clearly contemporary introductions, but since there was no opportunity for continuity of earlier landscape organisation into the eighth and ninth centuries, it is impossible to say whether this was simply the result of colonisation of a new landscape, or evidence for the emergence of a new system for land organisation.

There is evidence for late Anglo-Saxon reorganisation of nucleated settlements and fields at Raunds, Chalton Down, and Wharram Percy. The last two also demonstrate earlier, that is middle Anglo-Saxon, nucleation. At Chalton Down and Wharram Percy, field layouts appear to predate settlement nucleation. At Raunds the details of the origin and layout of middle Anglo-Saxon field systems and their relationship with the medieval field pattern are not known. In the special conditions of the silt fens, nucleated settlements and the fields around them appear to have been contemporary, although it is not known whether these fields were cultivated in severalty or as open fields.

Although it has been possible to suggest a chronological relationship between field systems and settlements at all of these sites, what still remains unknown is whether these fields were cultivated in the same way as medieval open or common fields. The problem is approached from a different direction below. There, we examine first the origins of nucleated settlement, and then of open/common fields, in order to try to establish the degree of overlap, and of relationship, between the two.

The Origins of Nucleated Settlement

Field survey and archaeological investigation suggest that there are many eleventh- or twelfth-century nucleated settlements whose origins post-dated the layout of open fields. Excavation results, the aratral curves of medieval ploughing fossilised in property boundaries, or the remains of medieval cultivation which persist within crofts, clearly establish the stratigraphic relationship between earlier fields and later settlement.

34 Robert J. Silvester, *The Fenland Project No. 3: Marshland and the Nar Valley, Norfolk, East Anglian Archaeology*, 45 (1988), at pp. 38–40, 76–9, 69 and 95.

Field and topographical evidence for settlements laid out over open/common fields is widespread, with examples at places like Wearne, Lopen and Limington (Somerset), Charlton (Wilts.), Caulcott and Charlcot (Oxon.), Charlock and Pytchley (Northants.), Chesterton and Comberton (Cambs.), and Tittleshall and Sutton (Norfolk).[35] So many settlements in West Lindsey (Lincs.) overlie ridge and furrow that it has been suggested their origin lay in the eleventh or twelfth centuries in a context in which open fields already existed.[36] Similar results have been derived from topographical analysis at Great Eversden and Toft (Cambs.), Copt, Hewick, Hemingbrough, Thornton-Le-Beans, Upper Poppleton, and Bulmer (all Yorks.), and Cockfield and Wolviston (Co. Durham).[37] There are further examples at Great Hammerton, Wressell, and Bickerton in the Central Vale of York, where it was argued that later 'villages were laid out within the boundaries of pre-existing [eleventh-century] field systems',[38] as at Haworth, Great Butterwick, and Marton in Craven, Appleton-le-Moors, Levisham, and Pockley (all Yorks.), and the Vale of Eden (Cumbria), where settlement is proposed to have begun in the first half of the twelfth century.[39] At Great Asby, Hayton, Gamblesby, and Cumwhitton (all Cumbria) 'the aratral curve within the furlong is clearly continued by the toft boundary within the compartment, sug-

35 Michael Aston, 'Rural settlement in Somerset: some preliminary thoughts', in *Medieval Villages: A Review of Current Work*, ed. Della Hooke (Oxford, 1985), 81–100, at pp. 87–9; Michael Aston, 'Settlement patterns and forms', in *Aspects of the Medieval Landscape of Somerset*, ed. Michael Aston (Taunton, 1988), pp. 76–7; N. Smith, 'Charlton, Wiltshire – the development of a chalkland settlement', in *Patterns of the Past*, ed. Paul Pattison, David Field and Stewart Ainsworth (Oxford, 1999), 77–84, at p. 82; C. James Bond, 'Medieval Oxfordshire villages and their topography: a preliminary discussion', in *Medieval Villages*, ed. Hooke, pp. 101–23, at pp. 112 and 117; RCHME, *South-West Northamptonshire* (London, 1982), pp. 1 and 3–4; RCHME, *Central Northamptonshire* (London, 1979), p. 123; Craig Cessford and Alison Dickens, 'The origins and early development of Chesterton, Cambridge', *Proceedings of the Cambridge Antiquarian Society*, 93 (2004), 125–42, at p. 130; Susan Oosthuizen, 'Medieval settlement relocation in west Cambridgeshire: three case studies', *Landscape History*, 19 (1997), 43–55; Peter Wade-Martins, 'Village sites in Launditch Hundred', *East Anglian Archaeology*, 10 (1980), at pp. 54–7.

36 Paul Everson, Christopher Taylor and Christopher Dunn, *Change and Continuity: Rural Settlement in North-West Lincolnshire* (London, 1991), pp. 14–15.

37 Oosthuizen, 'Medieval settlement relocation'; June Sheppard, 'Metrological analysis of regular village plans in Yorkshire', *Agricultural History Review*, 22, 2 (1974), 118–35, at p. 133; June Sheppard, 'Medieval village planning in northern England: some evidence from Yorkshire', *Journal of Historical Geography*, 2, 1 (1976), 3–20; Brian K. Roberts, 'Rural settlement in County Durham: forms, pattern and system', in *Social Organisation and Settlement: Contributions from Anthropology, Archaeology and Geography*, eds David Green, Colin Haselgrove and Matthew Spriggs (Oxford, 1978), 291–322.

38 Mary Harvey, 'The development of open fields in the central Vale of York: a reconsideration', *Geografiska Annaler*, 67B, 1 (1985), 35–44, at pp. 41–3, my addition.

39 Roberts and Wrathmell, *Region*, 92–4 and 113; Pamela Allerston, 'English village development', *Transactions of the Institute of British Geographers*, 51 (1970), 95–109, at pp. 97–8; Brian K. Roberts, 'Norman village plantations and long strip fields in northern England', *Geografiska Annaler*, 70B, 1 (1988), 169–77.

gesting that the village compartment has been superimposed over pre-existing strips', probably at some time in the twelfth century.[40]

Archaeological excavation in yet other places has uncovered no evidence for nucleation before the eleventh or twelfth centuries. In the Cotswolds, for example, the earliest pottery found within medieval villages dates from this period.[41] In Northamptonshire, the Royal Commission noted its 'continuing failure to discover any material earlier than the 10th century in the later medieval settlement sites examined in the area'.[42] A well-known example is that of Faxton (Northants.): the vill was mentioned in Domesday Book, but there is no evidence of occupation before the twelfth century.[43] Similar finds have been made at Riseholme (Lincs.), Anstey (Leics.), Chesterton (Cambs.), Laxton (Notts.), Wawne (Yorks.), and Thrislington (Co. Durham).[44] An innovative project of test-pitting within medieval settlements supports these conclusions at a wide range of sites including Great Easton (Leics.), Shelford, Ufford, Houghton, and Wyton (all Cambs.), Wiveton (Norfolk), and Coddenham and Hessett (Suffolk).[45] In just a few places, a slightly earlier date is proposed – tenth or eleventh centuries, rather than eleventh or twelfth – but not sufficiently different to do more than suggest some regional variation, for example, at Glaston (Rutland), Wheldrake (Yorks.), Wythemail and Upton (Northants.), and Barton Blount, Stanfield, and Weasenham St Peter (Norfolk).[46]

Field evidence, topographical analysis, and archaeological excavation all therefore indicate that there was substantial remodelling of medieval settlement in the eleventh or twelfth centuries in a landscape in which open- and, perhaps, common-field layouts already existed. They do not, however, demonstrate that nucleation itself is of that date – simply that nucleation was new

40 Brian K. Roberts, 'The great plough: a hypothesis concerning village genesis and land reclamation in Cumberland and Westmoreland', *Landscape History*, 18 (1996), 17–30, at p. 17.

41 Christopher Dyer, 'Villages and non-villages in the medieval Cotswolds', *Bristol and Gloucestershire Archaeological Society*, 120 (2002), 11–35, at p. 13.

42 RCHME, *Central Northamptonshire*, xlix.

43 RCHME, *North-West Northamptonshire* (London, 1981), at p. 122.

44 Christopher Taylor 'Medieval rural settlement: changing perceptions', *Landscape History*, 14 (1992), 5–17, at p. 6; John Thomas, 'The archaeology of historic/medieval village cores: evidence from Leicestershire and Rutland', *MSRG Annual Report*, 21 (2006), 34–36; Cessford and Dickens, 'Chesterton', p. 130; Ken Challis, 'Recent excavations at Laxton, Nottinghamshire', *MRSG Annual Report*, 10 (1995), 20–3, at p. 22; Colin Hayfield, 'Wawne, East Riding of Yorkshire: a case study in settlement morphology', *Landscape History*, 6 (1984), 41–67, at p. 50; Roberts, 'Rural settlement in County Durham', p. 297.

45 Carenza Lewis, 'Test pit excavation within occupied settlements in East Anglia in 2005', *MSRG Annual Report*, 20 (2005), 9–16; Carenza Lewis, 'Test pit excavation within currently occupied rural settlement in East Anglia – results of the HEFA Cors Project in 2006', *MSRG Annual Report*, 21 (2006), 37–44; also, see Lewis in this volume.

46 Thomas, 'Historic/medieval village cores', 34–6; June Sheppard, 'Pre-enclosure field and settlement patterns in an English township', *Geografiska Annaler*, 48B, 2 (1966), 59–77; Taylor, 'Changing perceptions', p. 8; Wade-Martins, 'Launditch Hundred', pp. 50–2 and 65–7.

on those particular sites then. Nor do they illustrate or explain whether such newly established medieval villages were preceded by dispersed settlement or had shifted from nucleated settlements elsewhere within each vill.[47]

Excavation of middle Anglo-Saxon sites has uncovered unexpected results. There are a growing number of high-status rural sites known in all parts of England on which rectilinear, planned nucleations were laid out in the late sixth or seventh centuries.[48] Some were certainly, or almost certainly, of royal or noble foundation, like the planned settlements established alongside the royal abbeys at Whitby (Yorks.) and Hartlepool (Cleveland) in the late seventh century, the nucleations associated with the royal complexes at Yeavering and Milfield (Northumberland), or the large, deliberately planned, settlement at Wicken Bonhunt (Essex) in the eighth century, which itself replaced an earlier nucleation.[49] The early bishops of East Anglia apparently oversaw the creation of a large, regular, planned settlement at North Elmham (Norfolk) which flourished between about 720 and 830, and was replanned several times thereafter.[50] The abbey at Ely may have been responsible for a substantial planned settlement at Brandon (Suffolk) which included a large industrial quarter for the weaving and dyeing of cloth, in part at least for export.[51]

Others, whose provenance is unknown, include the well-known, high-status, planned settlements of the sixth and seventh centuries at Cowdery's Down (Hants.), which was abandoned by about 800, and Foxley (Wilts.), which lay parallel to the road to Malmesbury and included an apsidal church, as well as the substantial timber 'great halls' laid out so carefully in the seventh century in alignment with each other at Sutton Courtenay (Berks.).[52] In Northamptonshire, high-status sites with good evidence for middle Anglo-Saxon nucleation include

47 cf. Taylor, *Village and Farmstead*, chapters 7 and 8.

48 Andrew Reynolds, 'Boundaries and settlements in later sixth- to eleventh-century England', *Anglo-Saxon Studies in Archaeology and History*, 12 (2003), 98–136, at p. 119.

49 Simon Denison, 'Anglo-Saxon 'planned town' revealed this month', *British Archaeology*, 64 (2002), 4; Rosemary Cramp and Robin Daniels, 'New finds from the Anglo-Saxon monastery at Hartlepool, Cleveland', *Antiquity*, 61 (1987), 424–32, at pp. 424–6; Chris Loveluck, 'Wealth, waste and consumption: Flixborough and its importance for Middle and Late Saxon rural settlement studies', in *Image and Power in the Archaeology of Early Medieval Britain*, eds Helena Hamerow and Arthur MacGregor (Oxford, 2001), pp. 79–130, at p. 108; Ken Wade, 'A settlement site at Bonhunt Farm, Wicken Bonhunt, Essex', in *Archaeology in Essex to AD1500*, ed. David G. Buckley (York, 1980), pp. 96–10, at p. 98.

50 Peter Wade-Martins, *Excavations in North Elmham Park 1967–1972*, *East Anglian Archaeology*, 9 (1980), at pp. 37–40, 94 and 103,

51 Robert Carr, Andrew Tester and Peter Murphy, 'The Middle Saxon settlement at Staunch Meadow, Brandon', *Antiquity*, 62 (1988), 371–7.

52 Martin Millet, 'Excavations at Cowdery's Down Basingstoke, Hampshire, 1978–81', *Archaeological Journal*, 140 (1983), 151–279; John Hinchliffe, 'An early medieval settlement at Cowage Farm, Foxley, near Malmesbury', *Archaeological Journal*, 143 (1986), 240–59; Helena Hamerow, Chris Hayden and Gill Hey, 'Anglo-Saxon and earlier settlement near Drayton Road, Sutton Courtenay, Berkshire', *Archaeological Journal*, 164 (2007), 109–96 at pp. 186–7.

Brixworth, Higham Ferrers, and Irthlingborough.[53] A huge, planned village, covering 40 acres, flourished between the late fifth and mid ninth centuries at West Heslerton (Yorks.), and a similar settlement of the early seventh to the early eleventh centuries at Flixborough (North Lincs.) underwent several phases of replanning before it was finally abandoned.[54]

Not all nucleations were necessarily associated with high status. A stock-rearing settlement at Pennyland (Bucks.) was nucleated in the late sixth or early seventh century. Other similar 'peasant' sites have been found at Cottenham (Cambs.), Thwing (E. Yorks.) and Bramford (Suffolk).[55] Fieldwork in West Norfolk, on the fringes of the 'central province', at places like Horningtoft, Wellingham, Longham, Mileham, and Weasenham All Saints, concluded that many settlements there originated in middle Anglo-Saxon nucleation, even if they were replanned on the same or nearby sites in the later Anglo-Saxon centuries.[56] In Lincolnshire, too, a mid-seventh century date has been proposed for the origins of many settlement nucleations, like that at Sempringham.[57]

A regional dimension might explain differences between such middle Anglo-Saxon nucleations and those in Whittlewood where, on lower-status sites, settlement nucleation at places like Great Linford (Bucks.), Leckhamstead, Lillingstone Dayrell, Lillingston Lovell, and Silverstone (all Northants.) began much later, sometime in the later ninth century, and became more common from the tenth century onwards.[58]

Planning was not an essential feature of such middle Anglo-Saxon nucleations. Many in Norfolk and Northamptonshire were 'apparently of a formless nature and unrelated in morphology to the subsequent layout' of the eleventh or twelfth centuries.[59] At Riby Cross Roads (Lincs.) and Catholme (Staffs.), trackways provided an underlying framework to each settlement, but the arrangement

53 Brown and Foard, 'Saxon landscape', pp. 79, 77 and 80; Michael Shaw, 'Saxon and earlier settlement at Higham Ferrers, Northamptonshire', *MSRG Annual Report*, 6 (1991), 15–19.

54 Dominic Powlesland, 'An interim report on the Anglo-Saxon village at West Heslerton, North Yorkshire', *MSRG Annual Report*, 5 (1990), 36–40, at pp. 37–8; Dominic Powlesland, 'West Heslerton settlement mobility: a case of static development', in *Early Deira*, eds Helen Geake and Jonathan Kenny (Oxford, 2000), pp. 19–26, at p. 22; Christopher Loveluck, 'A high-status Anglo-Saxon settlement at Flixborough, Lincolnshire', *Antiquity*, 72 (1998), 146–61; Loveluck, 'Wealth, waste'; Christopher Loveluck, *Rural Settlement, Lifestyles and Social Change in the Later First Millennium AD: Anglo-Saxon Flixborough in its Wider Context* (Oxford, 2007), at pp. 8–21.

55 Robert J. Williams, 'Pennyland and Hartigans', *Buckinghamshire Archaeological Society Monograph Series*, 4 (1993); Richard Mortimer, 'Village development and ceramic sequence: the Middle to Late Saxon village at Lordship Lane, Cottenham, Cambridgeshire', *Proceedings of the Cambridge Antiquarian Society*, 89 (2000), 5–34, at p. 9; Loveluck, 'Wealth, waste', p. 108.

56 Wade-Martins, 'Launditch Hundred', pp. 25, 73–5, 39, 42–4, 6 and 61.

57 Peter Hayes, 'Roman to Saxon in the South Lincolnshire fens', *Antiquity*, 62 (1988), 321–6, at pp. 324–5; Peter Hayes and Tom Lane, *The Fenland Project No. 5: Lincolnshire Survey, The South-West Fens, East Anglian Archaeology*, 55 (1992), at p. 215.

58 Jones and Page, *Medieval Villages*, pp. 89–91 and 103–4.

59 Taylor, *Village and Farmstead*, p. 122; Wade-Martins, 'Launditch Hundred', for example, pp. 26, Figure 15, 55, 62.

of structures and enclosures on common alignments so familiar in formal nucleations of the late Anglo-Saxon and medieval periods is lacking.[60]

It seems that a protracted process of settlement nucleation began in the middle Anglo-Saxon period, during the 'long' eighth century, and continued well into the post-Conquest period. Too little is understood about the factors which stimulated this process, although the grants of enormous estates to royal, ecclesiastical, and noble landholders, whose agricultural surpluses contributed to a burgeoning economy, may have been a major early influence.[61] That most nucleated settlements and most common fields are found in that part of Mercia in which arable cultivation was also predominant provides a proposition ripe for further research.[62] The central question is, of course, whether the origins of open and common fields might be found in the same period as the earliest post-Roman nucleations, and it is to this that we turn next.

The Origins of Open and Common Fields[63]

Irregular open fields were found across medieval England, while their more regular form, 'common' or 'Midland' fields, was restricted to the 'central province' (see Figs 6.2, 6.3).[64] They will be dealt with here in turn. The origins of open fields are explored below in an approach that is in part typological, that is, by listing the principal features of their layout and investigating their earliest occurrence. This approach is fraught with difficulty, both in terms of method and in terms of the limitations of physical evidence. Similarities in field layout between examples do not necessarily imply either that they were contemporary or that they were used in the same way; and it is just as possible that similar forms of land use might result in different forms of field layout in the same or different periods.[65] Furthermore, our understanding of common-field systems is almost entirely dependent on documentary evidence, since (as Taylor has observed) archaeologists 'would never realise the complex pattern of land-

[60] Ken Steedman, 'Excavation of a Saxon site at Riby Cross Roads, Lincolnshire', *Archaeological Journal*, 151 (1994), 212–306, at pp. 221 and 295; Stuart Losco-Bradley and Gavin Kinsley, *Catholme, An Anglo-Saxon Settlement on the Trent Gravels in Staffordshire* (Nottingham, 2002), pp. 125–7; Stuart Losco-Bradley, and H. Wheeler, 'Anglo-Saxon settlement in the Trent Valley: some aspects', in *Studies in Late Anglo-Saxon Settlement*, ed. Margaret Faull (Oxford, 1984), pp. 101–14.

[61] John Moreland, 'The significance of production in eighth-century England', in *The 'Long' Eighth Century*, eds Inge L. Hansen and Christopher Wickham (Leiden, 2000), pp. 69–104; Hamerow, *Early Medieval Settlements*, pp. 122–3.

[62] Susan Oosthuizen, 'The Anglo-Saxon kingdom of Mercia and the origins and distribution of common fields', *Agricultural History Review*, 55, 2 (2007), 153–80.

[63] For a fuller discussion of the origins of open and common fields, see Susan Oosthuizen, 'Anglo-Saxon fields', in *Oxford Handbook of Anglo-Saxon Archaeology*, eds David Hinton, Helena Hamerow and Sally Crawford (Oxford, forthcoming).

[64] Roberts and Wrathmell, *Region*, pp. 124 and 144.

[65] Alan R. H. Baker and Robin Butlin, *Studies of Field Systems in the British Isles* (Cambridge, 1973), p. 31 (my addition).

holding, communal cultivation and social organisation just from the physical remains themselves'.[66] Nonetheless, in the absence of other forms of evidence (and especially that of excavation), the typological approach is followed, with caution and reservation, in the first instance.

Throughout the Anglo-Saxon period and after, arable field layouts took two main forms, based on curvilinear ovals or rectilinear frameworks. Examples of enclosed fields based on an irregular circle or oval, and enclosed by a substantial hedge, bank, and/or ditch, have been identified at Brent, Cutcombe, and Withy (all Somerset), Daventry, Kislingbury, Hardingstone Hall, Raunds, Higham Ferrers, and Wollaston (all Northants.), Whaddon, Litlington, and Balsham (all Cambs.), Wenhaston and Hinton (Suffolk), Walpole St Andrew and West Walton (both Norfolk), Grewelthorpe (Yorks.), Crosby Ravensworth (Cumberland), and Cockfield (Co. Durham).[67] These enclosures were often subdivided, but their

66 Christopher Taylor, 'Archaeology and the origins of open-field agriculture', in *The Origins of Open-Field Agriculture*, ed. Trevor Rowley (London, 1981), pp. 13–21, at p. 16 (my addition).

67 Stephen Rippon, 'Medieval wetland reclamation in Somerset', in *The Medieval Landscape of Wessex,* eds Michael Aston and Carenza Lewis (Oxford, 1994), 239–53, at pp. 243–5; Anthony E. Brown, *Early Daventry. An essay in early landscape planning* (Leicester, 1991), p. 78; David Hall, 'Fieldwork and documentary evidence for the layout and organization of early medieval estates in the English Midlands', in *Archaeological Approaches to Medieval Europe*, ed. Katherine Biddick (Kalamazoo IL, 1984), 43–68, at pp. 51–2; Hall, 'Late Saxon countryside', pp. 114–15; David Hall, 'Fieldwork and field books: studies in early layout', in *Villages, Fields and Frontiers*, eds Brian K. Roberts and Robin E. Glasscock (Oxford, 1983), pp. 115–31, at pp. 117–19; Shaw, 'Saxon and earlier frontiers', pp. 16–17; Susan Oosthuizen, 'Saxon commons in South Cambridgeshire', *Proceedings of the Cambridge Antiquarian Society*, 82 (1993), 93–100, at pp. 95–7; Susan Oosthuizen, 'Unravelling the morphology of Litlington, South Cambridgeshire', *Proceedings of the Cambridge Antiquarian Society*, 91 (2002), 55–61; Susan Oosthuizen, *Cambridgeshire From the Air* (Stroud, 1996), at p. 28; Peter Warner, *Greens, Commons and Clayland Colonization* (Leicester, 1987), at pp. 30 and 33; Silvester, 'Fenland Project', pp. 69 and 95; Brian K. Roberts, 'Village patterns and forms: some models for discussion', in *Medieval Villages*, ed. Hooke, 7–25, at p. 25; Roberts, 'Great plough', p. 26; Brian K. Roberts, 'Townfield origins: the case of Cockfield, County Durham', in *Origins*, ed. Rowley, 145–61 at p. 149. The form continued to be used into the Middle Ages and later. Eleventh-century and later examples survive at Puxton (Somerset), South Radworthy (Devon), Tetsworth (Oxon.), Hathersage (Derbys.), Hunsterson in Wybunbury (Cheshire), Tunley in Wrightington (Lancs.), Wheldrake (Yorks.), Cockfield (Co. Durham), and Waitby (Westmoreland). Stephen Rippon, 'Infield and outfield: the early stages of marshland colonisation and the evolution of medieval field systems', in *Through Wet and Dry: Essays in Honour of David Hall*, eds Tom Lane and John Coles (Lincoln, 2002), 54–70, at pp. 60–3; Hazel Riley and Robert Wilson-North, *The Field Archaeology of Exmoor* (Swindon, 2001), p. 97; Bond, 'Medieval Oxfordshire', p. 115; Roberts and Wrathmell, *Region*, pp. 98–9; Margaret A. Atkin, 'Some settlement patterns in Lancashire', in *Medieval Villages*, ed. Hooke, 170–85; Sheppard, 'Field and settlement patterns', at pp. 69–71; Roberts, 'Townfield origins', p. 149; Brian K. Roberts, 'Five Westmoreland settlements: a comparative study', *Transactions of the Cumberland and Westmoreland Antiquarian and Archaeological Society*, 93 (1993), 131–43.

internal divisions do not appear to have provided physical barriers to movement from one subdivision to another, and they seem therefore to have been 'open'.[68]

At least some middle or late Anglo-Saxon curvilinear enclosures in Gloucestershire, Warwickshire, Northamptonshire, Yorkshire, Cambridgeshire, and Suffolk may represent those blocks of demesne land or 'inland' which were a feature of later medieval open-field systems but which were generally not found in common-field layouts.[69] They seem to have existed both inside and outside the 'central province' in the pre-Conquest period, although they had disappeared from 'Midland' England by about 1300, suggesting that they may be indicative of open-field systems that predate the emergence of more specialised common fields.

Curvilinear enclosures for arable had a history that pre-dated the Anglo-Saxon period by many centuries, however, and cannot have been an innovation of the sixth century or later.[70] Iron Age examples have been identified at sites like Park Brow (Sussex), Grateley South (Hants.), Alrewas (Staffs.), and High Knowes (Northumberland), and at the Roman farmstead at Royston Grange

[68] Rippon, 'Medieval wetland reclamation'; Stephen Rippon, Ralph Fife and Anthony Brown, 'Beyond villages and open fields: the origins and development of a historic landscape characterised by dispersed settlement in South-West England', *Medieval Archaeology*, 50 (2006), 31–70, at pp. 66–7; Atkin, 'Some settlement patterns'; Roberts and Wrathmell, *Region*, pp. 96–115.

[69] Herbert P. R. Finberg, 'Anglo-Saxon England to 1042', *The Agrarian History of England and Wales, I, ii, AD 43–1042*, ed. Herbert P. R. Finberg (Cambridge, 1972), 385–525, at p. 416; Rosamund Faith, *The English Peasantry and the Growth of Lordship* (Leicester, 1997), pp. 170–4; Barbara Yorke, *Wessex in the Early Middle Ages* (Leicester, 1995), p. 268; Faith, *English Peasantry*, pp. 171–2; Della Hooke, *Anglo-Saxon Landscapes of the West Midlands, The Charter Evidence* (Oxford, 1981), p. 207; Hall, 'Fieldwork', pp. 51–2, Hall, 'Saxon countryside', pp. 114–15; Hall, 'Layout', pp. 117–19; Roberts, 'Village patterns', p. 25; Oosthuizen 'Saxon commons'; Susan Oosthuizen, 'Prehistoric fields into medieval furlongs? Evidence from Caxton, South Cambridgeshire', *Proceedings of the Cambridge Antiquarian Society*, 86 (1998), 145–52; Oosthuizen, *Cambridgeshire from the Air*, p. 28; Warner, *Greens, Commons,* pp. 29–33.

[70] While the discussion below concentrates on continuities with the past, discontinuities should also be noted. In many places prehistoric or Roman field systems disappeared to be ignored by medieval open- or common-field landscapes. There are many examples of this process across the 'central province' from Wiltshire to Hampshire, Berkshire, Cambridgeshire, Essex, Northamptonshire, Nottinghamshire, and Derbyshire. For details see David McOmish, David Field and Graham Brown, *The Field Archaeology of Salisbury Plain* (Swindon 2002), p. 111; Della Hooke, 'Early forms of open field agriculture in England', *Geografiska Annaler*, 70B (1988), 121–31; Cunliffe, 'Evolution', pp. 183–8; Hooke, *Anglo-Saxon Landscape*, p. 64; Brown and Foard, 'Saxon landscape', p. 74; David Hall, *Medieval Fields* (Aylesbury, 1982), pp. 54–5; Gill Campbell, 'The preliminary archaeobotanical results from Anglo-Saxon West Cotton and Raunds', in *Environment and Economy in Anglo-Saxon England*, ed. James Rackham (York, 1994), 65–82, p. 65; Peter Addyman 'A Dark Age settlement at Maxey, Northants.', *Medieval Archaeology*, 8 (1964), 20–73, at p. 24; Catherine Hall and Jack R. Ravensdale, *The West Fields of Cambridge* (Cambridge, 1974); Susan Oosthuizen, 'New light on the origins of open field farming?', *Medieval Archaeology*, 49 (2005), 165–93; P. Tim H. Unwin, 'Townships and early fields in north Nottinghamshire', *Journal of Historical Geography*, 9, 4 (1983), 341–6.

(Derbys.).[71] What is not understood is whether this continuity from the first millennium BC into the first and second millennia AD is simply coincidence, or whether it represents continuity of arable management.

Other Anglo-Saxon fields were unenclosed, laid out on a roughly geometric framework often following the local topography. Late Anglo-Saxon examples have been found as far apart as Berkshire, Oxfordshire, and Yorkshire, while middle Anglo-Saxon examples have been identified at Dorchester and Sherborne (Dorset), Kempston (Beds.), and in the Bourn Valley (Cambs.).[72] Many appear to incorporate and/or adapt earlier prehistoric or Roman rectilinear layouts, and therefore imply continuous use, whether as arable or pasture, throughout the Anglo-Saxon period, like those at West Chisenbury, Fyfield Down, and Wylye (all Wilts.), Strettington (Sussex), Sutton Walls (Herefs.), Compton Beauchamp (Oxon.), Castle Ashby and Walgrave (both Northants.), Burton Lazars (Leics.), Lichfield (Staffs.), Tadlow, Caxton, and in the Bourn Valley (Cambs.), and at Scole and Dickleborough (Norfolk), Grantham and Goltho (Lincs.), and Wharram Percy (Yorks.).[73] Other large-scale examples of continuity between

71 Peter Drewett, David Rudling and Mark Gardiner, *The South-East to A.D.1000* (London, 1988), p. 135; Barry Cunliffe, *Wessex to A.D.1000* (London, 1993), p. 221; Peter Topping, 'Landscape narratives: the South-East Cheviots Project', *Proceedings of the Prehistoric Society*, 74 (2008), 323–64; Richard Hodges, *Wall-to-Wall History* (London, 1991), p. 84; Christopher Smith, 'The historical development of the landscape in the parishes of Alrewas, Fisherwick and Whittington: a retrogressive analysis', *Transactions of the South Staffordshire Archaeological and Historical Society*, 20 (1978–79), 1–14, at p. 12.

72 Hooke, 'Early forms'; Ernest A. Pocock, 'The first fields in an Oxfordshire parish', *Agricultural History Review*, 16, 2 (1968), 85–100; Mary Harvey, 'Regular field and tenurial arrangements in Holderness, Yorkshire', *Journal of Historical Geography*, 6, 1(1980), 3–16; Mary Harvey, 'Planned field systems in eastern Yorkshire: some thoughts on their origin', *Agricultural History Review*, 31, 2 (1983), 91–103; Mary Harvey, 'Open field structure and landholding arrangements in eastern Yorkshire', *Transactions of the Institute of British Geographers* (new series), 9 (1984), 60–74; Harvey, 'Central Vale of York'; Dominic Powlesland, 'Excavations at Heslerton, North Yorkshire 1978–82', *Archaeological Journal*, 143 (1986), 53–173, at p. 165; Campbell, 'West Cotton and Raunds', p. 65; Laurence Keen, 'The towns of Dorset', in *Anglo-Saxon Towns in Southern England*, ed. Jeremy Haslam (Chichester, 1984), 203–48, at p. 236; Hall, *Medieval Fields*, p. 46; Märit Gaimster and John Bradley, 'Medieval Britain and Ireland, 2002', *Medieval Archaeology*, 47 (2003), 199–340, at p. 221; Oosthuizen, *Landscapes Decoded*, pp. 91–113.

73 McOmish *et al.*, *Salisbury Plain*, p. 111; Peter J. Fowler, *Landscape Plotted and Pieced: Landscape History and Local Archaeology in Fyfield and Overton, Wiltshire* (London, 2000), pp. 235–7; Hooke, 'Early forms', 123–5; Alan Nash, 'The medieval fields of Strettington, West Sussex, and the evolution of land division', *Geografiska Annaler*, 1982B, 1 (1982), 41–9, at p. 42; June Sheppard, *The Origins and Evolution of Field and Settlement Patterns in the Herefordshire Manor of Marden* (London, 1979), at p. 33; Anthony E. Brown, 'Burton Lazars, Leicestershire: a planned medieval landscape?', *Landscape History*, 18 (1996), 31–45, at p. 43; RCHME, *Central Northamptonshire*, lxii; RCHME, *West Cambridgeshire* (London, 1968), p. xxx; Oosthuizen, 'Prehistoric Fields'; Oosthuizen, *Landscapes Decoded*, pp. 81–3; Christopher C. Taylor and Peter J. Fowler, 'Roman fields into medieval furlongs?', in *Early Land Allotment in the British Isles*, eds H. C. Bowen and P. J. Fowler (Oxford, 1978), pp. 159–62, at p. 159; Stephen Upex, 'Landscape continuity and fossilisation of Roman fields', *Archaeological Journal*, 159 (2002), 77–108, at pp. 87–94; Stephen Bassett, 'Medieval Lichfield: a topographical review',

prehistoric and medieval field layouts have been identified in Buckinghamshire, central, western, and southern Hertfordshire, and in the Elmhams and Ilketshalls (Suffolk).[74] As Williamson has observed, they appear to result from a process in which 'centuries of piecemeal alteration have preserved the essential orientation of field layout but not in every case the original boundaries'.[75]

The use of both curvilinear and rectilinear structures in the layout of fields from the prehistoric into the medieval periods suggests at least some continuity in 'traditional' forms of the division of land between cultivators. By the post-Conquest period, such fields were characteristically sub-divided first into furlongs and then into strips. If early open fields were also subdivided in these ways, then the similarities with medieval layouts would be more striking.

The earliest documentary references to furlongs date from the early tenth century.[76] Topographical analysis, however, indicates the possibility that they may have been an integral part of proposed eighth-century unenclosed fields in Dorset and Cambridgeshire.[77] Such suggestions gain support from the frequent lack of discernible differences in regularity between the structure of furlongs in many medieval field systems which incorporate prehistoric or Roman rectilinear field layouts, compared with those which do not.[78]

Middle Anglo-Saxon examples of strips, the smallest subdivisions of medieval open and common fields, have been identified in Somerset, at West Walton and Walpole St Andrew (Norfolk), and Milfield (Northumberland).[79] Their presence has been suggested on topographical grounds in the Bourn Valley (Cambs.).[80]

Transactions of the Staffordshire Archaeological and Historical Society 22 (1980–81), 93–121; Stephen Bassett, 'Beyond the edge of excavation: the topographical context of Goltho', in *Studies in Medieval History Presented to R. H. C. Davis*, eds Henry Mayr-Harting and Robert I. Moore (London, 1985), 21–39, at pp. 32–4; Tom Williamson, 'Early co-axial field systems on the East Anglian Boulder Clays', *Proceedings of the Prehistoric Society*, 53 (1987), 419–31; Märit Gaimster and John Bradley, 'Medieval Britain and Ireland, 2000', *Medieval Archaeology*, 45 (2001), 233–379, at pp. 294–5; Beresford and Hurst, 'Wharram Percy', p. 82.

74 E. J. Bull, 'The bi-axial landscape of prehistoric Buckinghamshire', *Records of Buckinghamshire*, 35 (1993), 11–27, at p. 16; Tom Williamson, *The Origins of Hertfordshire* (Manchester, 2000), at pp. 144–52; Peter Warner, *The Origins of Suffolk* (Manchester, 1996), pp. 44–53; Rackham, *British Countryside*, p. 158.

75 Williamson, 'Early co-axial field systems', at p. 425.

76 For example, Seebohm, *English Community*, pp. 107–8; Hooke, 'Early forms', p. 126; Della Hooke, *Anglo-Saxon Landscapes of the West Midlands, The Charter Evidence* (Oxford, 1981), pp. 190–1.

77 Keen, 'Dorset'; Oosthuizen, 'New light', pp. 165–93.

78 Stephen Bassett, 'Medieval Lichfield'; Brown, 'Burton Lazars'; Upex, 'Landscape continuity'; Oosthuizen, 'Prehistoric fields'; Bassett, 'Goltho'; see for comparison, for example, Robert Hartley, *The Medieval Earthworks of Rutland* (Leicester, 1983); Robert Hartley, *The Medieval Earthworks of North West Leicestershire* (Leicester, 1984); Robert Hartley, *The Medieval Earthworks of Central Leicestershire* (Leicester, 1989).

79 Rippon *et al.*, 'Beyond villages', pp. 59 and 66; Silvester, 'Fenland Project', pp. 95 and 69; J. Bradley and Märit Gaimster, 'Medieval Britain and Ireland, 1999', *Medieval Archaeology*, 44 (2002), 235–354, at p. 299.

80 Oosthuizen, *Landscapes Decoded*, pp. 99–107.

Prehistoric examples of the division of arable land into strips, whether for cultivation or tenure, or both, have been found on St David's Head (Pembrokes.), Sawtry (Cambs.), and in Northumberland, while Roman examples have been identified at Roystone Grange (Derbys.), Frocester (Glos.), King's Worthy (Hants.), Great Wymondley (Herts.), in Somerset, Dorset, Nottinghamshire, and Lincolnshire, and perhaps at Burnham Market (Norfolk). [81]

Some of the most characteristic elements which made up open-field layouts – curvilinear and rectilinear structures, furlongs and strips – can therefore be shown to have much earlier antecedents. The question is therefore whether the arable within them was managed in the same way.

The earliest, generally accepted, documentary reference to an open-field system appears in the late seventh-century laws of Ine, king of Wessex:

> If *ceorls* have a common meadow or other land divided into shares to fence, and some have fenced their portion and some have not, and [if cattle] eat up their common crops or grass, those who are responsible for the gap are to go and pay to the others, who have fenced their part, compensation for the damage that has been done there.[82]

This clause was interpreted by both Finberg and, later, Fox as a field in shared ownership bounded by a single hedge.[83] Fox argued convincingly that the description of the field as 'common', and the damage that a stray cow might do to crops belonging to a number of people, could only be explained if the field was open.[84] Did the law address such problems of liability and responsibility because they were new or perennial? There is some evidence to suggest the latter, although it is by no means conclusive. The curvilinear enclosures at Alrewas (Staffs.) and Royston Grange (Derbys.), for example, were both internally subdivided, but not in a way which impeded access across them and they have the appearance of open fields.[85] It is possible, therefore, but by no means certain, that some kind of open-field system predated the nucleations of the middle Anglo-Saxon period.

There is growing evidence for infield/outfield cultivation on early and middle Anglo-Saxon sites. Infields can often (but not always) be identified straightfor-

81 Ken Murphy, 'A prehistoric field system and related monuments on St David's Head and Carn Llidi, Pembrokeshire', *Proceedings of the Prehistoric Society*, 67 (2001), 85–99, at p. 94; Peter Topping, 'Early cultivation in Northumberland and the Borders', *Proceedings of the Prehistoric Society*, 55 (1989), 161–79; Topping, 'Landscape narratives', 323–64; Richard Newman, pers. comm.; Hodges, *Wall-to-Wall*, p. 79; Eddie Price, *Frocester, A Romano-British Settlement its Antecedents and Successors* (Gloucester, 2000), p. 242; Shimon Applebaum, 'Roman Britain', in *Agrarian History of England and Wales, I, ii, AD 43–1042*, ed. Herbert P. R. Finberg (Cambridge, 1972), 5–267, at pp. 90–5; Chris J. Arnold, *Roman Britain to Saxon England* (London, 1984), at p. 57; Williamson, *Shaping Medieval Landscapes*, 81.

82 *English Historical Documents c.500–1042*, ed. Dorothy Whitelock (London and New York, 1979), p. 403.

83 Finberg, 'Anglo-Saxon England', pp. 416–7; Fox, 'Approaches', pp. 87–8.

84 Fox, 'Approaches', p. 87.

85 Smith, 'Historical development', p. 12; Hodges, *Wall-to-Wall*, p. 84.

wardly from archaeological evidence because they were manured more intensively, carrying higher densities of the broken pottery added to middens rather than the outfields.[86] They have been found, for example, at Chalton (Hants.), Barnsley Park (Glos.), Eton Rowing Lake and Dorney (Berks.), Higham Ferrers and Raunds (Northants.), Chellington (Beds.), Peterborough (Cambs.), and Barton Bendish, Witton, Hales, and Loddon (all Norfolk).[87] (In Somerset, the absence of pottery between the fourth and tenth centuries means that differential manuring in that period is difficult to establish; in Shapwick during the tenth century, however, only the fields across the centre of the parish were manured, suggesting that the area to the north was being used as pasture.)[88] It is a pattern of land management in which core arable (the infield) was cultivated continuously without a fallow period, and therefore needed annual manuring; the outfield was pasture, on small areas of which short-lived arable fields were sometimes cultivated before returning to grassland for periods of up to twenty years or more. Infield/outfield agriculture was found across Britain throughout the prehistoric and Roman periods, and continued in some places well into the Middle Ages and beyond.[89]

The layout, open-ness, and methods of arable management of middle Anglo-Saxon fields therefore show sufficient continuities with prehistoric and Roman-period field systems to suggest that, at the very least, the origins of some elements of open fields are likely to have had ancient antecedents. It is possible that the major innovations of the Anglo-Saxon period – the colonisation of large areas of heavy land, the introduction of new and higher-yielding crops, innovations in ploughing technology, and a managed approach to the maintenance of

86 cf. Angus Winchester, *Landscape and Society in Medieval Cumbria* (Edinburgh, 1987), pp. 74–6.

87 Cunliffe, 'Chalton, Hants.', p. 185; Graham Webster, 'Excavations at the Romano-British villa in Barnsley Park, Cirencester, 1961–1966', *Transactions of the Bristol and Gloucestershire Archaeology Society*, 8, 6 (1967), 4–83; Peter J. Fowler, 'Continuity in the landscape', in *Recent Work in Rural Archaeology*, ed. Peter J. Fowler (Bath, 1975), 123–32; Jonathan Hiller, David Petts and Tim Allen, 'Chapter 5, Discussion of the Anglo-Saxon archaeology', in *Gathering the People, Settling the Land*, eds Stuart Foreman, Jonathan Hiller and David Petts (Oxford, 2002), 57–72, at p. 65; Brown and Foard, 'Saxon landscape', p. 78; Parry, *Raunds*, p. 93; Anthony E. Brown and Christopher Taylor, 'Chellington field survey', *Bedfordshire Archaeological Journal*, 23 (1993), 98–110, at p. 106; Upex, 'Landscape continuity', pp. 84 and 90–4; Andrew Rogerson, Alan Davison, David Pritchard and Robert Silvester, 'Barton Bendish and Caldecote: fieldwork in south-eest Norfolk', *East Anglian Archaeology*, 80 (1997), pp. 19–20; Andrew Lawson, 'The archaeology of Witton, near North Walsham, Norfolk', *East Anglian Archaeology*, 18 (1983), pp. 73–7; Alan Davison, *The Evolution of Settlement in Three Parishes in South-East Norfolk*, *East Anglian Archaeology*, 49 (1990), pp. 18–19.

88 Michael Aston, '"Unique, traditional and charming": the Shapwick Project, Somerset', *Antiquaries Journal*, 79 (1999), 1–58, at p. 27; Christopher Gerrard with Michael Aston, *The Shapwick Project, Somerset: A Rural Landscape Explored* (London, 2007), pp. 154–6.

89 cf. Catherine Stoertz, *Ancient Landscapes of the Yorkshire Wolds* (Swindon, 1997), pp. 67–9; Timothy Darvill, *Prehistoric Britain from the Air* (Cambridge, 1996), pp. 41–81; Tom Williamson, 'The development of settlement in north-west Essex: the results of a recent field survey', *Essex Archaeology and History*, 17 (1986), 120–32.

soil fertility – took place within field systems in which some elements of open-field organisation already existed.[90]

Middle and late Anglo-Saxon nucleation appears to be a development which was unconnected to the origin of open fields. Might it instead be related to the introduction of common-field systems? The possibility is particularly attractive since both nucleated settlement and common fields are more prevalent in the 'central province' where surpluses derived from specialisation and improved efficiency on large, arable estates contributed to the burgeoning national and international trading networks of the 'long' eighth century.[91]

There are, alas, some strong arguments to suggest that common fields developed later than the first phases of settlement nucleation in the seventh and eighth centuries. Such arguments turn on the development of the communal regulation of fallowing which both Thirsk and Fox regarded as a key indicator of common-field cultivation.[92] In open-field systems sufficient grazing existed on the outfield to allow continuous cultivation of the infield. In those places where arable was gradually added to the infield over successive centuries until almost all the land of a vill was under cultivation, the consequent shortage of pasture for the plough-beasts and other animals of the community became, it is argued, a serious problem. Both Thirsk and Fox argued that the communal regulation of fallowing was a response to this difficulty. It involved the setting aside of half or a third of the arable for fallow in each year to compensate for grazing lost to the plough. The fallow phase would be rotated from one field to another from one year to the next as common-field replaced infield/outfield systems. In order for all cultivators to benefit from this system, and to assure co-operation between them, it was necessary not only for each man's holdings to be distributed more or less equally between each arable field, but also for all cultivators to agree on the sequence of spring- or autumn-sown crops across the fields. Such co-ordination of sowing and harvest would ensure that flocks and herds could be let onto the field to graze on the stubbles without endangering growing corn. Thirsk suggested that a lack of documentary evidence for such *communal regulation* of fallowing indicates that 'we can point to the twelfth and first half of the thirteenth century as possibly the crucial ones in the development of the first common-field systems'.[93]

The argument that common fields were a later introduction receives support from recent work which concluded that, even in the later eleventh century, only between thirty and forty per cent of many Midland vills were cultivated, compared with closer to seventy per cent by the late thirteenth century.[94] If this is

90 cf. Hamerow, *Early Medieval Settlements*, pp. 152–5; Oosthuizen, 'Mercia', pp. 171–4; see also Susan Oosthuizen, 'Anglo-Saxon fields', in *Oxford Handbook of Anglo-Saxon Archaeology*.

91 Moreland, 'Significance of production'; Oosthuizen, 'Anglo-Saxon kingdom'.

92 Thirsk, 'Common fields', pp. 5–7; Fox, 'Approaches', p. 66.

93 Thirsk, 'Common fields', p. 23.

94 Roberts and Wrathmell, *Region*, p. 187; Mary Hesse, 'Domesday land measures in Suffolk', *Landscape History*, 22 (2000), 21–36; Oosthuizen, *Landscapes Decoded*, p. 44.

the case, then sufficient pasture for the community livestock outside the arable fields would mean that there was no impetus for the introduction of a regulated period of fallow in the arable fields, nor the introduction of common-field systems. Such arguments have received archaeological support from evidence for the continued use of infield/outfield cultivation methods within the 'central province' at Raunds and Whittlewood (Northants.) and Whittlesford (Cambs.) in the later Anglo-Saxon period.[95]

The conclusion that the introduction of common-field systems was delayed until the eleventh century or later is not, however, entirely straightforward. As Taylor has pointed out, only documentary evidence really allows us to distinguish between common-field and open-field landscapes. Since historical evidence becomes both increasingly rare and decreasingly explicit as its age increases, the paucity of documentary evidence for common-field introduction cannot in itself be taken as cast-iron support for its late emergence. Second, even if an eleventh-century (or later) date is correct for the introduction of common-field systems, the differences in organisation of layout, tenure, and cropping between such systems and open fields make it difficult to argue that they emerged over a short period. It seems likely that the social structures and agricultural improvements which either stimulated progress towards or coalesced in common-field systems were present not only in the later Anglo-Saxon period but possibly much earlier. At this stage, however, all that can be concluded is that settlement nucleation pre-dated recognisable common fields by a considerable period.

The work reported here has had an unexpected outcome in reminding us of the establishment of new, planned nucleations over existing open or common fields at the same time as common-field systems first emerge in the documentary record. The argument was proposed by Brown and Foard in 1998, and a detailed example has been explored at Burton Lazars (Leics.) where, it has been argued, the settlement was laid out over existing fields, in which tenure was reallocated to take into account the pattern of holdings in the new, planned settlement.[96] The arable fields of both Segenhoe (Beds.) and Dry Drayton (Cambs.) were also entirely reorganised by a 'new partition' in the mid-twelfth century.[97] Rather than a late adoption of the Midland system, as was previously suggested, perhaps these records are one of our few insights into a process of grand remodelling of both fields and settlements in the 'central province' in the early Middle Ages which Rackham has described as a tide which left 'the English Midlands submerged … [while parts of the ancient countryside] such as south Essex were not reached at all'.[98] They offer little insight, however, into common-field origins.

95 Parry, *Raunds*, p. 93; Jones and Page, *Medieval Villages*, p. 93; Christopher Taylor and Ashley Arbon, 'The Chronicle Hills, Whittlesford, Cambridgeshire', *Proceedings of the Cambridge Antiquarian Society*, 96 (2007), 21–40, at p. 38.

96 Brown and Foard, 'Saxon landscape' pp. 90–2; Brown, 'Burton Lazars'.

97 Fox, 'Approaches', pp. 95–8.

98 Rackham, *British Countryside*, p. 178, my additions.

Conclusion

There is, it seems, no clear relationship between the origins of nucleation and of open or common fields. Open-field layouts appear to have evolved from prehistoric or Romano-British field systems, although little is known about the similarity of their organisation and cropping to medieval open or common fields. The process of settlement nucleation appears to have begun in the middle Anglo-Saxon period and continued for several centuries thereafter, becoming most intense in the 'central province'. In a yet later period, open-field systems in the 'central province' evolved into or were replaced by common fields. The concentration of nucleated settlement and common fields within the 'central province' indicates that a connection between the two is likely, even though they do not appear at this stage to have been contemporary, but we still do not know what that relationship was.

7

The Environmental Contexts of Anglo-Saxon Settlement

TOM WILLIAMSON

Introduction

It has become unfashionable in recent decades to seek to explain spatial patterns in the archaeological or historical record – whether distributions of artefacts or particular social or religious practices, on the one hand, or patterns of farming or settlement, on the other – in terms of environmental influences. Indeed, such approaches are castigated by many archaeologists as 'environmental determinism' and, in a discipline strongly influenced by post-modern and post-processual approaches, viewed as a negation of individual 'choice', and thus of the essential humanity of the past peoples whose lives it is our task to study.[1] Instead, patterns in the data are generally viewed as representing shared lifestyles which were effectively the consequence of elective choice, the boundaries of which were essentially arbitrary in character. The limits of the 'central province' – that area of medieval England characterised by nucleated villages and regular open-field systems – have thus been interpreted as the edges of a zone where a 'fashion' for a particular mode of agrarian organisation simply petered out; while, at a more detailed level, the particular characteristics of the Whittleswood landscape have been attributed to the cumulative consequences of numerous individual decisions, with boundaries again largely unrelated to any other, non-social factors.[2]

This assertion of the primacy, or even autonomy, of the social is not in itself new. An older generation interpreted many past spatial patterns as signifying the settlement areas of particular ethnic groups, which had maintained and perpetuated traditions and practices forged elsewhere when they came to live in new regions with very different environmental characteristics. Howard Gray for example saw the distribution of different kinds of field system and settlement

1 For a recent discussion of the limitations of post-processual approaches to landscape and settlement see Andrew Fleming, 'Post-processual landscape archaeology: a critique', *Cambridge Archaeological Journal*, 16, 3 (2006), 267–80.

2 Christopher Taylor, 'Nucleated settlement: a view from the frontier', *Landscape History*, 24 (2002), 53–71; pp. 53–4; Richard Jones and Mark Page, *Medieval Villages in an English Landscape: Beginnings and Ends* (Macclesfield, 2006), pp. 240–2.

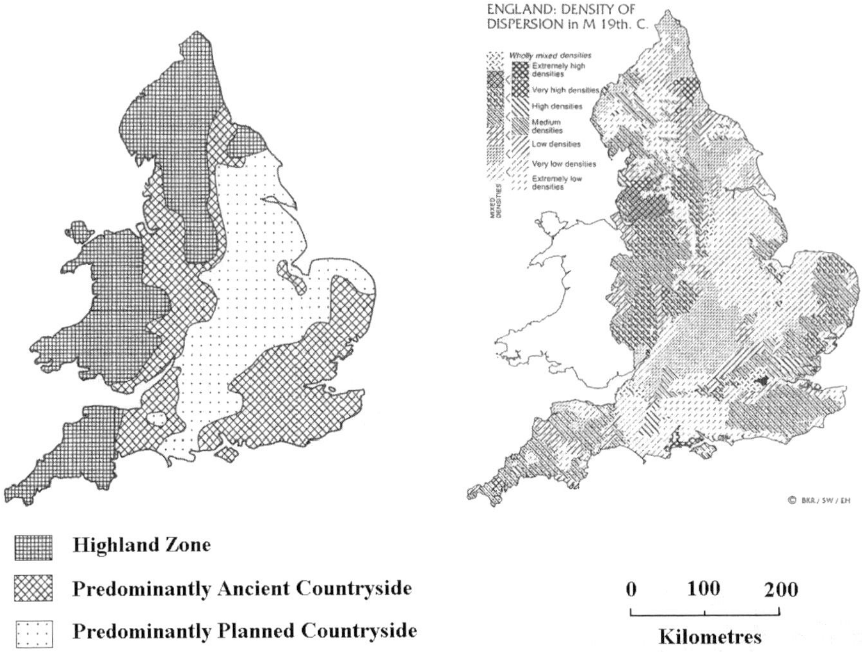

Figure 7.1. Patterns of settlement nucleation in the nineteenth century. Throughout the Middle Ages and into early modern times a broad band of England, extending from the north east to the south coast, was characterised by more nucleated patterns and settlement, and more communal systems of farming, than the districts lying to the south and east or the north and west. The open fields here generally survived well into the post-medieval period, creating the 'planned countryside' rectilinear fields identified by Oliver Rackham. Even in the nineteenth century, as Roberts and Wrathmell's meticulous mapping makes clear, the 'central province' was still characterised by more nucleated patterns of settlement than the regions lying to either side of it.

pattern in medieval England largely as the consequence of variations in the intensity of Anglo-Saxon or Danish settlement; the predominance of free tenures in eastern England at the time of Domesday has often been seen as a result of Danish settlement in the ninth of tenth centuries; while spatial variations in early Anglo-Saxon burial practices, and in the distribution of dress fittings, have since the time of Leeds been interpreted as a reflection of the settlement areas of Bede's 'three powerful nations' of the Angles, Saxons and Jutes.[3] Many of these ethnic interpretations have, of course, fallen from favour. But the patterns

3 Howard L. Gray, *English Field Systems* (Harvard, 1915); Barbara Dodwell, 'The free peasantry of East Anglia in Domesday', *Norfolk Archaeology*, 7 (1941), 145–57; Samantha Lucy, *The Anglo-Saxon Way of Death: Burial Rites in Early England* (Stroud, 2000), pp. 11–14.

remain, and in the current intellectual climate it is often difficult to explain them other than as the result, in effect, of chance.

In this short chapter an alternative view is offered which goes against much current orthodoxy and argues that many of the spatial patterns apparent in Anglo-Saxon England were, in fact, structured by environmental and topographic influences. In so doing it is not suggested that individuals were 'pawns of nature', helpless in the face of the 'titanic forces' of the environment. Nature in itself cannot 'determine' social practice. But the choices made by individuals and societies in the past about the ways they should live were not taken in an environmental vacuum. It is no denial of the principle of individual choice to assert that it is simply impossible to grow certain crops in certain places. Nor is it to deny the role of the individual to suggest that topography helped shape the boundaries of human societies: that language, traditions and beliefs were more likely to be shared between people living in the same valley than those living on different sides of a high mountain range. Climate, geology, soils and topography all affected choices made in the past and thus structured – often in ways infinitely subtle – the kinds of spatial variations in lifestyles, social structures and farming practices which we encounter in the archaeological and historical record.

Fields and Farms in Late Saxon England

I will begin with a complex issue, summarising all too briefly an argument presented in more detail elsewhere.[4] Historians, geographers and archaeologists have long pondered why, by the twelfth century, some areas of lowland England had come to be characterised by 'champion' landscapes of nucleated villages and extensive open fields, farmed in a highly communal manner, while others had a dispersed settlement pattern, and more irregular fields systems, or even landscapes of enclosed fields (Fig. 7.1). Older 'ethnic' explanations fell from favour in the 1960s and '70s partly because a wealth of documentary and archaeological research demonstrated that regional variations emerged later, rather than earlier, in the Saxon period, and may indeed have continued developing after the Conquest. The models which replaced them were more social, economic and demographic in character. According to that which is still most widely accepted, originally devised by Joan Thirsk but further developed by Christopher Dyer and his colleagues, the Midland landscape evolved as it did because this had long been the most densely settled, extensively cleared and intensively farmed area of England.[5] The expansion of arable at the expense of pasture, combined with the progressive fragmentation of peasant holdings through partible inheritance

[4] Tom Williamson, *Shaping Medieval Landscape: Settlement, Society, Environment* (Macclesfield, 2003).

[5] Joan Thirsk, 'The common fields', *Past and Present*, 29, 3–29; Carenza Lewis, Patrick Mitchell-Fox, and Christopher Dyer, *Village, Hamlet and Field: Changing Settlements in Central England* (Macclesfield, 2002).

Figure 7.2. It is likely that certain kinds of soils and terrain encouraged the development of communal farming systems in late Saxon England. 1. Areas of chalk and sand, with limited supplies of water and poor, easily leached soils in need of regular folding. 2. Areas of moderately fertile clay soils, capable of sustaining reasonable population densities but prone to puddling and compaction if ploughed wet, and thus with limited opportunities for spring cultivation (principally soils of the Denchworth, Ragdale, Dunkeswick, Foggarsthorpe and Clifton Associations).

and sale, precipitated a crisis of management (especially concerning dwindling reserves of grazing) which was resolved through the concentration of settlement in nucleated villages and the redistribution of farms as strips scattered evenly, and often very regularly, through the arable area of each township. This landscape of intermixed holdings was then farmed in such a way that half, or a third, of the arable area lay uncropped each year, in order to provide additional grazing for the stock (which also thereby manured the land). Where population levels were lower, and woods and pastures more extensive, none of this happened. Indeed, to many scholars the landscapes of the 'woodland' areas, lying outside the 'champion' Midlands, derived much of their character from the fact that they remained largely uncleared before the late Saxon or even post-Conquest periods.[6]

Scholars argue over whether the new modes of agrarian organisation were imposed from above, by powerful lords, or were developed from below, by peasant communities themselves, but, either way, versions of these 'resource crisis' models remain dominant. They have, however, one significant flaw: they fail to explain the distribution of 'champion' landscapes, for there is no reason to believe that the 'central province', as Brian Roberts and Stuart Wrathmell christened it,[7] ever represented the arable heartland of early England. Most of this area lies on heavy clays which, following enclosure in the post-medieval period, were often laid to pasture, thus fossilising the plough-strips of the open fields as the 'ridge and furrow' which today forms their most obvious archaeological trace. Our only evidence for the density of population in later Saxon England comes from Domesday Book and this, for all its admitted limitations as a source, leaves little doubt that this was *not* the most densely settled region of England (Fig. 7.3). Moreover, even the customary description of these landscapes as comprising, by the High Middle Ages, panoramas of near-continuous arable, with only tiny reserves of pasture, is misleading. On the Midland clays in western Northamptonshire for example *lacunae* in the distribution of ridge and furrow suggest that as much as 30% of the area of many vills remained under pasture, in parcels and ribbons scattered through the open fields, similar to the situation in many 'woodland' areas. Moreover, while the bulk of the 'central province' comprises clay soils, some parts lie on chalk or acid sands, and here great tracts of heath, down or wold usually remained unploughed until the time of enclosure in the post-medieval period. Shortage of pasture, in other words, was not a universal characteristic of 'champion' landscapes.

An alternative approach is to see the distribution of different kinds of early medieval landscape largely as a consequence of rational choices made by farming communities, or their masters, in response to specific agrarian conditions. In some parts of England, that is, it simply made more sense for farmers to live together in nucleated villages, and cultivate their fields in common, rather than

6 Brian K. Roberts and Stuart Wrathmell, 'Dispersed settlement in England: a national view', in *The Archaeology of Landscape*, eds Paul Everson and Tom Williamson (Manchester, 1998), pp. 95–116.

7 Brian K. Roberts and Stuart Wrathmell, *Region and Place* (London, 2002).

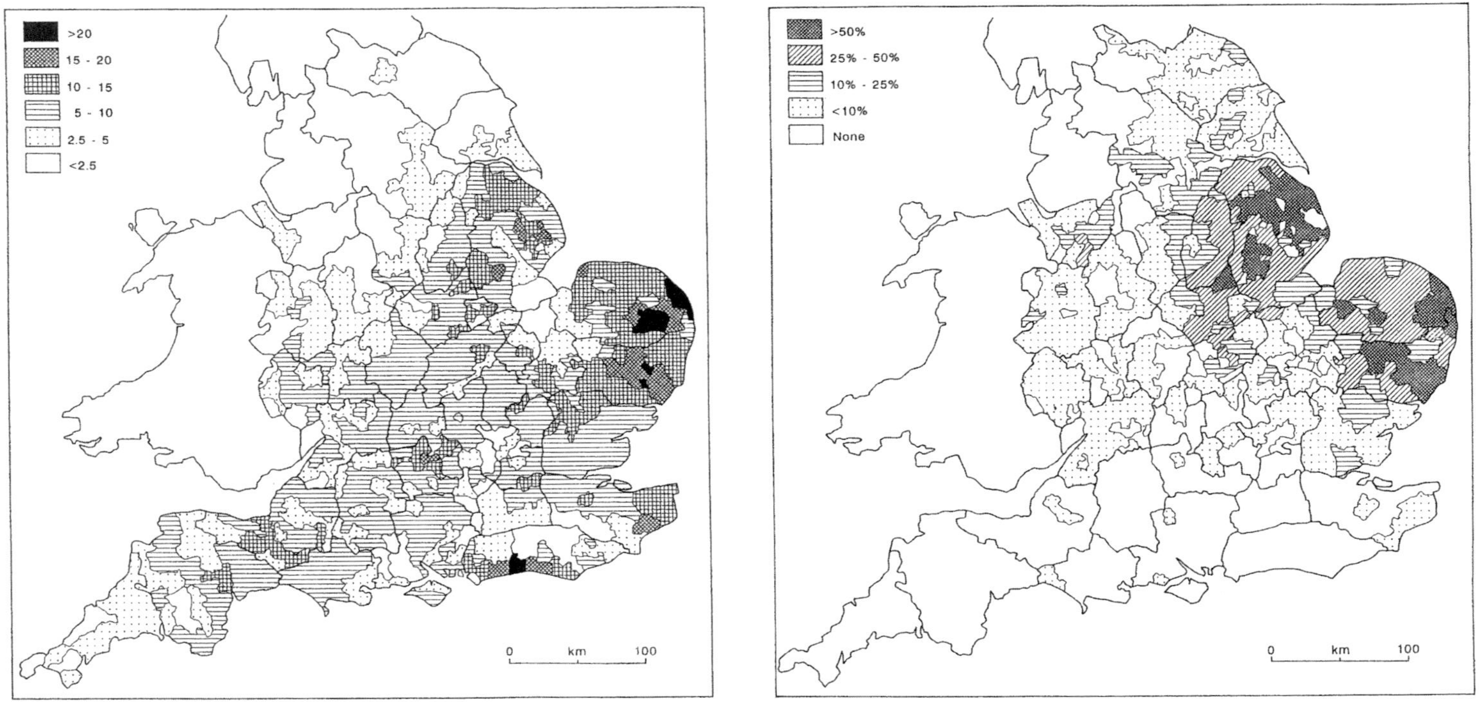

Figure 7.3. Domesday population (left) and free tenures (right), as mapped by H.C. Darby (1977).

in small hamlets or isolated farms. It is true that in some districts of marginal land, 'woodland' landscapes of scattered settlement and irregular open fields and enclosures may indeed have arisen as a consequence of very late colonisation and clearance. In districts such as the Weald of Kent or parts of the Forest of Arden in Warwickshire population remained too low for the emergence of significant nucleations of settlement before the thirteenth century, and much land remained uncleared until a period when, due to the changes in the law arising in part from the Statute of Merton, it could be assarted in severalty in the form of ring-fence farms.[8] But across much of England 'woodland' areas were not noted for late clearance and settlement, and were already relatively densely settled in later Saxon times, while, conversely, many 'champion' districts were not.

Much of the Midlands, as already said, are occupied by heavy clay soils. The same, somewhat problematically for 'environmental' and agrarian explanations for landscape variation, is true of most 'woodland' districts. But there are some subtle differences. Most of the 'central province' is either wetter (with rainfall above 650mm *per annum*) or else has clay soils which, while comparatively fertile, are particularly susceptible to structural damage when ploughed in wet conditions – pelostagnogleys which are silty or clayey to the upper horizons, such as those of the Denchworth, Oxpasture or Ragdale Associations (Fig. 7.2).[9] Climate and geology together ensured that there was a very short period during which the land could be safely cultivated, especially in the spring, something which remains true to this day on the worst Midland soils. Ploughs and ploughteams were, like modern combine harvesters, expensive pieces of equipment which were only used at limited times of the year. Even at the time of Domesday they were evidently shared between cultivators: on average, each villein owned 2.9 oxen.[10] In such a situation it is easy to see how, as larger and heavier ploughs, drawn by large teams of six or eight oxen, came into widespread use in the course of the later Saxon period,[11] and as cultivation expanded onto the more difficult ground, a landscape of clustered farms and intermingled holdings might have evolved. Proximity of farmsteads allowed rapid mobilisation of shared ploughs and teams, while intermingled holdings, scattered across land of varying aspect and drainage potential, allowed each cultivator a reasonable chance of getting their holding ploughed in time for seeding.[12]

This model, proposed in 2003, is currently under investigation (along with other matters) in Northamptonshire, as part of an AHRC project, and is being modified accordingly, although not as yet seriously challenged. Much 'champion'

8 Brian K. Roberts, 'Field systems of the West Midlands', in *Studies of Field Systems in the British Isles*, eds Alan Baker and Robin Butlin (Cambridge, 1973), pp. 195–205, at p. 229.

9 C. Hodge, R. Burton, W. Corbett, R. Evans, and R. Scale, *Soils and their Uses in Eastern England* (Harpenden, 1984).

10 Reginald Lennard, 'The economic position of the Domesday *Villani*', *Economic Journal*, 56 (1946), 244–64, at p.256.

11 Peter Fowler, *Farming in the First Millennium AD: British Agriculture between Julius Caesar and William the Conqueror* (Cambridge 2002), pp. 203–4.

12 For a more detailed statement of this argument see Williamson, *Shaping Medieval Landscapes*, pp. 141–59.

landscape, however, was found on much lighter land, such as on the Chiltern escarpment, the Yorkshire and Lincolnshire Wolds, and the Wessex chalklands. These are districts of easily cultivated, freely draining soils where none of the above arguments can apply (Fig. 7.3). Yet here, too, the rather less closely nucleated villages, and sometimes less regular field systems, may well have been a response to agrarian and environmental factors. On light lands, in contrast to the situation in many clayland districts, there were often extensive areas of grazing, in the form of heaths, wolds or downs, beyond the open fields. In part this was because such land was so marginal it was not worth cultivating, but it also reflected the low fertility of the light soils more generally, easily leached of nutrients and in need of regular, intensive manuring. Flocks of sheep, grazed by day on the pastures (and on the fallow weeds and harvest residues), were close-folded on the arable by night, in order to dung the land.[13]

In such districts there was a natural tendency for settlement to cluster in certain locations, for reliable supplies of running water and good meadowland were limited to major valleys, spring lines, or adjacent deposits of clay. This pattern was always present to some extent, but seems to have intensified from the seventh century, again perhaps because of the adoption of larger ploughs, pulled by larger teams of oxen which needed to be adequately fed and watered. Where farmsteads were forced to cluster in such ways any equitable division of land – whether holdings were being divided through partible inheritance, or allocated to bond tenants – could hardly take the form of enclosed and discrete blocks, for land lying close to the farm was generally of higher value and fertility than that at a distance. This was because in many of these districts the land on the lower ground where farms generally clustered was naturally more fertile than the thinner and often more acid soils on the intervening uplands, while, being closer to the main areas of settlement, it had generally received more farmyard manure than that located at a distance. It could also be reached more quickly, something which might be of critical importance at harvest time. When property was divided, each individual parcel would therefore tend to be split, leading over time to the emergence of intermixed holdings, which would have been further extended as cultivation expanded. Farmers who had formerly grazed an area of heath or downland in common, and who worked together to convert it to arable, would naturally have divided it between them equitably in the form of strips.[14]

The farming of intermixed holdings cultivated from clusters of farmsteads would in turn have encouraged some degree of communal management, especially for the management of the folding flocks.[15] The most efficient way of manuring was to pen sheep tightly together each night in moveable folds, a difficult procedure had each cultivator been obliged to move his own small flock every day from the open pastures to a fold erected on one of his scattered strips. In addition, as Kerridge astutely commented, the farmer would also have had 'all the

13 Eric Kerridge, *The Agricultural Revolution* (London, 1967), pp. 42–51.

14 Williamson, *Shaping Medieval Landscapes*, pp. 123–40.

15 Kerridge, *The Common Fields of England*, pp. 74–86.

lambing and shearing to attend to. All this would have preoccupied him to such an extent as to leave him little time for growing cereals.'[16] Common flocks under the control of communal shepherds were the solution, leading in turn to the adoption of various forms of communal crop rotation, in order to create continuous blocks of strips under the same 'season' which could be conveniently grazed or folded in turn. In some cases, the imposition of such rotations may have been accompanied by a reallotment of peasant holdings in more regular form.

In other words, there were a number of circumstances in which, over time, particular regions and districts of England might have come to develop communal forms of farming based on settlements which, to varying extents, took the form of nucleated villages. And other factors may well have been important. It is noticeable, for example, how far the distribution of meadowland in medieval England corresponds with the essential division between 'woodland' and 'champion' districts. In the latter, the configuration and topography of major river valleys and the character of the sediments they contained evidently ensured that meadowland could be created with relative ease, and in Campbell's words, 'From Somerset and east Devon in the south-west to the Vale of Pickering in Yorkshire's north Riding in the north-east, it was in the clay vales of this broad diagonal band of country that meadowland was most consistently represented. Except on the wolds, few demesnes were without at least some meadow ...'.[17] Concentrations of meadow may have further encouraged nucleated settlement in order to facilitate the rapid mobilisation of men and equipment required for cutting, turning and stacking the hay in the short window of opportunity often provided by the English summer.

I have summarised here, rather baldly, arguments stated at much greater length elsewhere. The critical point in the present context is that variations in early medieval settlement and field systems – not simply the general division between 'woodland' and 'champion', but the infinitely varied and subtle subdivision and hybrids of these two broad landscape types – can often be explained in a fairly straightforward manner in terms of variations in soils, topography and, to a lesser extent, climate. Early medieval farmers (or their masters) made realistic choices which, over time, produced landscapes which were best suited to the prevailing environmental, as well as to the prevailing social and economic, circumstances in which they found themselves.

The Gradient of Freedom

The second example I would like to discuss takes us further back in time, for although the distinction between 'champion' and 'woodland' areas, and other variations in settlement patterns and field systems, may have had their origins in the Saxon period, they were probably still only crystallising in the late eleventh

16 Kerridge, *The Common Fields of England*, p. 26

17 Bruce M. S. Campbell, *English Seigniorial Agriculture, 1250–1450* (Cambridge, 2000), pp. 75–6. Williamson, *Shaping Medieval Landscapes*, pp. 160–79.

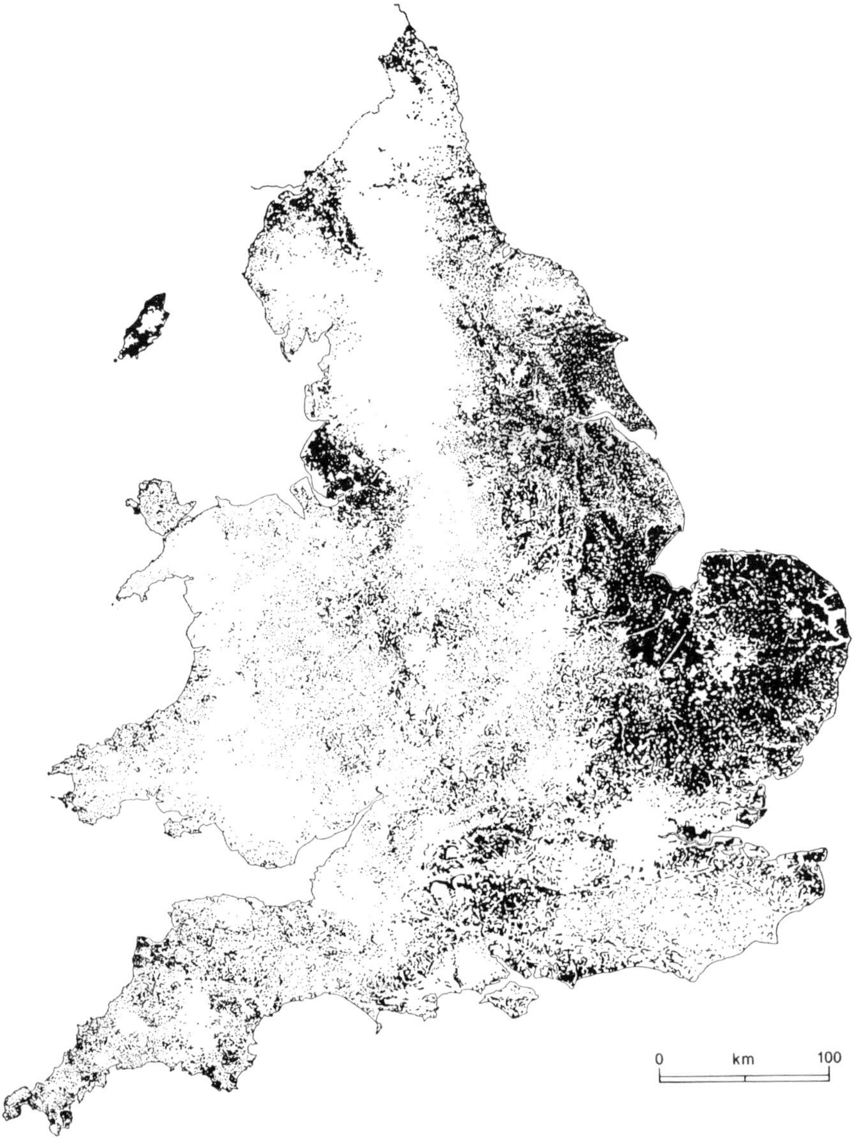

Figure 7.4. The distribution of arable land use in *c*.1940, as mapped by the Land Utilisation Survey. Compare with Figure 7.2.

or twelfth centuries. By this time another important pattern was well established, and is clearly apparent in Domesday Book, a pattern which, intriguingly, cuts right across the woodland/champion divide. The eastern areas of England, especially the counties of Lincolnshire, Cambridgeshire, Norfolk and Suffolk, but also parts of Nottinghamshire and Leicestershire, and other areas of the east, were characterised by high densities of 'free tenures' – by peasants described as 'free men' and 'socmen' in the pages of the great survey (Fig. 7.3). These were also districts – although this is more difficult to map from Domesday Book – in which patterns of manorial organisation were in general more complex than in the west, with a plethora of small manors and, in some districts, large numbers of diminutive vills.

Debate still continues over the meaning of the terms 'free man' and 'socman', and the nature of the differences between these classes of people. It is evident that the variations in their distribution apparent in Domesday were to some extent a consequence of the varying practices employed by those responsible for compiling the survey. In general terms, however, there is agreement among historians that free men in particular, and socmen perhaps to a lesser extent, enjoyed greater personal freedoms – especially from regular labour services on demesnes – than their villein, border or cottar neighbours. There was thus, again to oversimplify, a 'gradient of freedom' extending across England, not so much from east to west, but rather from the east towards the west and south: in the former areas, in other words, a lower proportion of the peasantry had been absorbed into demesne economies in the course of the middle and later Saxon periods than elsewhere. This distinction is arguably reflected in other aspects of tenurial organisation; it is, for example, noteworthy that comparatively few early charters are known from these same eastern areas of England. These social and tenurial idiosyncrasies have often been explained as the consequence of the Viking invasions of the ninth century. In Frank Stenton's words, it was no accident that 'a social organisation to which there is no parallel elsewhere in England occurs in the one part of the country in which the regular development of native institutions had been interrupted by a foreign settlement'.[18] The relative paucity of early charters has been similarly explained.[19] One possibility would be that the free men and socmen of Domesday represented the lineal descendants of demobbed Viking armies, or of Scandinavian peasants who migrated in the wake of conquest. Another is that the disruptions brought about by raiding and conquest allowed the inhabitants of the Danelaw to escape the increasing oppression suffered by their fellows in areas which remained under Saxon control.[20] Yet there is very little evidence that early medieval social and tenurial patterns, and Viking settlement, were in fact causally connected. Indeed, the concept of 'Viking freedom' is arguably the last vestige of the ethnic

[18] Frank M. Stenton, *Anglo-Saxon England* (3rd edn, Oxford, 1971), p. 519.

[19] Oliver Rackham, *The History of the Countryside* (London, 1986), p. 10.

[20] Dodwell, 'Free peasantry of East Anglia'; Frank M. Stenton, 'The historical bearing of place-name studies: the Danish settlement of eastern England', *Transactions of the Royal Historical Society*, 24 (1942), 1–24.

and invasionist models once prevalent in Anglo-Saxon studies. In reality there is no real reason to assume that the Danes were, by definition, lovers of freedom in a way that the English were not: Stenton believed that the settlers injected a fresh dose of 'Germanic freedom' into society,[21] but few historians would today be happy to accept such a simple notion. Moreover, the scale of Scandinavian settlement, and its distribution, remain contested,[22] and there is often in fact a measure of circularity in the arguments of those who believe it was a major factor in the social and tenurial development of eastern England, with the distribution of 'free peasants' being seen as a consequence of Viking settlement, but at the same time being presented as evidence for the scale and extent of that settlement. While there are certainly dangers in minimising the scale of Scandinavian immigration and influence,[23] it is difficult to see the social and tenurial peculiarities of eastern England simply as their consequence, not least because of the very real differences between the northern and southern Danelaw 'not only in law, but also in religion, administration, and the extent of Danish place names'.[24] In Lincolnshire, place-name evidence does seem to suggest intense Scandinavian settlement, but in East Anglia this is not the case. Moreover, the distribution of Danish place names, and that of 'free peasants', is poorly correlated, both in national terms and in detail. Socmen and free men were thus dense on the ground across much of Norfolk where, outside the district called Flegg to the north of Yarmouth, Danish place names are rare. Socmen, and to a lesser extent free men, are commonly recorded across much of northern Essex and eastern Hertfordshire where Scandinavian place names are unknown, and in general 'free peasants' are found far to the west of any of the suggested boundaries of Danish settlement. For all these reasons it might be useful to examine the distribution of 'free tenures' without the preconception that these had anything to do with Viking invasions, and to consider whether it correlates with any other feature of the human or natural environment.

In this context, it is striking that the closest contemporary parallel is with the overall population densities recorded in Domesday Book: that is, there was a broad coincidence between areas in which free men and socmen comprised more than 25% of the population, and areas with recorded Domesday population densities of ten or more per square mile (Fig. 7.3). It is hard to see how Viking settlement could have engendered this demographic pattern, suggesting in turn that both distributions had some third cause. What this might have been is best indicated by a third map, from a very different period: the distribution of arable land recorded by the Land Utilisation Survey in the 1930s (Fig. 7.4). By the

21 Stenton, *Anglo-Saxon England*, pp. 502–25.

22 Dawn Hadley, '"Cockle amongst the wheat": the Scandinavian settlement in England', in *Social Identity in Early Medieval Britain*, eds William Frazer and Andrew Tywell (Leicester, 2000), pp. 111–36.

23 Dawn Hadley, '"And they proceeded to plough and to support themselves": the Scandinavian settlement of England', *Anglo-Norman Studies*, 19 (1996), pp. 69–96.

24 Ralph H. C. Davis, 'East Anglia and the Danes', *Transactions of the Royal Historical Society*, 5 (1955), pp. 23–39: p.38.

later nineteenth century, enclosure, the widespread adoption of improvements like marling and under-drainage, and the continued elaboration of the transport infrastructure had ensured that arable land use was generally concentrated in those parts of the country best suited to the cultivation of cereals. Over the next half century, moreover, a long-lived agricultural depression led to the retreat of cultivation from all but the most suitable environments, enhancing and intensifying this pattern. By the 1930s the principal arable farming areas in England were strikingly similar to those in which Domesday suggests both the overall population density, and the density of free tenures, were greatest. This modern dominance of cereal cultivation in the east reflected not so much the inherent suitability of soils for this form of enterprise but rather (as remains the case today) particular climatic factors: dry summers made for reliable harvests. It is easy to see how these same environmental circumstances would, in an early medieval context, have encouraged a greater rate of population growth in the east than in the west of the country, where it would be unchecked by periodic harvest failure and dearth. But these same factors evidently likewise encouraged the survival, or enhancement, of peasant freedoms. In Stenton's words, they would have been less often 'compelled to put themselves and their households at the disposal of lords who could at least offer them food in evil days'.[25] To judge from numerous ethnographic parallels, frequent harvest failures may have encouraged bondage because peasant cultivators were obliged to fall into dependence on social superiors with greater command of resources, and greater facilities for the storage of surpluses. In contrast, in the expanding economy of late Saxon England a prospering peasantry may have been better able to assert or expand their ancient rights against a rising class of thegns than those living in less agriculturally favoured areas. Such favourable environmental conditions, and the high population densities resulting from them, may also have encouraged the more minute partition of estates, because every sub-unit had to be capable of supporting a thegn to the required level, thus leading to that tenurial complexity at manorial level which is also a feature of most eastern regions.

It is not at the present time possible to 'prove' the hypothesis that the social and tenurial differences between the east and west of England apparent in Domesday were a function of environmental circumstances, and I would not want to suggest here that they were *only* a consequence of such factors (see below, pp. 154–5). But it is surprising that this kind of explanation has not, so far, been given any serious consideration by scholars of Anglo-Saxon England.

Cultural Provinces in Anglo-Saxon England

My third example mainly concerns an earlier period, and a rather different range of environmental influences. Some readers may be aware of the kinds of models of social and territorial evolution which have been developed by historians of the

[25] Stenton, *Anglo-Saxon England*, p.471.

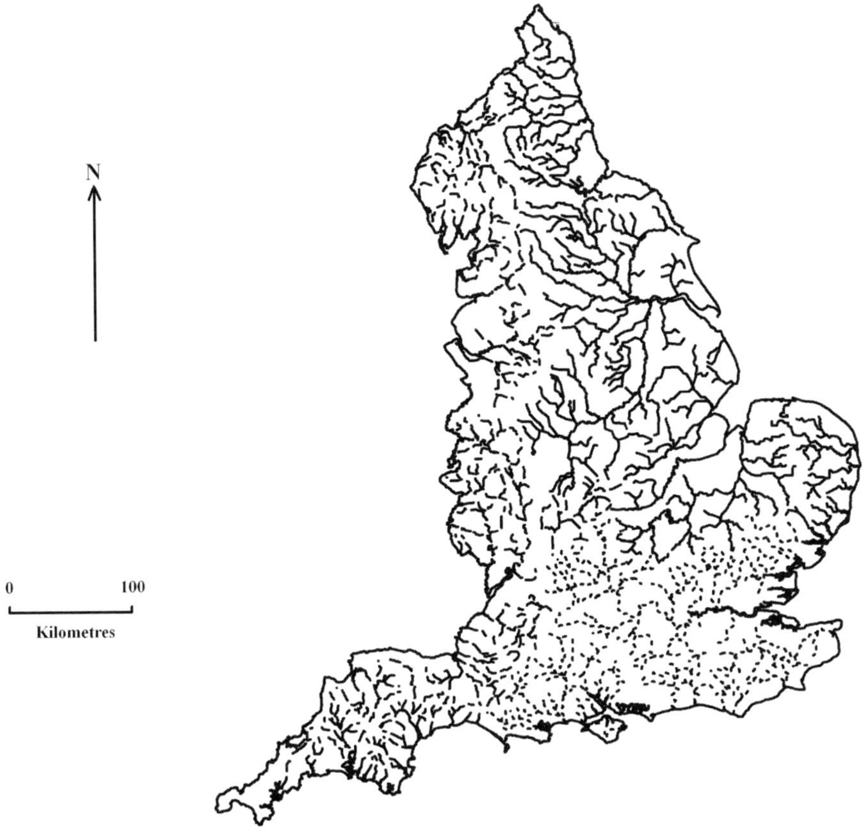

Figure 7.5. In topographic terms, England can be divided into three 'provinces', comprising rivers draining into the North Sea, the Thames and English Channel, and the Atlantic and Irish Sea respectively.

'Leicester School' and in particular by Alan Everitt, Charles Phythian-Adams and the late Harold Fox.[26] Put simply, from the later Iron Age through to the early medieval period the main areas of clearance, cultivation and settlement were to be found in the major river valleys. The high interfluves lying between were less intensively (and often less permanently) settled, and were more likely to be occupied by woods and pastures. Major valleys not only provided a reliable supply of water and meadowland, they also normally contained the most tractable and often the most fertile soils. The interfluves in contrast often lacked reliable supplies of water and were characterised by soils derived from heavy

[26] Alan Everitt, 'River and wold: reflections on the historical origins of regions and *pays*', *Journal of Historical Geography*, 3 (1977), 1–19; Charles Phythian-Adams, *Rethinking English Local History* (Leicester 1987); Harold S. A. Fox, 'The people of the wolds', in *The Rural Settlements of Medieval England: Studies Presented to Maurice Beresford and John Hurst*, eds Mick Aston, David Austin, and Christopher Dyer (Oxford 1989), pp. 77–104.

clays or acid, infertile drift. Given these essential constraints, according to the model, interfluves and watersheds tended to form cut-off points in patterns of human interaction; conversely, drainage basins and river systems tended, over time, to approximate to social territories.

This general model, often referred to as 'river and wold', has been employed on a number of occasions to throw light on the development of landscape and settlement at both a local and a regional level, most elegantly, perhaps, in Fox's famous paper on the 'People of the Wolds'. It has not, however – at least to my knowledge – been used at a *national* level. But it is arguable that the larger-scale configuration of major watersheds, and drainage basins, determined wider patterns of communication and contact, patterns which shaped many of the distributions mapped by archaeologists and, perhaps, helped structure wider senses of identity at various times in the Saxon period.

As most readers will be aware, the Anglo-Saxons in the fifth, sixth and early seventh centuries disposed of their dead in two main ways: by inhumation, usually with grave goods; or by cremation, with the burnt bones and ashes (together with the remains of grave goods and food put on the pyre) placed in the ground in a pottery urn or other receptacle. In very general terms, in the course of time cremation tended to decline in favour of inhumation.[27] It is possible that this indicates – like the changes in the character of grave goods in the later sixth and seventh centuries discussed by Helen Geake – the increasing influence of ideas from the Frankish and Mediterranean worlds, where cremation was rarely practised, and the decline in traditions deriving from north Germany and Scandinavia, where cremation had long been widespread.[28] All this was apparently part of a wider shift in the character of European cultural influences upon southern and eastern England, which arguably climaxed in the adoption of Christianity in the course of the seventh century. Of more interest in the present context, however, are the *spatial* variations in the relative importance of these two rites of disposal. Cremation, and in particular large cemeteries in which cremation is the sole or overwhelmingly dominant rite, is a feature of East Anglia, the Midlands and East Yorkshire – although inhumation was of course also practised here, and became more important with the passing of time. Cremation cemeteries are by no means unknown in the south and in the Thames valley, but they are rare and generally small in size.[29] Here inhumation was, from the fifth century onwards, the overwhelmingly dominant rite recorded archaeologically. In addition, while across most of northern East Anglia, the Midlands and the north-east of England cemeteries – cremation, inhumation, or mixed – are widely scattered, and with gaps in their distribution which are usually explicable in terms of environmental factors (areas of high, drift-covered uplands, tracts of heavy, intractable clay, or waterlogged fens), this is perhaps less true in the south and south-east. Here large areas of fertile and relatively easily worked land, as in east Hertfordshire,

27 Lucy, *Anglo-Saxon Way of Death*.

28 Helen Geake, *The Use of Grave Goods in Conversion Period England, c.600–850*, British Archaeological Reports 261 (Oxford, 1997).

29 Lucy, *Anglo-Saxon Way of Death*, pp. 140–4.

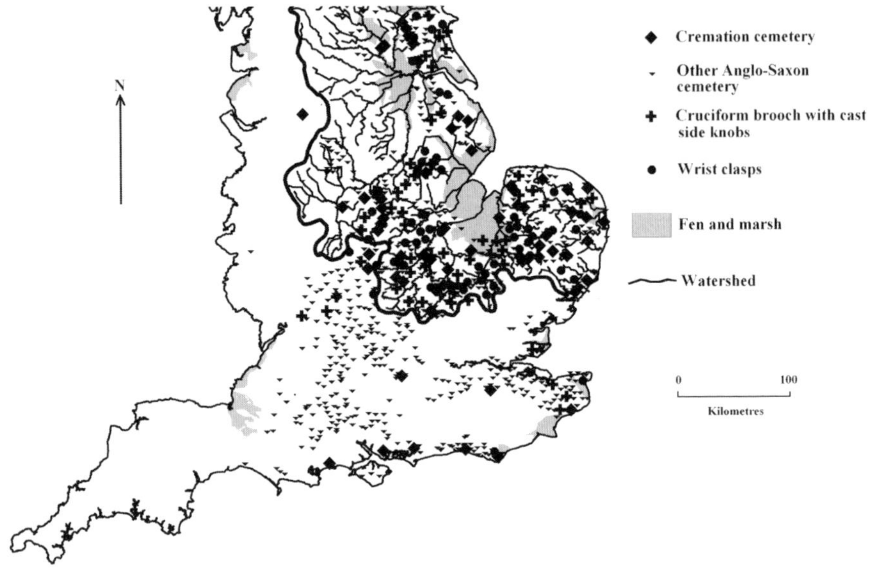

Figure 7.6. The distribution of 'Anglian' artefacts, and cremation cemeteries, correlates strongly with the 'North Sea Province'.

have failed to produce any kinds of 'Anglo-Saxon' burials, suggesting that some people in the fifth and sixth centuries may have employed forms of burial rite that have left no clear archaeological traces, like many of their predecessors in Roman Britain.[30]

Variations in Anglo-Saxon funerary practices used to be interpreted in fairly straightforward, ethnic terms:[31] they reflected the areas of settlement of the principal Germanic tribes in the fifth and sixth centuries, as famously described by Bede:

> The people of Kent and the inhabitants of the Isle of Wight are of Jutish origin, and also those opposite the Isle of Wight, that part of the Kingdom of Wessex which is still today called the nation of the Jutes. From the Saxon country, that is, the district now known as Old Saxony, came the East Saxons, the South Saxons, and the West Saxons. Besides this, from the country of the Angles, that is the land between the kingdoms of the Jutes and the Saxons, which is called *Angulus*, came the East Angles, the Middle Angles, the Mercians, and all the Northumbrian race … as well as the other Anglian tribes …[32]

Cremation cemeteries were thus concentrated within, although not entirely restricted to, those areas which Bede believed had been settled by people coming from *Angeln* – East Anglia, Mercia and Northumbria. This same general pattern

[30] Lucy, *Anglo-Saxon Way of Death*, p. 140.
[31] Lucy, *Anglo-Saxon Way of Death*, pp. 11–14.
[32] *HE*, I, 15.

is, moreover, reflected – albeit more weakly – in the distribution of certain kinds of artefact, especially those related to forms of dress, in the fifth and sixth centuries. So-called 'Anglian' material, largely restricted to East Anglia, the Midlands and the north-east, is typified by the artefacts known as 'wrist clasps' and by particular styles of brooch – those classified by archaeologists as 'equal armed', 'cruciform' and 'annular', together with most of the 'square-headed' variety. In 'Saxon' areas, in contrast – essentially, the south of England, including Essex, and the Thames basin – wrist clasps are largely absent and different forms of brooch predominate – a particular kind of square-headed ('Group VIII'), quoit, and radiate-headed types.[33] In fact, it has long been recognised that 'Saxon' material occurs widely in 'Anglian' areas, although the inverse is rather less true: but the patterns are intriguing nevertheless.

Modern archaeologists, for the most part, do not accept such neat ethnic labels, nor the elegant simplicity of Bede's account which was, after all, written nearly three centuries after the *Adventus Saxonum*. The modern orthodoxy is that the Germanic settlers were, in fact, culturally diverse and ethnically mixed. In the words of Sam Lucy:

> The immediate post-Roman period in Britain, and indeed in the whole of Europe, was a time when identities were in an extreme state of flux ... when charismatic leaders could gather strong bands of followers around them and gain control of often extensive tracts of territory ...[34]

In the process of migration people from a wide area of northern Germany and southern Scandinavia might become incorporated within the same war band. Nevertheless, the material culture of the period does display, at least to a degree, the kind of geographical character outlined above, and this requires some form of explanation. Whether or not these variations have any connection with the homelands of immigrant peoples settling in different parts of England, they certainly hint at regional variations in such matters as styles of dress in the fifth and sixth centuries. 'In East Anglia, the East Midlands and Yorkshire, women wore cruciform and annular brooches, and fastened their sleeves with metal clasps. In southern England, in Sussex, Wessex and Essex, they preferred round brooches and did not use clasps.'[35] A few archaeologists would, however, go further, still maintaining a 'traditional' view and equating these spatial variations in material culture fairly directly with patterns of ethnic settlement. Roger White for example has argued recently that the 'archaeological evidence bears out in large

33 Catherine Hills, 'Early historic Britain', in *The Archaeology of Britain: An Introduction from the Upper Palaeolithic to the Industrial Revolution*, eds John Hunter and Ian Ralston (London, 1998), pp. 176–93, at p. 184; Michael Parker Pearson, Robert van de Noort, and Alex Woolf, 'Three men and a boat: Sutton Hoo and the East Anglian kingdom', *Anglo-Saxon England*, 22 (1993), 27–50, at pp. 34–6; John Hines, *The Scandinavian Character of Anglian England in the Pre-Viking Period*, British Archaeological Reports British Series 124 (Oxford, 1984).

34 Lucy, *Anglo-Saxon Way of Death*, p. 4.

35 Hills, 'Early historic Britain', p. 184.

measure what he [Bede] tells us, with certain brooch types (along with the dress customs that they represent) and forms of burial associated with each group'.[36]

The real significance of these patterns becomes rather clearer when we consider them against the broad sweeps of regional topography, and in particular against the configuration of drainage basins and watersheds. For it was not only at a local level that patterns of cultural and social identity may have been influenced, or even moulded, by natural topography. It is arguable that at a much larger scale, situations in which contact and communication between individuals and groups of people were easy and regular tended to engender, if not a measure of social or political identity, then at least some sharing of beliefs, language and fashions. Where contact was restricted, in contrast – for topographic or other reasons – there was more divergence in social and cultural development. But there is another factor we need to bear in mind here – a necessary elaboration which we must make to the 'river and wold' model. In the fifth, sixth and seventh centuries England was, perhaps more than at any other time before or since, subject to the movement of people, artefacts and ideas coming from foreign lands – from Ireland, Scotland and above all from the European mainland. Where the principal English rivers entered the sea – which direction their valley-systems and associated hierarchies of social territories faced – is thus also a matter of some importance. Looked at in a wider European context England can thus usefully be considered as comprising three great 'provinces', facing the North Sea, the Irish Sea, and the Channel and the Thames estuary respectively (Fig. 7.5).

These three 'provinces' were, and indeed are, separated from each other by interfluves and watersheds of varying magnitude and significance. The boundary between the 'North Sea Province' and the 'Channel Province', for example, is defined all along its course between the area around Tring in Hertfordshire and a point a little to the south of Newmarket in Suffolk by the impressive escarpment of the Chiltern Hills and its more diminutive (but still physically striking) north-eastern extension, the so-called 'East Anglian Heights'. Much of the high watershed here is still occupied by tracts of woodland, and concentrations of 'woodland' place names indicate where more extensive areas were cleared and settled in the course of the Anglo-Saxon period. But at either end of this well-defined section the line dividing the two 'provinces' is less physically obvious. To the west, the line of division leaves the Chiltern escarpment and, tracking north through Buckinghamshire, follows the watershed dividing rivers like the Thame draining westwards into the Thames and those flowing eastwards into the Great Ouse, and picking a course along only moderately high ground, although ground peppered with a scatter of 'woodland' names – Wingrave, Stewkley, Mursley, Horwood – and on through Whaddon Chase. The line then swings south of Buckingham, and runs northwards through western Northamptonshire. To the east of the strongly defined Chiltern/East Anglian Heights section the boundary is more diffuse still. It makes its way, in a slightly convoluted manner,

[36] Roger White, *Britannia Prima: Britain's Last Roman Province* (Stroud 2007), pp. 197–9.

along the high ground of west Suffolk, passing to the south of Bury St Edmunds, but then turning northwards and following, to the south-east, the high ground lying just to the north of the river Gipping. The line continues towards the North Sea but becomes less distinct in this more muted topography, and fades out on the high ground lying between the Deben and the Orwell.

The other watersheds defining the boundaries of the topographic provinces are similarly varied. Sometimes they correspond to dramatic ranges of hills, obvious barriers to contact and communication, sometimes to more muted topographic incidents. But while the latter may have formed more permeable barriers to contact and movement, in all cases these major watersheds seem to have constituted the edges of major cultural distributions in the early Saxon period. 'Anglian' England – with its cremation cemeteries and distinctive artefacts like wrist clasps – thus clearly corresponds with the North Sea Province (Fig. 7.6). Its distinctive character must in part reflect the fact that it faces out across the North Sea to regions which had never been within the Roman *limes*. 'Saxon' England, in contrast – essentially, what I have defined here as the English Channel Province – faces France and the southern parts of the Low Countries, lands which had formed parts of the Roman Empire.[37] The absence of large cremation cemeteries from this region may, perhaps, indicate that it was less subject to major cultural influences from 'barbarian' lands, and perhaps less affected by 'barbarian' immigration in the immediate post-Roman period. Indeed, as a number of scholars have argued, the appearance in this region in the fifth century of cemeteries containing inhumations with grave goods may have been the consequence of indigenous developments within late Roman society, rather than representing, in any simple and straightforward way, the signature of 'invaders'. In Hills' words:

> Late Roman burials were mostly unfurnished inhumations, but the later fourth century saw the appearance in Britain and northern Gaul of inhumations accompanied by weapons and belt fittings. Although these have often been interpreted as the burials of Germanic mercenary soldiers, there is not really any reason to see them purely in ethnic terms, although it does seem to have been a fashion prevalent amongst a military elite, which included men of Germanic origins. These burials may have contributed to the development of the rite [i.e., inhumation burial with grave goods] seen throughout western Europe and southern Britain between the fifth and seventh centuries.[38]

Not that the appearance of *cremation* cemeteries, and other aspects of an intrusive culture, should be viewed even within 'Anglian' England simply as a sign that new people were arriving *en masse* from northern Europe. The fact that

37 In some ways this argument resembles that recently put forward by White, that different regions in the immediate post-Roman period received settlers from the nearest possible source. White, however, discusses these, and their archaeological signatures, mainly in terms of 'mercenaries': while the 'regions' with which he is concerned are not topographic zones, as argued here, but the various political units – the provinces of Roman Britain – that hired them. White, *Britannia Prima*, p. 199.

38 Hills, 'Early historic Britain', p. 184.

distributions of 'Anglian' material and cremation cemeteries tend to break at major watersheds suggests not that invaders found these some kind of insurmountable topographic obstacle to conquest, but rather that these aspects of material culture represent only the archaeologically visible aspect of a wider package of shared ideas and fashions that spread as much by emulation as by the actual displacement of one group of people by another. River systems, with their well-settled, fertile soils, evidently represented the arteries along which ideas, styles and fashions moved, exchanged from group to group and person to person; rivers themselves were, in their navigable lower reaches at least, physical paths of movement, for it was generally easier to transport men and materials by river than over land. In other words, the apparent correlation of archaeological distributions with aspects of the natural topography lends some support to those archaeologists who believe that the major changes in material culture apparent in the fifth and sixth centuries represent not so much outright conquest and a mass population movement from northern Europe, but rather the more general adoption of new fashions and beliefs, and new ways of life, derived from the barbarian north, as the social, economic and ideological influence of Rome and the south waned.[39] New people unquestionably arrived from the Continent, but not necessarily in vast numbers. Nor was this new pattern of cultural influences something operating over a short period of time; or even solely in one direction. As Hills again has noted:

> People did not get into their boats and sail to England, never to return. The communities on both sides of the North Sea remained in contact. The connections between them could have owed as much to the exchange of ideas and goods through trade, religion and political relationships as to migration.[40]

As John Hines has shown, contacts between Scandinavia and 'Anglian' England continued through the sixth and into the seventh centuries, and perhaps beyond.[41] Indeed, it is arguable that the distinction between the 'North Sea' and 'Channel' Provinces reappeared even more strongly in the ninth century. In the 860s and '70s, following more than seven decades of summer raiding, Viking forces from Denmark began to remain for longer periods in England, occupying East Anglia in 865 and Northumbria and Mercia in 866. In 870 the 'host':

> rode across Mercia into East Anglia, and took winter-quarters at Thetford: and the same winter King Edmund fought against them, and the Danes won the victory, and they slew the king and overran the entire kingdom.

From here they raided into the east Midlands, sacking the monastery at Peterborough, and into Wessex, fighting armies led by Æthelræd and Alfred at a number of places, before making peace. The 'Great Army' then withdrew to

39 R. Hodges, *The Anglo-Saxon Achievement: Archaeology and the Beginnings of English Society* (London, 1989).

40 Hills, 'Early historic Britain', p.183.

41 Hines, *Scandinavian Character of Anglian England*, pp. 286–301.

London and made peace with the Mercians. But the following year it was on the move again, progressing first to Northumbria, and then into Lindsey, before dividing, one portion returning to Northumbria, the other (under Guthrum) going on to Cambridge. This phase of activity culminated in systematic land grabbing. Northumbria was 'shared out' in 876; Mercia was partitioned in 877, and the Danish portion similarly 'shared'; while East Anglia was 'shared out' in 879. We have no certain way of knowing precisely what the *Chronicle* means by this phase – whether estates and revenues were being partitioned amongst a warrior elite, or whether a peasant folk-movement was under way in the wake of the conquering armies – but the 'Great Army' wandering across the country, from winter quarters to winter quarters, is not heard of again.

It is often stated that the division between English England and the 'Danelaw' was fixed by a treaty made in 886 between Alfred and Guthrum, the terms of which survive: the frontier was to run along the river Thames, then up the river Lea, and then along the line of Watling Street. In fact, as David Dumville has cogently argued, this treaty probably represents not the terms of a permanent settlement drawn up at Wedmore in 886, but only a temporary peace made following the battle of Edington in 878. More importantly, Dumville has drawn attention to the fact that the Anglo-Saxon Chronicle, while making it clear that eastern Mercia and East Anglia were overrun and settled by the Danes in the 870s and '80s, is much more circumspect in its treatment of Essex. Danish armies are mentioned in the north-east of the county, but 'When they wanted a safe base for their women or chattels, Essex was not [the Vikings'] first choice but East Anglia.... Essex was territory that was being debated.'[42] Most of the county seems to have remained in English hands, and one Chronicle entry, for 896, looking back to events earlier in the 880s and 890s, recalled the deaths of 'many of the king's best thegns' – including Brihtwulf, Ealdorman of Essex. Essex had effectively been incorporated into the West Saxon kingdom in the 820s, and that control was never subsequently relinquished, except in the north-east of the present county in the area around Colchester. It is noteworthy that in 921, during the 'reconquest' of East Anglia from the Danes, Edward was able to gather a great force 'from Kent, Surrey, *and Essex*', to attack Colchester (my italics).

The fact that Essex should have remained largely under English control while Suffolk and Norfolk were lost to the Danes is at first sight remarkable, given the fact that the area lay some way from the main centres of West Saxon power, had a long exposed coast facing the North Sea, and was not divided from East Anglia proper by impassable hills or a major watercourse. Looked at in the topographic contexts already discussed, however, this situation becomes much more explicable. Essex, and probably south-western Suffolk, continued to form part of the 'Channel Province'; the core of Danish influence always remained within the 'North Sea Province'. This relationship between natural topography

42 David Dumville, *Wessex and England from Alfred to Edgar: Six Essays in Political, Cultural and Ecclesiastical History* (Woodbridge, 1992), p. 9.

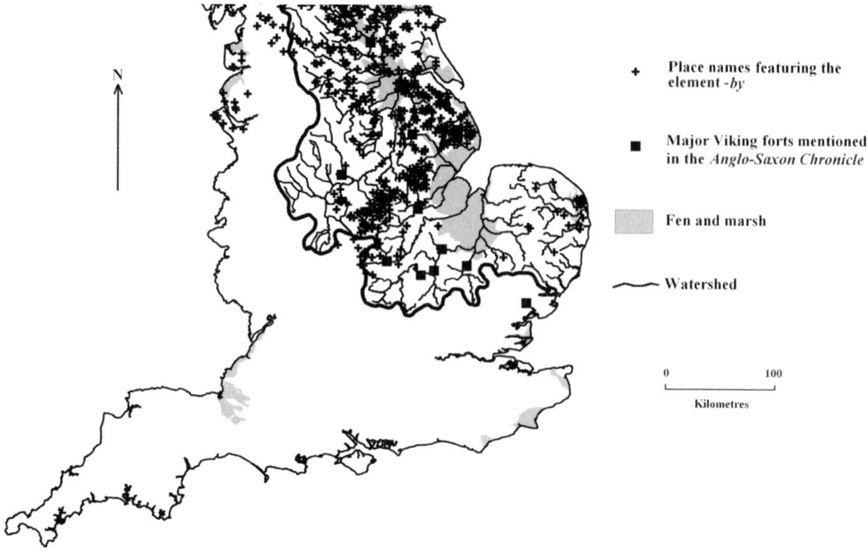

Figure 7.7. Although a less striking correlation, major Scandinavian place names and principal 'Viking' strongholds are also largely restricted to the 'North Sea Province', largely avoiding (in particular) the county of Essex.

on the one hand, and patterns of ethnicity and political power on the other, is clear when the distribution of major Scandinavian place names, and of the forts and towns described by the *Anglo-Saxon Chronicle* as major Viking strongholds, is mapped against the pattern of drainage basins and river catchments (Fig. 7.7). The same pattern of rivers and watersheds which arguably structured aspects of cultural variation in the fifth and sixth centuries now clearly affected patterns of Danish influence and settlement. This is not the place to discuss what this might imply about the true character of the 'Viking invasions': the point here is simply that, in the ninth century as in the fifth and sixth, the movement of people, artefacts and ideas coming from across the North Sea was strongly channelled within lowland England by the structures of natural topography.

Conclusion

This is a wide-ranging and perhaps over-ambitious chapter but the point it makes is simple enough. Spatial aspects of Anglo-Saxon settlement and society need to be examined within the contexts of topographical and environmental frameworks of all kinds, if we are fully to appreciate their significance. One major difficulty in doing this must, however, briefly be noted. To a significant extent the varied frameworks and patterns exhibited by soils, topography and climate are overlapping. A range of hills might thus constitute, at one and the same time, a boundary to social contact, a junction of soil types and a climatic division (with, for example, a rain shadow in its lea). The northern parts of East Anglia, and Lincolnshire, may thus derive much of their late Anglo-Saxon character from the fact that they lie in the dry east of England, but the fact that they lay within the 'North Sea Province' may also have been significant. Relative population density, peasant 'freedom' and tenurial complexity, that is, may have owed much to the expansion of the North Sea economy in the tenth and eleventh centuries, as well as being the consequences of climatic and agrarian factors. Such complexities do not negate the essential argument, but they do present archaeologists and historians with important interpretative challenges.

8

Calendar Illustration in Anglo-Saxon England: Realities and Fictions of the Anglo-Saxon Landscape

CATHERINE E. KARKOV

In the introduction to his edited volume *Landscape and Power*, W. J. T. Mitchell outlined the ambiguity of the term 'landscape'. 'Landscape is', he noted, 'both a natural phenomenon, a real place, and an object of cultural mediation, a representation, even a simulacrum.' As almost all the essays in that book went on to demonstrate, landscape is above all 'an ideological "class view" to which "the painted image" gives "cultural expression"'.[1] Mitchell's book deals exclusively with modern landscapes and modern (that is post-Renaissance) art, but the conclusions drawn are equally applicable to the Anglo-Saxon landscape and its representation – when and where it exists it reflects ideology as much as, if not more than, it reflects the natural world.

This is particularly evident in the two surviving Anglo-Saxon cycles of calendar illustrations contained in the early eleventh-century British Library, Cotton Julius A.vi,[2] and the *c*.1025–50 British Library, Cotton Tiberius B.v. Both manuscripts have been tentatively attributed to Christ Church, Canterbury. In both, the illustrations accompany metrical verse-calendars with signs of the zodiac and, in both, the calendar material is combined with computistical matter. In the case of Tiberius B.v, the computistical material is lengthy, and the contents of the manuscript extend to genealogies and lists, a zonal and world map, Ælfric's *De temporibus anni*,[3] Cicero's *Aratea*, and the Marvels of the East – the latter two texts illustrated by the same artist responsible for the calendar illustrations.[4] Both manuscripts are thus concerned with the mapping of time and space (earthly and celestial), and the locating of the Anglo-Saxon reader

1 (Chicago, 1994), p. 8.

2 The early eleventh-century calendar is combined in this manuscript with a post-Conquest hymnal in Latin with Old English gloss.

3 Nicholas Howe notes that this text includes a listing of the signs of the zodiac and a translation of the Latin name for each sign into English, providing a 'prose summary' of what the reader has seen depicted earlier in the manuscript. See Nicholas Howe, *Writing the Map of Anglo-Saxon England: Essays in Cultural Geography* (New Haven, 2008), p. 160.

4 For a detailed list of the contents see *An Eleventh-Century Illustrated Miscellany: British Library Cotton Tiberius B.v, Part 1*, eds Patrick McGurk, David N. Dumville, Malcolm R. Godden and Ann Knock, Early English Manuscripts in Facsimile 21 (Copenhagen, 1983).

in relation to the cycle of time – and in the case of the Tiberius manuscript, to other lands and their inhabitants both past and present. Indeed, Nicholas Howe has described Tiberius B.v as a book of 'elsewhere'.[5]

We know from place names, charter bounds and the like that the Anglo-Saxons did have a keen awareness of the physical landscape they inhabited, and could make subtle distinctions in the nature of its physical features – the various words used to distinguish different types of hills being but one example[6] – but this is in no way reflected in the landscape settings of Anglo-Saxon art in general, and those of the calendar illustrations in particular. What we see in the latter is strictly formulaic: patterned lumps and hillocks, streams flowing out of classical vessels, and trees and vines that grow in patterns similar to those of decorated initials. In the Tiberius manuscript there is virtually no difference between the way in which the land on which the figures stand is depicted in the calendar and the way in which it is depicted in the Marvels of the East. The difference lies primarily in the productivity of, and signs of civilization apparent in, the former. Indeed, art historians have often dismissed the calendar illustrations in both the Tiberius and Julius manuscripts as derivative of imported Carolingian calendars illuminated in the Rheims style, and ultimately indebted to late antique prototypes, despite the fact that surviving Carolingian calendars look nothing like those in either of the Anglo-Saxon manuscripts. Both Carolingian and Ottonian calendars show us single figures holding tools or attributes that signify the labour identified with each month, but they do not show us either the landscape or the carrying out of the labour.[7] One exception to the standard art historical approach was that of Meyer Schapiro, who, in his often overlooked review of J. C. Webster's *The Labours of the Months in Antique and Medieval Art to the End of the Twelfth Century*, stressed the originality of the Anglo-Saxon manuscripts and their difference from earlier traditions. The drawing style of the Anglo-Saxon manuscripts may ultimately show the influence of Carolingian art, and the landscape settings may indeed be somewhat formulaic, but the miniatures themselves are filled with an 'extraordinary activism and episodic richness'.[8] Schapiro was here referring primarily to style; nevertheless, he was the first to draw attention to the fact that the two manuscripts represent a break with the earlier traditions of calendar illustration, and that that break has to do with the artists' creation of a visual narrative carried by human activity. This is land that is in the process of being landscaped, and it is the fruits of the labour of landscaping that are the primary subject of both

[5] Howe, *Writing the Map of Anglo-Saxon England*, p. 154.

[6] See Kelley M. Wickham-Crowley, 'Living on the *Ecg*: the mutable boundaries of land and water in Anglo-Saxon contexts', in *A Place to Believe In: Locating Medieval Landscapes*, eds Clare Lees and Gillian Overing (University Park, PA, 2007), pp. 85–110, at 89.

[7] See e.g. Vienna, National Library, Codex 387, fol. 90v; Munich, State Library, Clm. 210, fol. 91v. Roman calendars also depicted single figures representative of particular activities often accompanied by isolated symbols of the land and/or its produce, such as birds, flowers, or vine sprouts. See Michele Renee Salzman, *On Roman Time: the Codex Calendar of 354 and the Rhythms of Urban Life in Antiquity* (Berkeley, 1990).

[8] *Speculum*, 16 (1941), pp. 131–7, at 137.

Anglo-Saxon cycles. In their focus on labour and the productivity of the land, the Anglo-Saxon manuscripts stand at the start of a new tradition, one that would culminate in the far more famous calendar illustrations of the Luttrell Psalter (London, British Library, Add. 42130) made for Sir Geoffrey Luttrell *c.*1340, or the early fifteenth-century Très Riches Heures of the Duc de Berry, now in the museum in Chantilly.

There is certainly a common model lying somewhere behind the Julius and Tiberius calendars as most of the depictions of the labours of the months – for example, the two scenes of pruning vines in February (Pl. VIII.1a, VIII.1b) – have strikingly similar compositions, but that model is now generally believed to have been Anglo-Saxon rather than Carolingian, though admittedly there can be no certainty in this regard, and the evidence either way is entirely circumstantial. We are left having to deal with the evidence as it survives. The text of the metrical calendars in the two manuscripts is, however, completely different, as are the style of the illustrations, many of the details within the individual miniatures, and the basic layout of the pages – the pictures in Julius being at the bottom of the page and those in Tiberius at the top. The labours assigned to each month are also not all depicted in the same order, as the following list demonstrates.

	Julius	*Tiberius*
January	ploughing & sowing	ploughing & sowing
February	pruning vines	pruning vines
March	digging & sowing	digging & sowing
April	feasting	feasting
May	tending sheep	tending sheep
June	**cutting wood**	**reaping**
July	**mowing**	**cutting wood**
August	**reaping**	**mowing**
September	feeding hogs	feeding hogs
October	hunting with falcon	hunting with falcon
November	stacking firewood/warming	stacking firewood/warming
December	threshing	threshing

Patrick McGurk has speculated that the artist of Tiberius may have accidentally skipped two pages in his model at June and, when he realized his mistake, simply gone on to illustrate July and August with the labours appropriate to June and July.[9] This is possible, but there was as yet no standard model assigning specific labours to particular months; for example, warming is the labour for January in the Carolingian calendars,[10] but ploughing (Pl. VIII.2a, VIII.2b) is

[9] *An Eleventh-Century Illustrated Miscellany*, pp. 41–2.

[10] Schapiro, in his review of Webster's *The Labours of the Months in Antique and Medieval Art* (see above n. 8), notes that the labours for January and December in the Carolingian calendars are uniformly different from those depicted in the Anglo-Saxon calendars (p. 137).

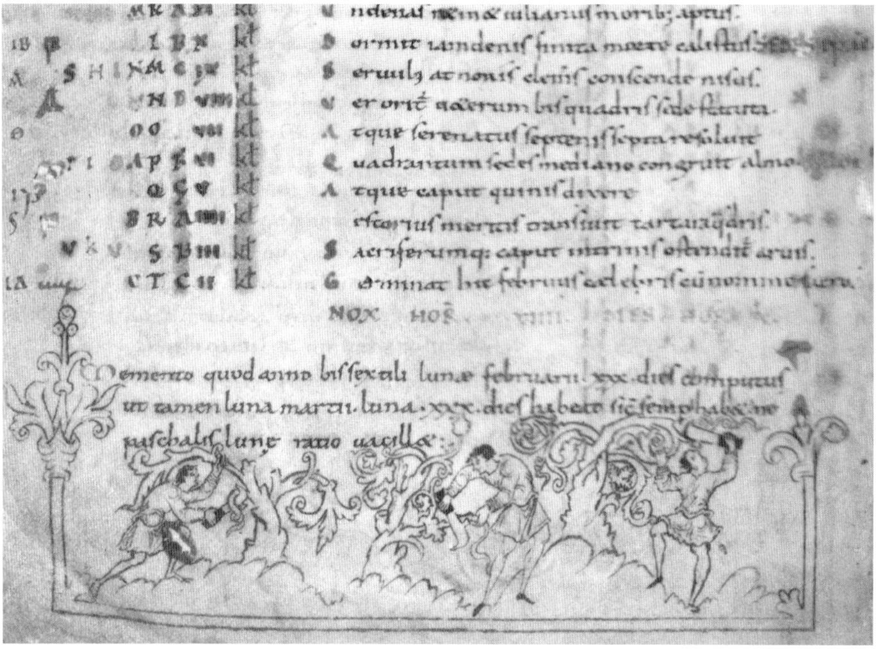

Plate VIII.1a. Pruning vines (February). British Library, Cotton Julius A.vi. © British Library Board

Plate VIII.1b. Pruning vines (February). British Library, Cotton Tiberius B.v. © British Library Board

Plate VIII.2a. Ploughing (January). British Library, Cotton Julius A.vi. © British Library Board

Plate VIII.2b. Ploughing (January). British Library, Cotton Tiberius B.v. © British Library Board

the labour in both Anglo-Saxon manuscripts, so it is equally possible that this is simply a variation rather than a mistake, a point to which I will return.[11] Similarly, the labours are not always in accord with the months in which they would have taken place (again, ploughing in January is the almost universally cited example). Fowler suggested that the scenes in the Anglo-Saxon calendars may have been changed to reflect the practices of a colder climate, but that seems unlikely.[12] The explanation for the primacy of ploughing may lie within the concerns of Anglo-Saxon society itself, or at least those of an important group within it, especially as it is likely that in general the scenes depicted do reflect real English practices. Della Hooke notes that pigs really did forage in

11 On the mistakes in Webster's identification of a 'tradition' see Schapiro's review as in n. 8.

12 J. Fowler, 'On medieval representations of the months and seasons' *Archaeologia*, 54 (1873), pp. 137–8, 198–200.

the woodlands in autumn,[13] and estate records show that woodcutting, mowing and reaping were all undertaken in the summer months, just as the calendars suggest.[14]

Interpretations of the depictions of the labours tend to centre not on any resemblance they might have to real agricultural practices but on their meaning within the larger religious and social order. Patrick McGurk, Derek Pearsall and Elizabeth Salter, and Nicholas Howe read them within the divine order imposed on the world with the fall of Adam and Eve. The passing of time and the labours which represented it formed 'a trenchant commentary upon man's loss of that original garden of everlasting life and spring',[15] and a persistent reminder of a system of punishment and reward. Working the soil is, in Howe's words, the 'fundamental condition for fallen man' and ploughing appears first in the calendar because it represents that condition. He cites God's order that the fallen Adam live by the sweat of his brow and the production of his own bread as recounted in lines 931b–935 of the Junius 11 Genesis, in support of his argument.[16] But in the Junius 11 manuscript Adam does not plough the earth, but digs it (the occupation for the month of March in both calendars).[17] Ploughing appears later as a labour of the descendants of Adam,[18] but by tradition it was Noah who was identified as the first farmer.[19] A strictly biblical interpretation of the calendars is not necessary for the observation to ring true that the regularity of the cycle depicted also provided comfort through its reassurance of the existence of a harmonious world in which labour brought forth food from a fruitful earth free from storms, crop failure, starvation and other such disasters.[20]

For Pearsall and Salter neither the Julius nor Tiberius illustrations could be considered 'landscape art'. Indeed, they saw their focus on manual labour as a deterrent to the development of landscape painting, that is, the depiction of landscape as an object of aesthetic enjoyment.[21] Yet almost in contradiction to their own argument they saw the illustrations for May as opening up the possibility of just such a development. The occupation for May is tending sheep, and both manuscripts include, to the right of the labouring shepherds, a group

13 Della Hooke, *The Landscape of Anglo-Saxon England* (Leicester, 1998), pp. 142–3, 162. It may be going too far, however, to suggest that the woodcutting scenes depict pollards – the trees are far too formalized – or that the timbers engulfed in flames in the labour for November are having their ends charred to prevent decay (p. 164).

14 Andrew Reynolds, *Later Anglo-Saxon England, Life and Landscape* (Stroud, 1999), p. 155.

15 Derek Pearsall and Elizabeth Salter, *Landscapes and Seasons of the Medieval World* (London, 1973), p. 122. See also McGurk, *An Eleventh-Century Illustrated Miscellany*, pp. 40–3; Howe, *Writing the Map of Anglo-Saxon England*, pp. 154–68.

16 *Writing the Map of Anglo-Saxon England*, p. 168.

17 See Oxford, Bodleian Library, Junius 11, pp. 45, 46, 49.

18 Tubal-Cain is shown ploughing on p. 54 of the Junius 11 manuscript.

19 Daniel Anlezark, *Water and Fire, the Myth of the Flood in Anglo-Saxon England* (Manchester, 2006), p. 25.

20 Pearsall and Salter, *Landscapes and Seasons of the Medieval World*, p. 124.

21 Pearsall and Salter, *Landscapes and Seasons of the Medieval World*, p. 129.

of two or three spectators whose dress and leisurely poses set them apart from the workers. By introducing these figures Pearsall and Salter believed that the Anglo-Saxon artists had opened a space 'for the appreciation of a scene which originally recorded only participation'.[22]

It is doubtful, however, that these figures are engaged in the pure aesthetic enjoyment of the scene that Pearsall and Salter's description implies. Their clothes identify them as members of a higher class, and whatever their attitudes within this scene, they are representatives of the aristocratic classes for whom the shepherds would in reality have laboured; yet they too are engaged in a labour of a sort, the labour of observing the productivity of their land, the abundance of their flocks and the diligence of their workers. Even if we trace the formal arrangement of this group of spectators back to the bucolic landscapes of classical art, there can be no doubt that their activity in these miniatures parallels that of the readers of the two manuscripts, who would have enjoyed a similar status whether they were members of the Church or the laity. By the twelfth century it was standard to include aristocratic as well as peasant labours amongst the labours of the months, with aristocratic labours consisting of such things as smelling flowers, feasting and hunting. Based on their dress and attributes, it seems likely that the figures representing February, March and May in the Carolingian calendars represent aristocrats rather than peasants, but the Anglo-Saxon calendars are the earliest surviving manuscripts in which their participation is expanded. Aristocratic and peasant labour would never be equally balanced, and both Julius and Tiberius include aristocratic labour at just two other points: the feasting of April and the hunting with falcons of October (Pl. VIII.3a, VIII.3b).

Alternatively, it is possible to understand the calendar images within the more narrow ideology of Benedictine monasticism, especially if both the Julius and Tiberius manuscripts are products of post-reform Canterbury. Earl Anderson has read the *Colloquy* of Ælfric, a text to which the calendar illustrations are sometimes related, in just such a way. The *Colloquy*, he writes, reflects 'an orderly and well-regulated life within the confines of an economically self-sufficient community'.[23] John Ruffing takes this idea further, noting that there is a particular order to the occupations of the *Colloquy*, with the workers beginning on the monastic grounds, venturing out 'to the edge of the known world' and ending up back in the monastic kitchen'.[24] The agricultural workers, he observes, are as tied to the monastic lands as the animals they tend or hunt.[25] Similar observations can be made with regard to the calendar illustrations, even though while both manuscripts are likely to have been produced in a monastery, Tiberius B.v is generally described as a secular manuscript (what exactly that means is poorly defined) and the figures depicted in both calendars are exclu-

22 Pearsall and Salter, *Landscapes and Seasons of the Medieval World*, p. 132.

23 Earl R. Anderson, 'Social idealism in Ælfric's *Colloquy*', *Anglo-Saxon England*, 3 (1974), pp. 153–62, at 153.

24 John Ruffing, 'The labor structure of Ælfric's *Colloquy*', in *The Work of Work*, eds Allen J. Frantzen and Douglas Moffat (Glasgow, 1994), pp. 55–70, at 59.

25 Ruffing, 'The labor structure of Ælfric's *Colloquy*', p. 60.

Plate VIII.3a. Hunting with birds (October). British Library, Cotton Julius A.vi. © British Library Board

Plate VIII.3b. Hunting with birds (October). British Library, Cotton Tiberius B.v. © British Library Board

sively secular.[26] The order of the calendar illustrations is not identical to that of the *Colloquy*, but in the *Colloquy* the ploughman is the first of the workers to speak, and ploughing, as we have seen, is the first of the labours depicted in Julius and Tiberius, something that distances them from the Carolingian calendars in which warming oneself by the fire (a much more appropriate occupation for January) comes first.[27] Significantly, in the New Minster Charter (London, British Library, Cotton Vespasian A.viii), one of the key monuments of reform ideology, the monastery is described in chapter 7 as *Domini cultura* ('the Lord's

[26] This is true of calendar illustrations in general, including those that decorate church portals; see further J. J. G. Alexander, '*Labeur* and *Paresse*: ideological representations of medieval peasant labor', *Art Bulletin*, 72.3 (1990), pp. 436–52.

[27] As calendar illustrations became standardized, feasting was to become the labour for January, and warming by the fire would shift to February.

ploughland'), and in chapter 18 as *Christi cultura* ('Christ's ploughland').[28] As in Ælfric's *Colloquy*, the calendars provide a sense of movement through space as well as through time. The preparation of the earth and the vines leads up to the scene of feasting in April, and then we move out again to a depiction of the plentiful fruits of the land (be they sheep, crops, wood, pigs or game), before ending in December with the threshing of grain bound ultimately for the table. And as in that text, the workers in the calendars are every bit as tied to the land as the animals and crops that they tend, something that is made even more apparent in these pictures by the often stooped posture of the figures, the curves of their backs echoing the curves of the land beneath their feet or the branches and vines that they cut (Pl. VIII.4a, VIII.4b). One might also cite in comparison Exeter Book Riddle 21 in which the plough itself expresses a similar sort of relationship between the burden of the labour practised and the form the labourer is forced to take on, describing the ploughman as its lord, who goes stooping at its tail and who allows the plough to do its job as long as he (the ploughman) serves the plough properly.[29] The riddle inscribes an interesting, almost Hegelian, scheme of social hierarchies in that the worker here becomes the lord, but he is a lord who stoops to serve an object which is also his master.

A great deal of attention is also paid in the calendar miniatures to tools and animals so that the focus is not only on the production of the land but on property – tools, oxen, sheep, game, crops, wood and men. This is not yet individualized property as it is in the Luttrell Psalter or the Très Riches Heures, but it is property all the same – just as the manuscripts that contain the calendars were also property.[30]

Property and possessions bring us back finally to the act of ploughing (Pl. VIII.2a, VIII.2b) and the possible reasons for its primacy amongst the calendar illustrations. In their respective analyses of Ælfric's *Colloquy* and the Luttrell Psalter, both John Ruffing and Michael Camille emphasized the relevance of ploughing to book production.[31] Vellum, the skin of a calf, was the material favoured for luxury manuscripts,[32] while the Old English verb for to plough,

28 Sean Miller, ed., *Charters of the New Minster, Winchester*, *Anglo-Saxon Charters IX* (Oxford, 2001), pp. 98 and 101.

29 neol ic fere / ond be grunde græfe, geonge swa me wisað / har holtes feond, ond hlaford min / who færeð weard æt steorte … / ic toþum tere, gif me teala þenaþ / hindeweardre, þæt biþ hlaford min; *The Exeter Book*, ed. G. P. Krapp and E. V. K. Dobbie, ASPR III (New York, 1936), p. 191, lines 1b–4, 14–15 ('I burrow and cut deep into the ground as I go guided by the old enemy of the forest, and my lord stooping at my tail … I tear with my teeth if from behind he who is my lord serves me well').

30 On property in the Luttrell Psalter and Très Riches Heures see Michael Camille, *Mirror in Parchment: the Luttrell Psalter and the Making of Medieval England* (Chicago, 1998); idem, '"For Our Devotion and Pleasure": the sexual objects of Jean, Duc de Berry', *Art History*, 24.2 (2001), pp. 169–94. See also Jane Welch Williams, *Bread, Wine and Money: the Windows of the Trades at Chartres Cathedral* (Chicago, 1993).

31 Ruffing, 'The labor structure of Ælfric's *Colloquy*', p. 60; Camille, *Mirror in Parchment*, p. 193.

32 It has yet to be determined whether this particular manuscript was written on vellum or parchment.

Plate VIII.4a. Chopping wood (June). British Library, Cotton Julius A.vi. © British Library Board

Plate VIII.4b. Reaping (June). British Library, Cotton Tiberius B.v. © British Library Board

arare, was a synonym for the act of writing. One could add that the pigments used to make the ink and colours of the text and miniatures came primarily from the land. Ground-breaking and land-clearing tools, of the sort that we see in the illustrations for the spring and summer months, were also essential to the demarcation of boundaries between estates, territories, kingdoms and countries. This may seem a bit much to read into a simple calendar illustration, but it should be remembered that the charter bounds that map the demarcation, division and ownership of land record a sequence of landscape features in the order in which they would have been encountered by a walker in the landscape,[33] just as the calendars provide a sequence of activities which would have been immediately recognizable parts of the real, lived landscape. Moreover, in the Tiberius manuscript the calendar illustrations are combined with texts and images that map history, the skies and the lands of the East; the Marvels that exist in or inhabit the East are distinguished from the Anglo-Saxons by their distance from England and by the different activities enacted in and upon the land. The Anglo-Saxon landscape, for example, produces food, while in the landscape of the Marvels trees produce gems rather than fruit, and a traveller runs the risk of becoming food for cannibals. While rich, the foreign landscape is not necessarily productive. It may also be significant in this regard that the calendar miniatures were used early on by historians to illustrate the making of England and the English people.[34] They do not portray landscapes, but rather fields of production that extend from food to a people to a nation and its history.

In his discussion of the depiction of agricultural labour in the Luttrell Psalter, Michael Camille interpreted the de-emphasis on landscape in its miniatures as reflecting a situation in which the land was valued for what it was able to produce rather than in and of itself,[35] and surely the Anglo-Saxon calendars provide a precedent for just such a view. Yet if we wish to situate them in terms of the larger history of calendar illustration, they can also be understood as marking a shift from a tradition in which the cycle of the year was signified by the human figure alone to one in which it was represented by the introduction of the human figure into a landscape setting, however simple and formulaic that setting may have been at first. In making the change, the Anglo-Saxon manuscripts also mark the transition from the representation of labour as abstract personification to its representation as physical work, and hence the opening up of the class division between those depicted and those for whom they were depicted, those who really did chart the passing of time by labouring on the land and those who charted it through computistical tables, astronomical and historical texts, and the idealized productivity of the calendar landscapes.

33 A point stressed by Wickham-Crowley, 'Living on the *Ecg*', p. 89.

34 See for example H. D. Traill and J. S. Man, eds, *Social England: a Record of the English People in Religion, Laws, Learning, Arts, Industry, Commerce, Science, Literature and Manners: from the Earliest Times to the Present Day* (London, 1901–04), or J. R. Green, *Short History of the English People* (London, 1915), ill. 155, 157, 159.

35 Camille, *Mirror in Parchment*, pp. 180–1.

9

The Anglo-Saxon Plough: A Detail of the Wheels

DAVID HILL

A small but important group of illustrations of the plough and other agricultural equipment survives from late Anglo-Saxon and early Anglo-Norman England.[1] This has been discounted as contemporary evidence as to what was actually happening in the English countryside by several scholars, on the grounds that manuscript illustration rested heavily on the repetition of pre-existing manuscript models dating ultimately back to the Ancient World.[2] This somewhat nihilistic view has, however, been cautiously challenged by Martin Carver,[3] and more forthrightly by the author in 1998,[4] making the case that the *Gerefa*, an eleventh-century guide to estate management in Old English, demonstrates the relevance to the English countryside of the Labours of the Months as set out in the calendar illuminations. As regards the evidence for the plough, I have already published a discussion and overall assessment.[5] What follows, therefore, should be read very much as an addendum to the papers published in 1998 and 2000 regarding just one problem thrown up by the illustrations, namely the size and nature of the wheel(s) depicted in representations of the plough, which has emerged in the course of a current project by Derek Seddon and myself to build a scale-model of an Anglo-Saxon plough. Such a three-dimensional effort raises all kinds of questions of reality. Words can come easily and lead to facile explanations, but models raise hard problems, as we found when we built a model of an Anglo-Saxon wagon, with which we were greatly assisted by the late Bob Beech of the Guild of Model Wheelwrights. Much rests on the series of late Anglo-Saxon illustrations and also the depiction of a plough

1 London, British Library MS Cotton, Julius A.VI, ff. 2–17v; London, British Library MS Cotton, Tiberius B.V. (Vol. I), ff. 2–19.

2 See in particular David N. Wilson, 'Anglo-Saxon rural economy: a survey of the archaeological evidence and a suggestion', *Agricultural History Review*, 10 (1962), 65–79, whose argument was in large part followed by Peter J. Fowler, *Farming in the First Millennium AD* (Cambridge, 2002), pp. 182–204.

3 Martin O. H. Carver, 'Contemporary artefacts illustrated in Late Saxon manuscripts', *Archaeologia*, 108 (1986), 117–45.

4 David H. Hill, 'Eleventh-century labours of the month in prose and pictures', *Landscape History*, 20 (1998), 29–39.

5 David H. Hill, '*Sulh* – The Anglo-Saxon Plough *c.*1000 AD', *Landscape History*, 22 (2000), 5–19.

Figure 9.1. upper: the sequence of agricultural activities illustrated in the lower margin of the Bayeux Tapestry; lower: the Bayeux Tapestry plough in more detail, both after *Vetusta Monumenta*, 6 (1886).

in the Bayeux Tapestry. The view chosen by the artist commonly illustrates only one wheel of the pair with the second hidden behind the first; this is also true of contemporary illustrations of the wheels of Anglo-Saxon wagons.

Only one of these illustrations is from a viewpoint where both wheels are shown and this is the plough on the Bayeux Tapestry. There is a series of linked vignettes in the lower border which carries a sequence of cultivation, from ploughing the soil through seeding and harrowing to scaring birds off the growing crop (Fig. 9.1a). The sequence runs from left to right (as do the majority of scenes on the tapestry, although this sequence can be broken as with the crossing of the River Cousenon which is a mirror image; one assumes that the artist did not wish to break the flow of the narrative). It is possible that the original artist used the ploughing scenes in the tapestry illustrations to indicate that the arrival of Harold was in early spring; we may also wonder whether the mule pulling the plough was intended to show that rural society in Normandy was pauperized at that time.

Consideration of this image, although it is executed in wool on a linen background, appears to show that the far wheel is markedly larger than its fellow (Fig. 9.1b). This is a feature of many medieval and later ploughs and I am indebted to Roy Brigdon of the Agricultural Museum at the University of Reading, and author of *Ploughs and Ploughing* (Shire Books), for a discussion of this point. He also drew our attention to Peter Michelsen's illustrations of wheeled ploughs held in Danish museum collections,[6] and notably to the fact that the majority of these nineteenth-century examples have wheels of two different sizes. We, Derek Seddon and I, went to Denmark to study the surviving

6 Peter Michelsen, *Danish Wheel Ploughs: An Illustrated Catalogue* (Copenhagen, 1959).

Figure 9.2. Schematic illustration of the action of the plough.

examples, particularly those at Sonderborg, in April 2008, and we are most grateful for the assistance we received there.

The plough is a machine, a moving processor of the soil and a vital link in the Anglo-Saxon economy, and it is essential that we understand how it worked. The first stage was the slicing of the furrow via the action of the coulter, followed immediately by the second stage in which the share cut horizontally so that the whole block was isolated. One of the major problems is that there are very few pictorial sources for the period, just three relevant illustrations with perhaps another two with something to offer but in a confusing format; there are also glancing references in some documents, poems and riddles. There is, however, a mass of relevant material in the thousands of acres of fieldworks which can be shown to date back to our period by the detailed work of scholars such as Della Hooke.[7] These fields are long in comparison to their width and are clearly not the product of the 'ard' or simple plough which lent itself to turning across the field, giving rise to rectangular blocks, the so-called 'Celtic Fields'. Much of what we know of tenth-century agriculture is of the long strip fields, the product of the wheeled plough.

The reason for the disparity of height in the two wheels would seem to be that if they were the same the whole plough would cant over, as one wheel would

7 Della Hooke, *The Landscape of Anglo-Saxon England* (London, 1998), passim.

Plate IX.1. Nineteenth-century Danish plough.

be lower (in the furrow) than the other (on the unploughed ground). Thus with wheels of different sizes the plough would be level and stress on the implement lessened. It is a reminder that careful and informed study of our few examples can still yield useful insights into the agricultural uses of the day and a clear understanding of our sources.

It should be noted that once the initial cut has been made, with the still unploughed land on the left (Fig. 9.2), the furrow remains clear of soil with the ploughed earth turned to the right, leaving an unencumbered track for the lead oxen to walk down as they cultivate the next furrow. The earth has already been ploughed and the furrow builds; of particular importance is the fact that there is no pressing need for a mould board, so arguments about this useful part of the plough can be relegated to a later point in the discussion of its development.

The devil is in the detail, which I discussed both for these drawings and other aspects of Anglo-Saxon agricultural life in 2000. But is this a minor piece of parochial detail or is there something else that might be discerned from the fact of the asymmetrical wheels? Yes, the wheels are asymmetrical and therefore so are the plough and the ploughed field. It is common for medieval ploughs, wheeled or unwheeled, to be asymmetrical and therefore to throw the furrow onto one side, meaning that they commonly ploughed one way. The medieval plough could not turn easily, especially with a team of four or six oxen, so the longer the furrow the fewer the turns and the more efficient the ploughing. We must always remember that this is an active, mobile process; line drawings tend to disguise the fact of a dynamic system. The plough moved the soil, leaving the furrow to the left. By ploughing up one way and down the other the plough-soil

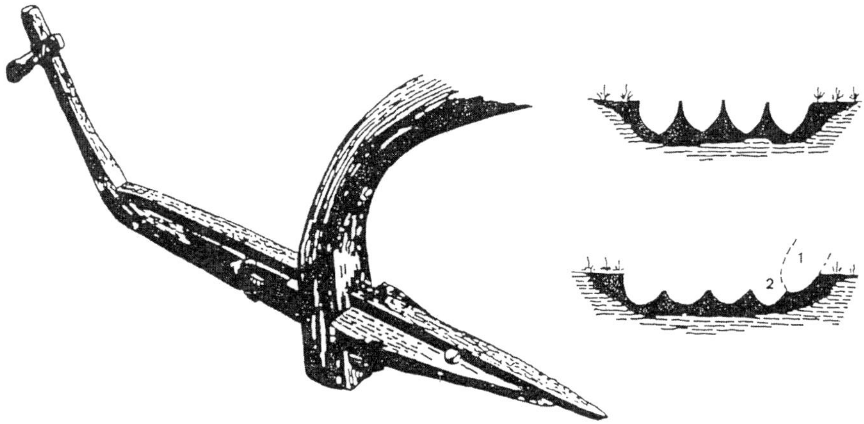

Figure 9.3 A light plough or ard (after H. C. Bowen, *Ancient Fields* (London, 1961)).

Figure 9.4. Light ploughs from BL, Harley 603 and Cambridge, Trinity College, R.17.1.

is moved to the centre and we finish up with the 'ridge and furrow' known to us all. The Bayeux Tapestry illustration allows us to project this type of plough back through the Middle Ages, at least to the late eleventh century, as the central equipment responsible for the system of strip fields and ridge and furrow.

The Mediterranean or 'primitive' plough shoves the soil to either side of the ploughshare and passes the earth not to one but to both sides, so it does not cut a clear furrow the way we would expect the Bayeux Tapestry plough to do; therefore what we are seeing is the turning action and the gathering of the furrows into a clear ridge, the *action* of a mould board without its early illustration.

If we turn from the plough as a machine to the effect it has on the worked soil we can see that a furrow is cut by the coulter, then the share lifts the soil from the furrow and deposits the slice to one side, turning it over to rest on the slice cut by the previous passage of the plough. The furrow is thus left vacant for the wheel to run up it; this would mean that to keep the plough upright it would be inches deep in the furrow with a wheel inches larger in diameter than its partner. Too much attention has recently been given to the 'ard', but many of the illustrations of light ploughs (Fig. 9.4) are clearly blind copying of Mediterranean models.

10

'In the Sweat of thy Brow Shalt thou eat Bread':[1] Cereals and Cereal Production in the Anglo-Saxon Landscape

DEBBY BANHAM

Introduction

Three major changes took place in arable farming during the Anglo-Saxon period. One was a change in the landscape, one in technology, and the third in the assemblage of crops that Anglo-Saxon farmers grew. The first, the reorganisation of much of England's arable land into open fields, is already the object of a substantial body of scholarly work, so it might seem redundant to venture yet another account of this transformation.[2] But the intention in this paper is to explore the relationship there might have been between this major landscape change and the two other developments mentioned above, namely the adoption of the 'heavy' mould-board plough and the transition from a largely barley-growing regime to one where wheat, and especially bread wheat, *Triticum aestivum* L., was the dominant cereal crop. A link between the open fields and the mould-board plough is hardly a novel proposition,[3] but the argument here will be that both of these innovations were made less for the sake of their own virtues than to facilitate the expansion of wheat cultivation. This shift from barley to wheat, although long recognised,[4] has received little scholarly attention, perhaps because Anglo-Saxon historians and landscape scholars have not

1 Genesis III:18.

2 For a comprehensive survey of scholarship on the origins of the open fields, see Tom Williamson, *Shaping Medieval Landscapes: Society, Settlement, Environment* (Macclesfield, 2003), pp. 1–21. In this paper I use the term 'open field(s)' to refer to the layout of arable land, without necessarily implying that such fields were held or cultivated in common.

3 It goes back at least to Charles S. Orwin and Christabel S. Orwin, *The Open Fields* (Oxford, 1938), pp. 30–3.

4 In 1972, Finberg believed it was lack of data which accounted for the paucity of wheat remains from the early period (H. P. R. Finberg, 'Anglo-Saxon England to 1042', in *The Agrarian History of England and Wales*, vol. 1.II: *AD 43–1042*, ed. Finberg (Cambridge, 1972), pp. 385–525, at p. 421), but subsequent accumulation of evidence has only confirmed the figures available at that time.

primarily been concerned with what are sometimes called 'foodways'.[5] What we are looking at here is essentially a change in diet. But this is a change that could not be made, in an economy in which the population was fed almost exclusively from consumers' own land, rather than from the market, without concomitant changes in farming practice. These changes, in turn, inevitably produced changes in the landscape. Thus the proposal offered here is that vast tracts of Midland England were transformed into a new kind of landscape primarily because the Anglo-Saxons preferred wheat bread to bread made of other cereals. This will seem eminently plausible to anyone (most anthropologists, for instance) who believes that food is one of the most important elements in human culture, if not *the* most important. But many historians (at least to judge by the paucity of work on this topic) would feel less comfortable with the idea, and so this paper, by examining each of these major changes in turn, along with some related developments, will attempt to convince a historical readership that the proposal is not in fact outrageous.

Diet

Having proposed to attribute wholesale landscape change to mere dietary preference, the next step is to expound the preference in question: the Anglo-Saxon taste for wheat bread, as opposed to bread made from barley or any other cereal. It would be wrong to suggest that the Anglo-Saxons did not have barley bread; to give just a couple of examples, it is used as the vehicle for treating a sick horse in the *Lacnunga*,[6] a medical text of around the year 1000, and it was what St Guthlac ate, in moderation, of course, to defeat the Devil, who was tempting him to the sin of pride in excessive fasting, that is, not eating anything at all.[7] So it is clear that barley bread was familiar and available, but not, in these instances, regarded as high-status food. No one gives their best bread to horses, even for medicinal purposes, and eating fancy food would have defeated Guthlac's purpose of demonstrating to the Devil that eating modestly is more humble than showing off by starving oneself.

If barley bread was not fancy food, what was? Unfortunately we cannot turn to the menus for Anglo-Saxon feasts to find this out, for from the whole of the Anglo-Saxon period, we have only one surviving, in fact more like a shopping list, for a series of funeral feasts, probably held at Bury St Edmunds.[8] Bread clearly formed a large part of these meals, but unfortunately we are not told

5 For a concise survey of the attitudes of various academic disciplines to diet, see Alan Davidson, 'Food history', in his *The Oxford Companion to Food* (Oxford, 1999), pp. 312–13.

6 Line 956 [entry 165]: *Anglo-Saxon Remedies, Charms and Prayers from British Library MS Harley 585: The Lacnunga*, ed. Edward Pettit (Lampeter, 2001), I.114.

7 *Felix's Life of St Guthlac*, ed. Bertram Colgrave (Cambridge, 1956), p. 100.

8 This is found in a fragment of an Old English will copied in the twelfth century at Bury onto Cambridge, Pembroke College 83, first flyleaf. *Anglo-Saxon Charters*, ed. A. J. Robertson (Cambridge, 1939), p. 252.

what kind of bread was required. More informative on that score, fortunately, are food-rents, the payments in kind that Anglo-Saxon peasants made to their landlords, and which were the main source of food for the landholding classes. These invariably include either bread or wheat.[9] When barley is mentioned, it is in the form of malt, for brewing (and if it is not mentioned, there is beer instead). The major ecclesiastical landlords of Kent were clearly fairly sophisticated in such matters, and documents from both Christ Church and St Augustine's, Canterbury, go into some detail about what kind of bread is required. Wheat bread is specified in two of these lists, some of it to be 'clean',[10] and two others require 'white' bread.[11] 'Clean' could mean various things, for instance unleavened,[12] or simply free from straw and mouse-droppings. But 'white', in reference to bread, must mean that it was made of wheat. It is relatively easy to make white flour from wheat, because the inner layers of bran and the germ, that is to say the coloured parts of the grain, break off in quite large chunks when wheat is stone-ground, and can thus be sieved out quite easily.[13] The resulting flour would not look very white compared with modern bleached flour, but wheat bread would be much whiter than bread made from barley or rye. However much you sieve rye or barley flour, the results always look greyish. In one food-rent where wheat, rather than finished loaves, was required, it is specified as *hlafhwæte*, wheat suitable for making bread.[14]

All these food-rents come from the latter part of the Anglo-Saxon period, from the ninth century onwards, which produced most of our surviving charters. Although the food-rents can be regarded as 'traditional', that is to say, a product of local custom rather than a royal imposition, and may therefore pre-date the documents containing them, there is no reason to suppose that they were unchanged over centuries. It is safest, therefore, to regard them as evidence for the dietary preferences of the landholding classes in later Anglo-Saxon England only. It is clear that those classes preferred wheat for their bread, and that, at least in some cases, the reason for this was that it could make a paler-coloured loaf.

But this taste was not a complete innovation in the late Anglo-Saxon period. The etymological connection between the words 'wheat' and 'white' in other

9 This discussion is based on work originally carried out for my thesis: Deborah A. R. Banham, 'The Knowledge and Uses of Food Plants in Anglo-Saxon England' (PhD dissertation, Cambridge, 1990), pp. 74–9.

10 For Nackington (S1239, *c*.850 AD) and Lymne (S1188, 805x810), both in Kent: *Charters of St Augustine's Abbey, Canterbury, and Minster-in-Thanet*, ed. Susan E. Kelly, AS Charters 4 (London, 1995), no. 25, and *Select English Historical Documents of the Ninth and Tenth Centuries*, ed. Florence E. Harmer (Cambridge, 1914), no. 1, respectively.

11 For Mongeham and Challock, again both in Kent, and both of uncertain date: *Select English Historical Documents*, ed. Harmer, nos. 4 and 2 respectively.

12 See Banham, 'Food Plants', pp. 74–5.

13 For an extensive discussion of the structure, chemistry, etc. of the wheat berry, see Harold McGee, *McGee on Food and Cooking: An Encyclopedia of Kitchen Science, History and Culture* (London, 2004), pp. 461–2, 467–8 and 521–31.

14 Hurstbourne Priors, Hampshire, *c*.900 AD: *Charters*, ed. Robertson, p. 206.

Germanic languages, as well as English, suggests that the pale colour of wheat flour had already been observed at a time when wheat was first known to the Anglo-Saxons' ancestors on the continent, and was probably the main feature that struck them about it, in contrast to the cereals they were used to.[15] And the preference for light-coloured bread certainly goes back to the conversion period in England, as Bede's famous story of the kings of Essex shows: three kings, brothers, apparently ruling jointly after the death of their father, Sæberht, who had converted to Christianity, demanded that Bishop Mellitus should give them 'the white bread that you gave our father', even though they themselves had not been baptised.[16] Bede, not being a food historian himself, neglects to tell us if this white bread, clearly the eucharist, was in fact made of wheat, but this seems virtually certain. At any rate, it was extremely attractive to these three kings, irrespective of its salvific properties.

Another reason for preferring wheat as one's bread-corn is that it makes a lighter loaf in another sense: the elastic proteins in wheat allow it to retain a lot of the gas produced by fermentation with yeast, so that it rises far better than bread made from rye or barley.[17] This is why barley is often made into unleavened breads such as bannocks, and rye is usually raised with sourdough rather than fresh yeast.[18] This property of wheat is not mentioned in any of the Anglo-Saxon sources, but it must have made wheat bread more palatable to those Anglo-Saxons who had a choice, all the same.

Hilary Cool, in her recent book on food and drink in Roman Britain, suggests that the Romano-British elite preferred wheat bread in emulation of Mediterranean diet.[19] It would be interesting to know whether that preference persisted in sub-Roman Britain. If it did, it must have been much more difficult to gratify without the organisational structures of the Roman state. Martin Jones, looking at the whole of Europe in his book *Feast*, sees bread wheat as being disseminated first of all by the Roman Empire, and subsequently by Christianity, which of course reconnected lowland Britain with Mediterranean culture.[20] This would also tie in with the association between a bishop, Mellitus, and the white bread so pleasing to East Saxon kings. The dating of the archaeobotanical evidence is not precise enough to suggest that bread wheat was introduced to Anglo-Saxon

15 German, for instance, has *Weizen*, beside *weiß*. The *Oxford English Dictionary*, sv 'wheat', traces OE *hwæte* back to an Old Teutonic **χwaitaz*, a derivative of **χwit-*, 'white'. Ferdinand Holthausen, *Altenglisches etymologisches Wörterbuch* (Heidelberg, 1934), sv *hwæte*, relates it to words in Germanic languages meaning 'light', 'lighten' and 'white'.

16 *HE*, II.5.

17 There is a photograph in Jane M. Renfrew, *Palaeoethnobotany: The Prehistoric Food Plants of the Near East and Europe* (London, 1973), plate 48, of loaves made of equal quantities of wheat, barley and rye, presumably by the same method, where the barley and rye loaves are about half the thickness of the wheaten one, and incidentally darker in colour.

18 Andrew Whitley, *Bread Matters* (London, 2006), pp. 83–4, for rye; Laura Mason and Catherine Brown, *Traditional Foods of Britain: An Inventory* (Totnes, 1999), pp. 228–9, for barley bannocks.

19 Hilary E. M. Cool, *Eating and Drinking in Roman Britain* (Cambridge, 2006), p. 79.

20 Martin Jones, *Feast: Why Humans Share Food* (Oxford, 2007), pp. 260–2 and 269–70.

England for the first time by the Church (although it might be nice to think that the early missionaries were responsible for an improvement in the Anglo-Saxons' diet, as well as the salvation of their souls). It is any case unlikely that cultivation of such a prestigious cereal would have died out altogether in sub-Roman Britain. Perhaps the flour for Mellitus' wafers was made not only from wheat, but also by a more effective refining technique than was known to the Anglo-Saxons.[21]

Archaeobotany, however, does provide a good deal of relevant information. The earliest evidence from the Anglo-Saxon period, such as the pottery impressions studied by Helbæk,[22] shows us that wheat was known, but barley was much more common, so, if wheat was already preferred at this time, it may not have been easy to get hold of. Looking at the whole of the Anglo-Saxon period, however, we do see a changing situation. The archaeobotanical evidence is much more plentiful for cereals than for any other kind of plant, but it is not so abundant as to allow an enormous amount of chronological precision, as already indicated. Nevertheless, if we divide the Anglo-Saxon period fairly broadly into three phases, we can say that in the early part (fifth–seventh centuries), barley was much more common than wheat (found on 88% of sites, as opposed to 63%), in the middle of the period (eighth and ninth centuries) wheat is already more popular (95%, against 64% for barley), and in the final phase (tenth and eleventh centuries), wheat is twice as common as barley (89%, as opposed to 42%).[23] Other cereals, rye and oats, are found, too, both becoming more popular, but nothing like as common as wheat or barley. One interesting thing about the wheat, though, is that the increase, especially in the tenth and eleventh centuries, is accounted for almost entirely by either bread wheat (*Triticum aestivum*, present on 38%, 59% and 73% of sites in each successive phase) or other free-threshing varieties. These are much easier to turn into bread than hulled types, which need to be roasted or parched to get rid of the inner chaff layers before they can be ground into flour. This does suggest that it was for bread-making that all this extra wheat was being grown and processed, rather than for cooking in stews and porridges, or even brewing into beer.

Climate

Clearly, then, there was a change in cereal production during the course of the Anglo-Saxon period. As it was a change in favour of the cereal that was more

21 Either the flour for the host, or else equipment for sieving or bolting it, may have been imported.

22 Knud Jessen and Hans Helbæk, *Cereals in Great Britain and Ireland in Prehistoric and Early Historic Times* (Copenhagen, 1944).

23 Banham, 'Food Plants', p. 38. These are simple 'presence' figures; no attempt has been made to allow for relative *amounts* of different crops on the individual sites. A similar progression is observed by Peter Fowler, *Farming in the First Millennium AD: British Agriculture between Julius Caesar and William the Conqueror* (Cambridge, 2002), pp. 212–13.

highly valued as food by the Anglo-Saxons, it seems reasonable to suppose that dietary preference was driving agricultural change. However, the questions then arise, how did it become possible for the Anglo-Saxons to indulge their preference on such a scale in the later period, or what was stopping them earlier on? An answer that might seem obvious nowadays would be the climate. Although climate history is hardly a precise science, even now that its importance is more widely recognised, broad developments have been agreed on for some time: the climate in Britain seems to have deteriorated at or after the end of the Roman period, but by the millennium it was improving again towards the 'Medieval Warm Period' or 'Little Optimum', giving an average temperature in the late Anglo-Saxon period about the same as the early twenty-first century.[24] Until recently, it was believed that there was a fairly steady amelioration in the climate in the late Anglo-Saxon period, which might have allowed an equally steady increase in wheat production: warmer (and drier) weather would mean more wheat, which is at the northern edge of its range in the British Isles. However, interesting new data on early medieval climate has recently been published, which has allowed exploration of this relationship in more detail.

This new data depends upon the assumption that a major factor in climatic variation through time is the changing level of sunspot activity, an assumption that seems to hold good at least from about 1600, when reliable records of both sunspots and weather begin, until the late twentieth century, when human activity became a more important factor.[25] The new work shows that the deposition of two radioactive isotopes, the familiar carbon-14, of carbon-dating fame, as found in tree-ring samples, and beryllium-10, found in polar ice-cores, varies in inverse relation to the level of sunspot activity. Thus, a graph of variations in these two isotopes, if inverted, will follow the sunspot curve, as shown in fig. 10.1. Thus, the two isotope curves, before the period where there are sunspot records, will act as a proxy for the sunspot data, and show what the effect on the climate is likely to have been.

The curves in fact reflect the 'Little Optimum' very clearly, lasting from the late eleventh century to the middle of the thirteenth, and then decline very steeply to the early fourteenth century, when there was a series of disastrous harvests and widespread hunger. But at the other end of the 'Little Optimum', we do not see the climate improving in such a straightforward way during the tenth and eleventh centuries. The curves in fact rise during the early tenth century, after a fall in the second half of the ninth, but then fall again during most of the tenth century to another low point early in the eleventh, and only then rise steadily but fairly steeply towards the 'Little Optimum'.

[24] See Petra Dark, *The Environment of Britain in the First Millennium AD* (London, 2000), pp. 27–8.

[25] Sami K. Solanki, *et al.*, 'Unusual activity of the Sun during recent decades compared to the previous 11,000 years', *Nature*, 431 (2004), 1084–7. The findings are summarised and elucidated by Sebastian Payne, 'New insights into climate history', *British Archaeology* (January–February 2007), p. 54.

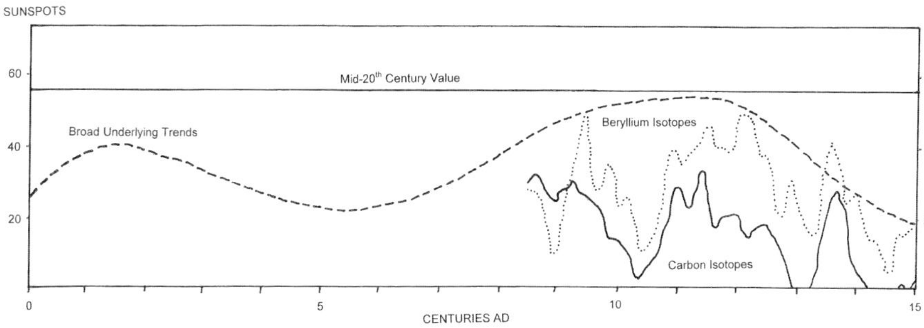

Figure 10.1. Climate in the Middle Ages. The vertical axis represents number of sunspots, reconstructed from beryllium (upper line) and carbon (lower line) isotopes, after Solanki *et al.*, 'Unusual activity of the sun'. The broken line shows broad underlying trends, based on Dark, *The Environment of Britain*, pp. 27–8. The horizontal line represents mid-twentieth-century value.

Crops

An interesting aspect of this climatic 'dip' in the early part of the eleventh century is that it would include the 'great hunger throughout the English people' recorded by the *Anglo-Saxon Chronicle* for the year 1005, 'such that no one ever remembered one so grim before', so bad that it almost certainly sent the Vikings home, something that King Æthelred rarely managed.[26] Of course, the *Chronicle* mentions other famines, not all corresponding with bad or worsening climate as represented by the new data. In 1042, for instance, there was a 'very heavy time … in bad weather and in crops of the earth', as well as a cattle-plague, and in 1044 'a very great hunger over the land of the English, and corn so dear as no one remembered before, so that the sester of wheat went up to 60 pence, and even further'.[27] In these years, however, the climate, according to the new information, was improving. The apparent discrepancy may simply be due to the difference between climate and weather: there can be bad years even during a period of generally warm, or warming, conditions. Or the changing patterns could have triggered extreme weather episodes, as at the present time. So recorded famines need not correspond with climatic dips in a straightforward manner. Nor were there necessarily simple relationships between climate and farming regimes, but relationships of some kind should be detectable.

One interesting point about the 1044 famine report is the way that the shortage of food is calibrated by the price of wheat. This clearly shows that

[26] *The Anglo-Saxon Chronicle: MS C*, ed. Katherine O'Brien O'Keefe, The AS Chronicle: A Collaborative Edition, eds David Dumville and Simon Keynes, 5 (Cambridge, 2001), p. 91.

[27] *The Anglo-Saxon Chronicle: MS E*, ed. Susan Irvine, The AS Chronicle: A Collaborative Edition, eds David Dumville and Simon Keynes, 7 (Cambridge, 2004), p. 77, and *ASC MS C*, ed. O'Brien O'Keefe, p. 108, respectively.

there was a market in agricultural products by this period, suggesting some kind of expansion or intensification in farming in the later Anglo-Saxon period. It is also interesting that the annalist is concerned with wheat, not barley or any other crop, which fits in with the archaeobotanical data showing that, by the eleventh century, wheat had replaced barley as the main bread corn in most of England. Nonetheless, there must have been large parts of the population for whom the price of wheat was of purely academic interest even by the eleventh century, since they would never have enough spare cash to buy in food on any scale: if their own harvest failed, they went hungry, and that was the end of it.

Returning to the climatic data, this shows us that the conditions for growing wheat, which originated in regions both warmer and drier than Britain, first improved during the early tenth century, then deteriorated again, and finally improved again during most of the eleventh. In these circumstances, it would not be surprising to find an increase in wheat production, or indeed an expansion of wheat production from areas more naturally favourable to its cultivation into areas where climate, terrain or soil made it a less reliable crop. But the new climatic data shows that neither increase nor expansion is likely to have proceeded at a steady pace. Rather, growth in production can be expected to be sporadic, and variable from place to place. It must also have been affected by factors other than climate, such as cultural expectations, or warfare. Thus changes such as the climate data suggest may not always be detectable, or their causes apparent, in the surviving sources. Nevertheless, taking climate into account helps make sense of the information that is available.

Agricultural Techniques

This is the point to turn to the open fields, or to be more precise, to ridge and furrow, the undulating profile we see where medieval arable lies under grass in parts of England today. It is true that there are places where there were open fields but there is no ridge and furrow, and that there are also examples of ridge and furrow occurring in fields which have always been closes.[28] The two can, however, be linked in terms of their origins, as well as their use, as will appear below. To begin, then, with the ridge and furrow in itself: the places where ridge and furrow (with or without open fields) occur are mainly on heavy soils, that is to say, soils that do not naturally drain freely, and thus a major function of ridge and furrow was almost certainly to facilitate drainage. On land that might otherwise be waterlogged for part of the year, the raised soil provided by the ridges would lift the growing plants above the water-table, while the furrows would contain the water, even where there was no proper drainage system to carry it away. Granted, nothing could be grown in that part of the field occupied by the

28 Some examples are given by Oliver Rackham, *The History of the Countryside* (London, 1986), pp. 168–70.

furrows, but that loss might be acceptable if it allowed a crop to be cultivated that would not otherwise grow at all in those particular fields.

If the origins of ridge and furrow can be located in the middle or late Anglo-Saxon period, the principal crop that the system allowed farmers to grow would be wheat. Improved drainage might allow wheat to be grown where the soil was otherwise too wet, or too wet at particular times of the year. This suggestion may seem counter-intuitive, since wheat in fact requires more moisture in the soil than barley,[29] but there is a difference between wheat and barley, at least as grown in England, that might make drainage especially important. In later medieval farming, wheat was winter corn, sown in the autumn, while barley was mainly sown in the spring.[30] Unfortunately, we cannot be certain that this was also the case in the early Middle Ages, but it seems likely. If changing from barley to wheat meant growing winter corn for the first time, improved drainage might be vital to prevent the young plants standing with their feet in water over the winter, even on soils which were not particularly wet in the spring and summer. To quote an expert writing in 1959, 'Good drainage is of prime importance in crop production … Continued excessive wetness will cause the death of plants as can be seen each spring on wet patches in fields sown to, say, an autumn cereal.'[31] We also have the testimony of the sixteenth-century agricultural versifier (and failed farmer) Thomas Tusser, for what it is worth, that this might be a particular problem in wheat cultivation: 'Where water all winter annoieth too much, bestow not thy wheat upon land that is such'.[32]It is worth pausing here, to explore why it seems likely that wheat was winter corn in the early Middle Ages, and why there cannot be greater certainly on this matter. There is no positive evidence for spring wheat at any time in the Middle Ages. According to Georges Comet, no medieval agronomist mentions spring-sown wheat.[33] Nor of course do classical writers on farming, who assume that all cereals are sown in the autumn (this is because they were writing in the Mediterranean region, where it is the hot, dry summer that threatens crops most, rather than a cold, wet winter, as in northern Europe).[34] For the early Middle Ages, we have no agricultural writers *per se*, only a brief reference in Isidore's *Etymologies*: '*Trimestre triticum* (three-months' wheat) is so-called because it is gathered three months after being sown; it is sought as a safeguard when, on account of water or some other reason, the sowing was not done at the usual time.'[35] Comet regards any spring sowing of wheat in the Middle Ages as being such an emergency measure, but also points out that the second half of Isidore's

29 Henry I. Moore, *Crops and Cropping* (5th edn, London, 1959), pp. 46 and 59.

30 See for instance Orwin and Orwin, *The Open Fields*, p. 55.

31 Moore, *Crops and Cropping*, p. 13.

32 Thomas Tusser, *Five Hundred Points of Good Husbandry* (Oxford, 1984) [reprinting the text of the 1580 edition], p. 45.

33 Georges Comet, 'Les Céréales du Bas Empire au Moyen Age', in *The Making of Feudal Agricultures?*, eds Miquel Barceló and François Sigaut, The Transformation of the Roman World 14 (Leiden, 2004), pp. 131–76, at p. 144.

34 Kenneth D. White, *Roman Farming* (London, 1970), p. 173.

35 XVII.iii.8: *Isidorus Hispalensis, Etymologiae XVII*, ed. J. André (Paris, 1981), p. 35.

sentence is lifted from Columella, in other words, this is a classical view of the subject, not a seventh-century one.[36] This should also remind us that Isidore was not himself a specialist in agricultural matters.

Taking a longer perspective, it is likely that all cereals were originally autumn-sown, since that reflects the life-cycle of their wild ancestors.[37] Spring-sown varieties may have been selected in order to facilitate cereal cultivation in areas with cooler and wetter climates than the 'Fertile Crescent' where agriculture began. Certainly it would be easier for spring-sown varieties to be adopted in places, like Britain, with harder winters than that eastern-Mediterranean crescent. If barley was spring-sown from an early date, and thus easier to grow in more northerly climes, that might explain why it was the majority cereal in early Anglo-Saxon England, and why wheat was slower to be adopted. It may be relevant here to cite the anecdote of St Cuthbert, who (admittedly with divine help) was able to raise a crop of barley on Little Farne Island after his wheat crop had failed.[38] His wheat was sown in the spring, no doubt a sensible precaution on an exposed island, but the story does show that barley was easier to grow in the north of England than wheat. Only after his time did the changes in agricultural techniques and technology discussed here make bread wheat as easy to grow, in some parts of England, as barley.

Under what circumstances, then, was ridge and furrow adopted in England, and when? The new climatic data does offer us a fresh perspective here. When the climate was thought to have improved steadily during the tenth and eleventh centuries, it seemed reasonable to attribute the spread of wheat cultivation, and therefore of ridge and furrow, to some kind of climatic tipping point, when the seasons were warm enough to allow wheat to be grown on well-drained soils in much of lowland England, but not on those that were waterlogged in the winter. It also seemed plausible that there might be a cultural tipping point, in that, when wheat was harder to grow in England, and thus rare, most farmers would not have minded not being able to grow it, since their neighbours were in the same position. But as the climate improved, there must have come a point when, in any given district, a considerable number of farmers were able to grow wheat, and thus their neighbours wanted to grow it too. And of course this desire would spread from areas better suited to growing wheat to less favoured ones. It would also be something that landlords encouraged, either deliberately or indirectly, since they would want wheat or wheat bread for their food-rents, as we have seen above.

This 'tipping point' idea still seems convincing, but it may not have been the only process in play. If, when the climate was improving in the earlier tenth century, more and more farmers were able to grow wheat, and more than their landlords took from them in rent, they may have got used to eating it. They may

36 Comet, 'Les céréales', p. 144.

37 See Norman T. Gill and Kenneth C. Vear, *Agricultural Botany*, vol. 2: *Monocotyledonous Crops* (3rd edn, London, 1980), p. 43.

38 Bede, *Vita sancti Cuthberti*, c. xix: in *Two Lives of St Cuthbert*, ed. Bertram Colgrave (Cambridge, 1940), p. 220.

have been selling wheat, too, since it was more popular with the prosperous classes than barley, and thus they could also have grown accustomed to having more disposable income. But when conditions grew cooler and wetter in the second half of the century, they would not have wanted to give up growing this favoured crop. When the climate deteriorated, some farmers, where it was simply no longer warm enough to grow wheat, or the season was too short, or the main problem was the lie of the land, may have had little choice but to revert to growing more barley or other crops. But some, at least, may have decided that their wheat was failing largely because their soil was too wet in the winter, and thus turned to improving their drainage by means of ridge and furrow. The same thing might have happened in the ninth century, too, but the published climatic data only goes back to 850. Wheat production was already expanding by then, as we have seen, but without detailed knowledge of the climate in the first half of the century, we can only guess what its effect might have been on farming.

Agricultural Equipment

Now the classic account of the origins of ridge and furrow, and of the open fields, in England is associated with the introduction of the mould-board plough.[39] Almost proverbially, there is no ridge and furrow without a mould-board to turn the sod to one side and build up the ridges (unless they are made with a spade), and the long, thin shape of the strips making up the open fields is attributed to the laboriousness of turning such a heavy plough, plus the yokes of oxen needed to pull it, meaning that a ploughman would want to carry on ploughing in the same direction for as long as possible. Put like this, it does sound as if the ridge and furrow came first, and the strips, and thus the open fields, were a by-product. One need not argue that it was the need for better drainage that led to the introduction of the mould-board plough to England in the first place, however, partly because heavy ploughs probably already existed in Britain in the Roman period.[40] Nonetheless, even if the plough was already here, it does not seem too far fetched to suppose that its use to improve drainage, for the purpose of growing winter wheat, could have resulted in the appearance of open fields for the first time in some parts of England with heavy, water-retentive soil. Let us examine the connection, then, between the plough together with ridge and furrow, on the one hand, and the open fields on the other.

The crucial feature of the so-called heavy plough is not, of course, its weight as such, or that it usually has wheels, but the curved board which turns the sod, that is, inverts the slice of soil that has been cut by the ploughshare, so that whatever was growing on that slice is now buried, and the soil that was underneath is exposed to the weather, which helps reduce heavy soils, especially, to a tilth suitable for sowing. A plough of this type is needed to produce ridge and furrow,

[39] As given by, for instance, the Orwins in *The Open Fields*, part 1.

[40] See Shimon Applebaum, 'Roman Britain', in *Agrarian History* 1.II, ed. Finberg, pp. 3–277, at pp. 83–7.

because the ard, or scratch-plough, which has no mould-board, only breaks the soil up; it does not turn it, and it leaves it level. The mould-board, on the other hand, inverts the soil by turning it sideways, and in the Middle Ages (and until recently) the mould-board was fixed, so that it always turned the soil the same way, to the right.

This means that if a ploughman ploughed one furrow across the field in one direction, and then ploughed back across the field to his starting point, alongside his original furrow, there would either be two furrows right next to each other, or two ridges. If he kept going back and forth across the field like that, the result would be a series of double furrows and double ridges. If his soil was poorly drained, and he noticed how the water lay in the furrows after rain, but the ridges dried out, he might decide to sow only on the ridges. The problem with that, of course, is that half his field would be furrows, and therefore unproductive. So the solution was to create bigger ridges, with furrows taking up less of the ground. This was done by ploughing in what was in effect an elongated spiral, so that a number of ridges lay against each other on either side, with just one furrow right at the edge. And if he went on doing that year after year, the argument goes, with the furrows always in the same places, the outcome would be that undulating profile of broad, high ridges, with even better drainage, and furrows between them.[41]

The connection between the mould-board plough and the open fields, as we have seen, lies in the shape of the strips, or selions, into which the fields were divided.[42] The mould-board plough, being heavy, needed a number of oxen to pull it (possibly as many as the eight of the standard Domesday plough-team, although they need not all have worked at once), and oxen do not turn round easily, as they cannot cross their feet like horses. So each time the plough was turned, and the oxen with it, a considerable space was required. And the farmer needed as much of his land as possible to be used for growing crops, not turning round. He would have wanted to plough for as long as he could before he turned, and the result would be a field made up of long thin strips of ploughing, with just a small area at either end for turning. Usually the strips lay alongside each other in furlongs, with a continuous headland, or balk, at either end for turning on. And those strips, of course, could easily be in the form of ridge and furrow, with one ridge per strip and furrows between. Or if that was unsuitable for the soil, or the shape of the field, there might be more than one ridge per strip. On the other hand, if the drainage was already quite good enough, ridges might not be necessary at all. The strips could just as well be flat.

So, the connection between the mould-board plough and ridge and furrow holds up, and so too does that between the plough and the open fields, but the functional link between ridge and furrow and open fields remains indirect. It is true that ridge and furrow is the most common form of evidence for open fields, especially where it lies in long, thin, reversed-S configurations like the shape of

41 See Orwin and Orwin, *The Open Fields*, pp. 33–4.

42 What follows is based on the account of the Orwins (pp. 30–6).

the classic open-field selion. Nonetheless, to maintain that open fields, not just ridge and furrow, owed their origin to the expansion of wheat cultivation, we would need to argue that the open fields originated in areas of poor drainage, where there might have been an equivalence between the ridges needed for drainage and the strips into which the work of ploughing was divided, but that this arrangement of arable land was then copied in areas where ridge and furrow was unnecessary for drainage purposes. We would need to explain why the spatial arrangement, with or without the ridge and furrow, was copied by farmers whose land was perfectly adequately drained to start with. Such an explanation might have to do with social organisation, with a desire to work the land in co-operation, or with the profit-driven schemes of landlords, who might see open fields as a more 'efficient' way of having their land cultivated, or it might have to do with the plough itself, whose advantages presumably extended beyond its usefulness in drainage, since it became the standard plough in the whole of England.[43]

However, it does seem plausible that improved drainage was the advantage that recommended this type of plough to English farmers, perhaps not originally, but to such an extent that ploughing in ridge-and-furrow style became standard practice in such large areas of the country. And the thing that made improved drainage, and the type of plough that made it possible, so attractive to so many farmers was the burgeoning fashion for growing wheat.

Date and Place

At this point, it seems apposite to quote some remarks of Miquel Barceló on early medieval farming:

> Tool improvement, selective changes in cereal crops … or variation in field shapes are … easily placed on the record, but the meaning of any of them in relation to the rest becomes blurred. Indeed, the more precise and tightly chronological the historical context in which we expect sets of related factors to have come together, the harder it is to establish the correlation.[44]

This presents a considerable challenge: to demonstrate that the various processes considered above coincide chronologically with enough precision to suggest a causal relationship between them. Equally challenging is the task of pinning these developments down in geographical space. Both must be attempted, however, to give the necessary rigour to the arguments put forward above that there was indeed a causal link between 'tool improvement … changes in cereal crops … [and] variation in field shapes' in early medieval England.

43 Perhaps only right at the end of the Middle Ages, however: John Langdon, *Horses, Oxen and Technical Innovation: The Use of Draught Animals in English Farming from 1066 to 1500* (Cambridge, 1986), pp. 244–5.

44 Miquel Barceló, 'Foreword', in *Making of Feudal Agricultures?*, eds. Barceló and Sigaut, pp. vii–ix, at p. vii.

The dating for the change from wheat to barley is, as we have seen, not very precise, and it is of course in the nature of such changes that it must have happened gradually, and at different paces in different places. It is even likely that the direction of change sometimes departed from the overall trend. The change certainly began in the middle Anglo-Saxon period, that is to say, between 700 and 900 AD, but that is about the limit of available precision.[45] As far as geography is concerned, the majority of the archaeobotanical data are from the East Midlands and South-East of England. This distribution may as it stands be an artefact dependent on the location of archaeobotanists, but it is nevertheless likely that the complex of changes described here was characteristic of those areas, and did not take place, or did not take the same form, in the West and North.

The new data suggests that climate change was not a steady progress in one direction either. Sometimes the trend was reversed for several years, and then reverted to its original direction. Sometimes change, in either direction, accelerated, and sometimes it slowed down. Sometimes there must have been a bad season, even when the climate was improving, and presumably there were good ones when it was deteriorating, too (although the sources do not consider it necessary to mention that). Nevertheless, the overall trend was clear: the climate was getting warmer between say 900 AD and the end of the Anglo-Saxon period, even if the peaks of the eleventh century were after the Conquest. Thus, climatic improvement, as far as we can tell, did not actually begin until after wheat production began to expand. Nevertheless, it will have facilitated that expansion enormously. The climatic data are of course global, not local to England, so we cannot make straightforward links between changes in the climate and developments in English farming. In fact, it is not impossible that global increases in average temperature might have led to deterioration in the weather in England, with the Gulf Stream moving away to the north, as it may be doing at present. At any rate, we can expect some discrepancies.

Indeed, fluctuations and variation in the climate were probably reflected in changes in cereal production. There must have been times when the amount of wheat being grown in England actually declined, as the weather deteriorated and farmers struggled to improve their drainage, and possibly other techniques, before they could increase it again. All this must also have been extremely local. For some farmers, drainage will not have been the main problem, but unusually wet and cold weather will still have made it harder for them to grow the more desirable crop. Or it may be that wheat cultivation had to be abandoned in some areas while in others, perhaps not far away, it continued to expand.

The dating of the origins of the open fields is not so much imprecise as controversial. Dates ranging from the *aduentus Saxonum* to close to the end of the Middle Ages have all been proposed at one time or another.[46] We can be rea-

[45] More recent work confirms the general outlines of the picture presented here, but there has been no quantified synthesis on which a detailed analysis might be based.

[46] The Orwins point out that 'It has generally been accepted by historians that the open-field farming system was introduced into England by Germanic settlers' (p. 3), and go on to list some of the historians concerned (Stubbs, Seebohm, *et al.*). Since their time, opinion

sonably certain, however, that these origins lie somewhere in the Anglo-Saxon period. The work of Della Hooke on charter bounds has shown that open fields did exist in some places in England by the later tenth century, and perhaps by the beginning of that century.[47] The laws of Ine of Wessex (688x94) refer to 'meadow or other land' which *ceorl*s might hold in common, and 'common crops or grass', showing some kind of co-operative farming going on, if not necessarily in open fields.[48] In the eleventh century the *Rectitudines singularum personarum* envisage a more clearly organised system of common agriculture, in which the hay-ward is required to have his arable land at the 'end' next to the pasture, so that, if his fencing is not well maintained, his will be the first crops to suffer.[49] Perhaps we would be justified in inferring something like 'classic' open-field farming by this stage. Unfortunately, the location of the *Rectitudines* is far from certain, and the author or compiler specifically warns us that customs vary from place to place. The text cannot therefore give us any clue as to *where* open-field farming might have originated, or might have spread to by the eleventh century. Nor can the charters identify its epicentre, for their survival is very much conditioned by subsequent events. However, between them the written sources do suggest that open-field farming existed in a period when wheat production was already expanding, and the climate had also begun to improve.

The dating of ridge and furrow is even more difficult to pin down: there are no written references to it from the Anglo-Saxon period, and the surviving remains, like many landscape features, are virtually undatable. There is of course the rule of thumb that those examples of ridge and furrow displaying a 'reversed S' formation were made by ploughs drawn by oxen,[50] but this does not allow us to distinguish the Anglo-Saxon period from after the Conquest, let alone make finer distinctions within the pre-Conquest centuries.[51] There are three examples of excavated ridge and furrow that probably date from within our period, from Gwythian, Cornwall (tenth–eleventh centuries), Sandal Castle, near Wakefield (also tenth–eleventh), and Hen Domen, near Montgomery (eleventh).[52] None can be dated with absolute certainty before the Conquest, but between them they at least support the idea that this technique was in use in the late Anglo-Saxon period. Their distribution (if three records can be said to have one) is

has been much more various, the main proponent of a late dating being Joan Thirsk, in a series of articles culminating in 'The origins of the common fields', *Past and Present*, 33 (1966), 142–7.

47 Della Hooke, *The Landscape of Anglo-Saxon England* (Leicester, 1998), pp. 121–2 and 126. See also Finberg, 'Anglo-Saxon England', p. 493.

48 Edited by Felix Liebermann, *Die Gesetze der Angelsachsen* (Halle, 1903), I, 88–123.

49 Ed. Liebermann, *Die Gesetze*, I, 444–53.

50 See for instance Michael Aston, *Interpreting the Landscape: Landscape Archaeology in Local Studies* (London, 1985), pp. 120–3.

51 Langdon, *Horses*, e.g. table 30, p. 208, shows that oxen were still in widespread use at the end of the Middle Ages.

52 There is a table showing all excavated medieval ridge and furrow in Grenville Astill, 'Fields', in *The Countryside of Medieval England*, eds Grenville Astill and Annie Grant (Oxford, 1988), pp. 62–85, at p. 74.

also interesting: none of them is within the core Anglo-Saxon cultural area, or indeed in that diagonal strip across the country (the 'central province') where we expect to see open-field systems. Nor can the distribution of ridge and furrow in the landscape add to our certainty, since it owes so much to post-medieval, and indeed post-enclosure, developments, which may have obliterated it even in places where it was originally just as common as where it survives to the present day.[53]

Finally, there is the question of when the mould-board plough was introduced. David Hill has presented both literary and iconographic evidence that people in later Anglo-Saxon England were familiar with mould-board ploughs.[54] Of the pictorial representations, the most detailed and convincing (it is hard to see how some of the others would stay in one piece, let alone work) are the two calendar illustrations discussed by Catherine Karkov in this volume, both dating from the first half of the eleventh century. These might well suggest that the illustrator had seen such machines, and even knew how they worked, but an important question here is how familiar the people who produced Anglo-Saxon manuscripts would have been with the everyday objects used in food-production that sometimes appear in those books. In other words, did they draw from life, or simply copy what they found in other books? I think we can safely argue that no one in eleventh-century England, however exalted, could have been as ignorant about how their food was produced as many people are today. That is not to say, however, that they would not have copied a picture of a plough from an exemplar simply because that picture looked nothing like any plough they had seen in real life. They might have believed this was the latest high-tech fashion in Francia, or wherever the exemplar came from, or they might have viewed it as a superior way of representing ploughs, even though not particularly naturalistic. It has always to be borne in mind that Anglo-Saxon manuscript illustrations might have been copied from overseas exemplars, even when no such exemplar can be identified among surviving manuscripts, and may therefore not be good evidence for what was going on in real life in England.

On the other hand, the Exeter Book of Old English poetry, dating from the later tenth century, contains a riddle on a plough, which has no known source, unlike many other riddles in the collection. This poem shows a clear understanding of how the mould-board plough works, not just what it looks like, describing it turning the sod to one side so that it leaves black on one side and green on the other.[55] This does suggest that such a plough was a familiar object in England around the turn of the millennium, in the fields and not just in books, and could be seen in operation, and makes it rather more plausible that the illustrations, too, draw upon the common experience of the people who

53 See Robert Liddiard, 'The distribution of ridge and furrow in Norfolk: ploughing practice and subsequent land-use', *Agricultural Historical Review*, 47 (1999), 1–6, and discussion by Williamson, *Shaping Medieval Landscapes*, pp. 151–3.

54 D. Hill, '*Sulh*: the Anglo-Saxon Plough c. 1000 AD', *Landscape History*, 22 (2000), 5–19.

55 *The Exeter Book*, eds George P. Krapp and Elliott van K. Dobbie, ASPR III (New York, 1936), 21.

made and looked at them. Between them, these two art forms hardly constitute incontrovertible evidence, but they do tend to confirm the inference from the existence of open fields by the late Anglo-Saxon period that the plough which determined their form must have existed, too. They can shed little light, however, on where in England it might have first been used. The question also remains whether this written and pictorial evidence, all from late in the period, coincides with the introduction of the mould-board plough, or rather portrays for the first time a piece of equipment that was already in use.

Conclusions

It is difficult, therefore, to make these various developments coincide closely enough, either in time or in space, to produce a watertight causal relationship between them. Perhaps it is best to abandon for the time being the hope of greater geographical precision, but it is possible to put our four developments in a very rough chronological order. Wheat production was already expanding by *c.*900 AD, and quite possibly by 700, the beginning of our broadly defined 'mid-Anglo-Saxon' phase. Climatic amelioration also took off *c.*900, but may have begun about a century earlier. Open fields, and perhaps by implication ridge and furrow, are attested by the later tenth century. The plough that must have created them is not clearly in evidence before the millennium, but it can certainly be inferred that it existed when the fields did, if not before.

Thus the expansion in wheat production seems to be the earliest of our four developments. It looks, in fact, as if it may have begun in what has been referred to as the 'long eighth century', to which various kinds of economic growth and innovation have been attributed. John Moreland sees this period (for him, *c.*670–750, earlier than most scholars' formulations) as a time when production was already expanding in rural England, ahead of the growth of the first trading settlements:

> One of the most significant features of all sites … is the evidence for … production at the beginning of the 'long eighth century'. This can take the form of intensified livestock or cereal production/processing, or of craft activities … but the crucial point is that it can now be seen as a reality in the English countryside at a time coincident with or, more probably, antedating the 'emergence of production' on the *emporia*.[56]

Here we see once again rural growth preceding another factor with which it is apparently closely linked. Just as this expansion in rural production must have originally been independent of the *emporia*, likewise, the increase in the cultivation of wheat cannot have been *caused* by climatic improvement, or by technological innovation (the plough, or indeed the mill, left out of the account

56 John Moreland, 'The significance of production in eighth-century England', in *The Long Eighth Century*, eds Inge Lyse Hansen and Chris Wickham, The Transformation of the Roman World 11 (Leiden, 2000), pp. 69–104, at p. 97.

here), or by new ways of organising the land, since all these developments, to judge by the evidence adduced above, began later. Increased wheat production must have been facilitated by all these other changes, but it was apparently underway before they could have had any effect. What then is the causal relationship? The climate of course must be left out of this calculation: if it did not cause agrarian change, the reverse certainly cannot be postulated, since, until recently, the climate has not been susceptible to human influence. For the other two facilitating factors, the plough and the open fields, on the other hand, there is no such objection to the proposal that they owed their popularity to precisely the property expounded above, namely that they allowed Anglo-Saxon farmers to continue the process that they, or their ancestors, had already begun, of expanding the production of wheat, even when the climate was against it. Thus these two developments, the one in agricultural technology and the other in the landscape, can be seen to owe their widespread adoption in England to the Anglo-Saxons' desire for that prestigious dietary item, light, white wheat bread.

11

The Early Christian Landscape of East Anglia*

RICHARD HOGGETT

Introduction

This paper explores aspects of the historical and archaeological evidence for the coming of Christianity to Anglo-Saxon East Anglia with a particular focus on the wide-scale restructuring of the landscape that the conversion precipitated (Fig. 11.1). In order to establish the historical framework within which these events sit, it begins with an examination of the evidence presented by Bede in the *Historia Ecclesiastica*. Bede draws our attention to some of the ecclesiastical sites established by the early churchmen; a broader consideration of the conversion-period landscape reveals many important sites that are not mentioned in the surviving historical sources. In particular, disused Roman enclosures and topographically distinct locations can be demonstrated to have been of particular significance to the conversion process. The coming of Christianity also caused a great upheaval in the sites chosen for cemeteries, argued to be a direct result of a changing attitude towards the dead, which resulted in the integration of cemeteries and settlements during the Middle Saxon period. Finally, this paper offers some suggestions about how we might take the study of the conversion-period landscape further.

The Historical Framework

One of the main themes of Bede's *Historia Ecclesiastica* is the gradual conversion of the Anglo-Saxon kingdoms – a feat most often achieved via royal patronage, the establishment of the episcopal sees and the encouragement of missionary activity.[1] East Anglia was no exception and Bede emphasises the role

* This paper is based on doctoral research undertaken at the School of History, University of East Anglia, between 2002 and 2007. The work was funded by a post-graduate scholarship from the School of History and I am grateful to my supervisors, Prof. Tom Williamson and Prof. Stephen Church. Plates XI.1, XI.2, XI.3 and Fig. 11.2 are reproduced with the permission of Norfolk Museums and Archaeology Service.

1 Leslie Barnard, 'Bede and Eusebius as Church historians', in *Famulus Christi*, ed. Gerald Bonner (London, 1976), 106–24; Robert Markus, *Bede and the Tradition of Ecclesiastical History* (Jarrow, 1975).

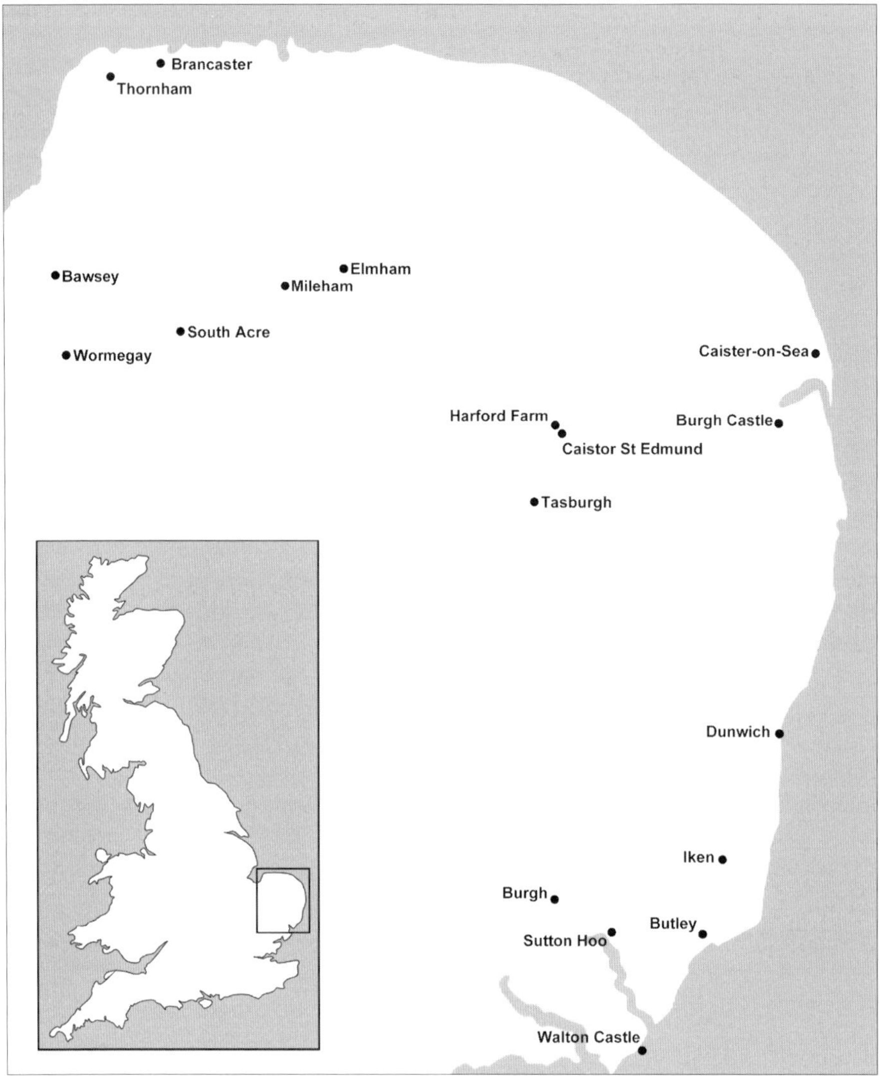

Figure 11.1. Sites mentioned in the text.

that the East Anglian kings played in the Christianisation of the region, the most important developments in his eyes being the establishment of the bishopric at *Dommoc* and the encouragement of the missionary Fursa.[2] Yet we must proceed with caution, for Bede was primarily a theologian and his motives for writing the *HE* were more than simply to provide an historical account, as we would

2 *HE*, II,15; III, 19.

understand it, of the English Church.[3] Consequently, we must be wary of taking the historical framework Bede presented at face value, but at the same time we must make the most of what information we do have.

It is clear from the text of the *HE* that very little of Bede's East Anglian material was derived from East Anglian sources, instead being drawn from Northumbrian sources as well as those of Wessex, Essex and Kent. Bede does not appear to have been in contact with any of the East Anglian bishops, and his episcopal lists and diocesan history doubtless came direct from Canterbury.[4] First-hand accounts were reportedly provided by Abbot Esi (about whom nothing else is known) and King Ealdwulf, while Bede's account of Fursa was clearly derived from a copy of the *Vita Fursae* in his possession.[5] Far from providing a comprehensive account of the East Anglian conversion, in Kirby's words 'Bede's account of the kingdom is fragmentary, the traditions scattered in time and space'.[6] Unfortunately, there are few other East Anglian sources to which we can refer, meaning that although the veracity of the material within the *HE* can be questioned in this fashion, it is still the only source available to us.

The first East Anglian king to come into contact with Christianity was Rædwald, who ruled the region in the first quarter of the seventh century and was baptised in Kent *c*.604.[7] Although a king in his own right, Rædwald was subordinate to Æthelberht of Kent at the time of his baptism and his acceptance of the new faith should perhaps be seen as much as a statement of allegiance as a genuine spiritual conversion. In either case, Rædwald's conversion did not last long and on returning to East Anglia he apparently lapsed, establishing a temple in which stood two altars, one to the Christian God and one for devils.[8] But was Rædwald really an apostate? Certainly, he did not adhere exclusively to his new faith, but he did not reject it outright either and it has been argued that Rædwald might have considered himself a Christian of sorts.[9] Whatever his personal circumstances, Christianity clearly did not become the dominant religion of East Anglia during his reign – no attempt was made to develop a diocesan infrastructure, for example – and if Rædwald was the individual buried

3 James Campbell, 'Bede I', in *Essays in Anglo-Saxon History*, ed. James Campbell (London, 1986), 1–28; Roger Ray, *Bede, Rhetoric, and the Creation of Christian Latin Culture* (Jarrow, 1997).

4 David Kirby, 'Bede's native sources for the *Historia Ecclesiastica*', *Bulletin of the John Rylands Library* 48 (1966), 341–71.

5 Charles Plummer, *Venerabilis Baedae Opera Historica* (Oxford, 1896) I, pp. 163–8; *Monumenta Germaniæ Historica, Scriptores Rerum Merovingicarum, 4: Passiones Vitaeque Sanctorum Aevi Merovingici*, ed. Bruno Krusch (Hannover, 1902), pp. 434–9.

6 Kirby, 'Bede's native sources', p. 363.

7 Frank Stenton, 'The East Anglian kings of the seventh century', in *The Anglo-Saxons*, ed. Peter Clemoes (London, 1959), 43–52; David Dumville, 'The Anglian collection of royal genealogies and regnal lists', *Anglo-Saxon England* 5 (1976), 23–50.

8 *HE*, II,15.

9 Sam Newton, *The Reckoning of King Rædwald* (Colchester, 2003); William Kilbride, 'Why I feel cheated by the term "Christianisation"', *Archaeological Review from Cambridge* 17.2 (2000), 1–17, at pp. 5–7.

in Mound 1 at Sutton Hoo, then those who buried him clearly did not consider him to be a Christian.[10]

Rædwald was succeeded by his surviving son, Eorpwald. In 627, Edwin of Northumbria converted to Christianity and, we are told, 'he also persuaded Eorpwald, son of Rædwald and king of the East Angles, to abandon his idolatrous superstitions and, together with his kingdom, to accept the Christian faith and sacraments'.[11] By then Edwin had become an overlord in his own right and Eorpwald's acceptance of Christianity should be viewed in the same context as Rædwald's baptism under Æthelberht. Again, there is no evidence to suggest that the East Anglian kingdom was converted in anything more than a nominal sense under Eorpwald and his conversion was literally short-lived; he was assassinated not long afterwards.[12]

Following a period during which the kingship seems to have been lost to Rædwald's family, Eorpwald was succeeded by his brother Sigeberht *c*.630. Described by Bede as 'a good and religious man'[13] and 'a devout Christian and a very learned man in all respects',[14] Sigeberht had been in exile in Gaul during his brother's reign, where he had become a Christian, and Bede states that 'as soon as he began to reign he made it his business to see that the whole kingdom shared his faith'.[15] Unlike the reigns of his predecessors, that of Sigeberht saw the true beginning of the East Anglian conversion. Not only was the king a devout Christian himself, he also set a number of religious developments in motion, not least the creation of an East Anglian diocese.

Sigeberht was aided in his efforts by Felix, a Burgundian bishop sent to East Anglia by Archbishop Honorius, perhaps in response to a request from Sigeberht. In 630/1 Felix became the first Bishop of the East Angles and Sigeberht granted him the site of *Dommoc* to establish his bishopric.[16] Felix died seventeen years later and *Dommoc* remained the sole East Anglian see until *c*.673, when Archbishop Theodore divided the diocese and consecrated two bishops.[17] One bishopric continued at *Dommoc*, while a new see was established at Elmham.[18]

Dommoc is traditionally identified with the east-coast town of Dunwich,

10 Howard Williams, 'Death, memory and time: a consideration of mortuary practices at Sutton Hoo', in *Time in the Middle Ages*, eds Chris Humphrey and W. Mark Ormrod (York, 2001), 35–71; Martin Carver and Christopher Fern, 'The seventh-century burial rites and their sequence', in *Sutton Hoo: A Seventh-Century Princely Burial Ground and its Context*, ed. Martin Carver (London, 2005), 283–313.

11 *HE*, II,15.

12 *HE*, II,15.

13 *HE*, III,18.

14 *HE*, II,15.

15 *HE*, II,15.

16 *HE*, II,15.

17 *HE*, IV,5.

18 Stuart Rigold, 'The Anglian cathedral of North Elmham, Norfolk', *Medieval Archaeology* 6 (1962), 67–108; Peter Wade-Martins, *Excavations in North Elmham Park 1967–1972*, East Anglian Archaeology 9 (Gressenhall, 1980), pp. 3–11.

although this association is largely unfounded.[19] The descriptive terminology used by Bede and by the signatories of the Council of *Clovesho* of 803 suggests that *Dommoc* was, in fact, a site with a significant Roman past, and twelfth- and thirteenth-century documents clearly identify the site as lying at Felixstowe.[20] This evidence and comparative examples from elsewhere suggest that the episcopal see was actually founded within the walls of the Roman fort at Walton Castle, situated in the heartland of the East Anglian kings. Sadly, Walton Castle was eroded by the sea in the seventeenth century, meaning that one of the potentially most significant conversion-period archaeological sites has been lost to us.

The establishment of *Dommoc* was not the only step towards the Christianisation of the region which occurred during Sigeberht's reign. Bede records that Sigeberht also welcomed the Irish missionary Fursa to the kingdom and encouraged him to found a monastery at *Cnobheresburg*.[21] The location of *Cnobheresburg* is also unknown, but is almost universally thought to have been the Roman fort at Burgh Castle (Pl. XI.1). There is no strong evidence to suggest that this identification is correct, but it is clear from archaeological evidence that Burgh Castle was a site of considerable religious significance during the conversion period, whether it was founded by Fursa or not.[22]

We know that Fursa's missionary activities were by no means unique, for we hear of other missionaries at work in East Anglia, the most notable being Botolph, whose founding of a monastery at Iken is recorded in the *Anglo-Saxon Chronicle* for the year 653.[23] Botolph is not mentioned in the *HE*, although Bede had almost certainly heard of him, and it is highly likely that Bede only included Fursa's story because he had access to a convenient source.[24]

Here then we begin to reach the limit of what can be inferred from the surviving documentary sources. Fortunately the corresponding archaeological record is very rich and a combination of historical, archaeological and landscape-based approaches yields far more significant results than any individual approach. Having been guided by the historical sources, we turn our attention to a recurring theme in the history of the conversion: the reuse of Roman enclosures.

19 Stuart Rigold, 'The supposed see of Dunwich', *Journal of the British Archaeological Association* 24 (1961), 55–9; Stuart Rigold, 'Further evidence about the site of "Dommoc"', *Journal of the British Archaeological Association* 37 (1974), 97–102; Jeremy Haslam, 'Dommoc and Dunwich: A Reappraisal', *Anglo-Saxon Studies in Archaeology and History* 5 (1992), 41–5.

20 *Councils and Ecclesiastical Documents Relating to Great Britain and Ireland*, eds Arthur Haddan and William Stubbs (Oxford, 1871), III, pp. 546–7; James Campbell, 'Bede's words for places', in *Names, Words and Graves*, ed. Peter H. Sawyer (Leeds, 1979), 34–54, at p. 40; Rigold, 'The supposed see', pp. 57–8; Rigold, 'Further evidence', p. 9.

21 *HE*, III,19.

22 Stephen Johnson, *Burgh Castle, Excavations by Charles Green 1958–61*, East Anglian Archaeology 20 (Gressenhall, 1983), pp. 60–5.

23 *The Anglo-Saxon Chronicle, A Collaborative Edition, Volume 7, MS. E*, ed. Susan Irvine (Cambridge, 2004), p. 26.

24 *English Historical Documents* c.*500–1042*, ed. Dorothy Whitelock, Eng. Hist. Documents I (2nd edn, London, 1979), pp. 758–70, at p. 759.

Plate XI.1. Burgh Castle looking west. Note the surviving walls of the fort to the left of the frame and the medieval parish church to the right of the frame. It would appear that the church was relocated when the fort was adapted into a castle in the eleventh century. © and reproduced with the permission of Norfolk Museums and Archaeology Service

The Reuse of Roman Enclosures

The association between early ecclesiastical sites and extant Roman ruins has long been recognised, but why should such sites have been considered by early ecclesiastics to be suitable locations?[25] One traditional explanation is that they provided a ready source of quarried stone for new churches, yet this cannot be the case in East Anglia where the building of stone churches did not begin in earnest until the Late Saxon period.[26] The real explanation for the association is to be found in the symbolic connotations and *romanitas* that such structures would have held in the eyes of the Christian missionaries, many of whom were of Mediterranean extraction.[27]

25 Stuart Rigold, 'Litus Romanum – the shore forts as mission stations', in *The Saxon Shore*, ed. David Johnston (York, 1977), 70–5; Richard Morris and Julia Roxan, 'Churches on Roman sites', in *Temples, Churches and Religion*, ed. Warwick Rodwell (Oxford, 1980), 175–209.

26 Richard Morris, *The Church in British Archaeology* (York, 1983), pp. 43–5; Tim Eaton, *Plundering the Past: Roman Stonework in Medieval Britain* (Stroud, 2000), pp. 10–35.

27 Helen Geake, *The Use of Grave-Goods in Conversion-Period England* c.*600*–c.*850* (Oxford, 1997), pp. 121–2, 132–3; Helen Geake, 'Invisible kingdoms: the use of grave-goods in seventh-century England', *Anglo-Saxon Studies in Archaeology and History* 10 (1999), 203–15, at pp. 209–12; Tyler Bell, 'Churches on Roman buildings: Christian associations and Roman masonry in Anglo-Saxon England', *Medieval Archaeology* 42 (1998), 1–18, at pp. 5–8; Tyler Bell, *The Religious Reuse of Roman Structures in Early Medieval England* (Oxford, 2005), pp. 16–22.

It is clear that a number of the region's walled Roman enclosures played an instrumental part in the evangelisation of East Anglia, as they did in other parts of the country.[28] Once the early ecclesiastics had occupied these Roman enclosures they became missionary stations from which the holy men could begin their work within the local population. A strong case can be made for the Roman fort at Walton Castle having become the site of the episcopal see, from which the authority of the bishop radiated across the region. Further north, the pair of forts which flanked the estuary of the River Yare, Burgh Castle and Caister-on-Sea, each became the focus of a Christian community, the archaeological evidence for which is clear, albeit heavily disturbed.[29] Still further north, the Roman fort at Brancaster may also have housed such a community, although the evidence is currently less certain.[30]

A good indication of the degree of success enjoyed by the early missionaries is provided by the extent of the seventh- and eighth-century cemeteries exhibiting typical Christian burial rites associated with these Roman sites.[31] Excavations at Burgh Castle revealed a cemetery containing perhaps 200 burials, with many more probably lost to plough-damage (Pl. XI.1).[32] The intramural cemetery at Caister-on-Sea was perhaps of a similar size to that at Burgh Castle, while the extensive extramural cemetery was much larger, comprising hundreds or perhaps even thousands of burials.[33] The fort at Brancaster has not been extensively excavated, but ploughed-up human bone might suggest the presence of a similar cemetery here.[34] It can be assumed that one or more cemeteries also formed part of the episcopal complex at Walton Castle.

From the sheer quantity of burials discovered it would seem that each of these missionary stations had a zone of influence which extended far beyond its walls, with individuals from the surrounding area being buried within or close to the fort. This interpretation is supported by the fact that these cemeteries contained a mixture of males and females ranging in age from childhood to old age, indicating that the cemeteries catered for whole communities, rather than any particular section of society.

Although no traces of missionary churches have been found in association with any of these cemeteries, something of the kind must surely have once existed (Pl. XI.1). In many parts of the country such churches were built of

28 Bell, 'Churches on Roman buildings'; Bell, *The Religious Reuse*.

29 Johnson, *Burgh Castle*; Margaret Darling with David Gurney, *Caister-on-Sea Excavations by Charles Green, 1951–55*, East Anglian Archaeology 60 (Gressenhall, 1993).

30 Derek Edwards and Christopher Green, 'The Saxon Shore fort and settlement at Brancaster, Norfolk', *The Saxon Shore*, ed. David Johnston (York, 1977), 21–9; John Hinchcliffe with Christopher Green, *Excavations at Brancaster 1974 and 1977*, East Anglian Archaeology 23 (Gressenhall, 1985).

31 Richard Hoggett, 'Charting conversion: burial as a barometer of belief', *Anglo-Saxon Studies in Archaeology and History* 14 (2005), 28–37.

32 Johnson, *Burgh Castle*.

33 Darling with Gurney, *Caister-on-Sea*.

34 Edwards and Green, 'The Saxon Shore fort'.

stone and many continued to develop on the same site into the medieval period.[35] There are no stone-built conversion-period churches in East Anglia, and their absence here may be explained by the organic nature of the original structures and the post-depositional disturbance which occurred at each of the sites. The East Anglian dioceses were disrupted by the Viking incursions of the tenth century and the fact that only the later diocese of Elmham was re-founded indicates that *Dommoc* had diminished greatly since its seventh-century heyday.[36] Despite this there is historical evidence to suggest that a church survived within the walls of Walton Castle until the eleventh century.[37] Similarly, both Burgh Castle and Caister-on-Sea appear to have floundered during the Late Saxon period and it is possible that they too fell victim to the Vikings, either directly or via precautionary measures taken against attack from the sea. We are left with only the most tantalising glimpses of their former glory.

The discussion so far might be taken to suggest that only Roman enclosures became missionary stations and that there were only a handful of East Anglian examples, but this was not the case. Roman sites were clearly attractive to the first wave of Christian missionaries, but that is not to say that they were occupied to the exclusion of all other sites. Many other sites were also put to a Christian use during the course of the conversion.

Other Enclosures and 'Isolated' Sites

In the absence of an appropriate Roman enclosure, other earthwork enclosures or a suitably defined topographical setting were often chosen for missionary centres.[38] Extant Iron Age earthworks were reoccupied and put to ecclesiastical use, such as was the case at Tasburgh in south Norfolk, where the parish church sits within an Iron Age enclosure which excavation has shown to contain much evidence for Middle and Late Saxon occupation (Pl. XI.2).[39] A similar situation might also be in evidence at Burgh in south-east Suffolk, where the church stands within a ploughed-out enclosure,[40] and at Thornham in north-

35 Bell, 'Churches on Roman buildings'; Bell, *The Religious Reuse.*

36 Dorothy Whitelock, 'The pre-Viking-Age church in East Anglia', *Anglo-Saxon England* 1 (1972), 1–22, at p. 1; Tim Pestell, *Landscapes of Monastic Foundation* (Woodbridge, 2004), pp. 72–6.

37 Stanley West, 'The excavation of Walton Priory', *Proceedings of the Suffolk Institute of Archaeology* 33.2 (1974), 131–52, at pp. 141–9; John Fairclough and Steven Plunkett, 'Drawings of Walton Castle and other monuments in Walton and Felixstowe', *Proceedings of the Suffolk Institute of Archaeology and History* 39.4 (2000), 419–59, at pp. 451–2.

38 John Blair, 'Anglo-Saxon minsters: a topographical review', in *Pastoral Care before the Parish*, eds John Blair and Richard Sharpe (Leicester, 1992), 226–66, at pp. 227–35.

39 Andrew Rogerson and Andrew Lawson, 'The earthwork enclosure at Tasburgh', in *The Iron Age Forts of Norfolk*, eds John Davies, Tony Gregory, Andrew Lawson, Robert Rickett and Andrew Rogerson (Gressenhall, 1986), 31–58, at pp. 31–5, 57–8.

40 Edward Martin, *Burgh: Iron Age and Roman Enclosure*, East Anglian Archaeology 40 (Ipswich, 1988).

Plate XI.2. Tasburgh fort looking south. The hedgeline in the foreground follows the earthworks of the fort. Note the parish church within the enclosure to the top of the frame. © and reproduced with the permission of Norfolk Museums and Archaeology Service

west Norfolk, where a conversion-period cemetery was found within a square earthwork enclosure.[41]

It has often been observed that a number of Anglo-Saxon churches are situated on low hills, promontories or islands in marshy floodplains.[42] Such sites, both topographically separate from the surrounding landscape and yet fully integrated into riverine communication routes, were ideally suited to those who were seeking to combine a traditional life of monastic devotion with the proactive conversion of the surrounding population.[43] Perhaps the best known East Anglian example (although one not mentioned by Bede) is Botolph's minster at *Icanho*, the foundation of which is recorded in the *Anglo-Saxon Chronicle* for the year 653.[44] *Icanho* has been firmly identified with Iken, in south-east Suffolk, where the church is situated on a spur of land which projects into the river, and excavation has confirmed the Middle Saxon foundation date of the

41 Tony Gregory and David Gurney, *Excavations at Thornham, Warham, Wighton and Caistor St Edmund, Norfolk*, East Anglian Archaeology 30 (Gressenhall, 1986), pp. 1–60.

42 Blair, 'Anglo-Saxon minsters', pp. 227–35; Pestell, *Landscapes of Monastic Foundation*, pp. 52–6.

43 Eric Cambridge and David Rollason, 'The pastoral organisation of the Anglo-Saxon church: a review of the "Minster Hypothesis"', *Early Medieval Europe* 4.1 (1995), 87–104, at pp. 93–4; Sarah Foot, 'What was an early Anglo-Saxon monastery?', in *Monastic Studies*, ed. Judith Loades (Bangor, 1990), 48–57, at p. 50.

44 See n. 23.

church.[45] A similarly isolated topographic situation was exploited at Burrow Hill, Butley, some 10km south of Iken, where excavation revealed a Middle Saxon cemetery containing over 200 inhumations.[46]

A number of island and promontory sites have also been identified on the west Norfolk fen edge, such as at Wormegay, where field-walking has revealed a substantial scatter of Middle Saxon pottery adjacent to the church, and at Bawsey, where field-walking, metal-detecting and limited excavation have revealed evidence for seventh-century occupation.[47] The major Middle Saxon site excavated at Brandon was similarly located on an island in a river valley and, in addition, demonstrated that it was possible for the ecclesiastical elements of a settlement – in this case a timber church and two cemeteries – to be fully integrated with river-borne trade, arable and pastoralism, and light industry.[48]

The sites referred to here are many and varied, but they are linked by a number of common themes: their symbolic connotations, similar locations, material remains and, in particular, their association with Christian burials. Indeed, burials are one of the most visible classes of evidence for the conversion period and we now turn to examine the place of the dead in the conversion-period landscape.

Cemeteries in the Landscape

The locations chosen for the burial of the dead were not arbitrary and cemeteries are a particularly good indicator of religious change. The contrasting types of site used for pre- and post-conversion cemeteries and the differing relationships between cemeteries and settlements of those periods suggest that the changes which occurred during the conversion period also affected where the dead were placed in the landscape.

Inhumation, cremation and mixed-rite cemeteries all existed in Early Saxon East Anglia and they varied greatly in the number of burials which they contained. It has frequently been observed that Early Saxon cemeteries were sited on higher ground, hilltops or terraces above river valleys, and that, while Early Saxon settlements and cemeteries might lie in close proximity, they remained separate entities in the landscape. It has also been observed that many cemeteries may have served large geographical areas containing numerous settlements.[49]

45 Stanley West, Norman Scarfe and Rosemary Cramp, 'Iken, St Botolph, and the Coming of East Anglian Christianity', *Proceedings of the Suffolk Institute of Archaeology and History* 35.4 (1984), 279–301.

46 Valerie Fenwick, 'Insula de Burgh: excavations at Burrow Hill, Butley, Suffolk, 1978–1981', *Anglo-Saxon Studies in Archaeology and History* 3 (1984), 35–54.

47 Andrew Rogerson, 'Six Middle Anglo-Saxon sites in West Norfolk', in *Markets in Early Medieval Europe*, eds Tim Pestell and Katharina Ulmschneider (Macclesfield, 2003), 110–21.

48 Robert Carr, Andrew Tester and Peter Murphy, 'The Middle-Saxon settlement at Staunch Meadow, Brandon', *Antiquity* 62 (1988), 371–7.

49 Catherine Hills, 'The archaeology of Anglo-Saxon England in the pagan period: a review', *Anglo-Saxon England* 8 (1979), 297–329, at p. 310; Howard Williams, 'Placing the dead:

Middle Saxon cemeteries, by contrast, are not frequently excavated and, as such, are more poorly understood. This scarcity is partly due to their relative archaeological invisibility, as the vast majority of Middle Saxon cemeteries were unfurnished, but is largely owing to changes in the landscape setting of cemeteries which occurred during the Middle Saxon period. These changes resulted in most becoming obscured by later settlement features, in particular churchyards and churches. The exceptions to this pattern are those cemeteries which contain so-called 'Final Phase' burials, generally interpreted as the Christian successors to Early Saxon cemeteries, founded on fresh sites in the seventh century and eventually superseded by a churchyard located elsewhere.[50]

This 'Final Phase' model has proved very popular and is widely accepted, but it is not without its critics. There were undoubtedly significant changes in the types of grave-goods deposited during the seventh century (argued to reflect the Christian beliefs of those using the cemeteries),[51] but the argument for a linear development of cemetery types – an Early Saxon cemetery succeeded by a 'Final Phase' cemetery and replaced in turn by a churchyard – simply cannot be maintained. This is not least because the total number of 'Final Phase' inhumations falls far short of representing even a fraction of the seventh-century population, meaning that the vast majority of seventh-century burials remain unaccounted for.[52] Indeed, so great is this disparity that 'Final Phase' burial must be viewed as the exception rather than the rule and other explanations for the whereabouts of the seventh-century dead must be sought.

The environs of *Venta Icenorum*, the Roman town at Caistor St Edmund, south-west of Norwich, provide an illustrative case of many of the arguments presented thus far. Roman occupation of the town continued into the fifth century and a degree of continuity into the Early Saxon period is attested by the presence of two Early Saxon cemeteries on the hillsides overlooking the town (Pl. XI.3).[53] Both cemeteries contained substantial numbers of cremations and inhumations and both fell out of use in the early seventh century, in accordance with patterns observed elsewhere in East Anglia. Yet, it is clear that

investigating the location of wealthy barrow burials in seventh-century England', in *Grave Matters*, ed. Martin Rundkvist (Oxford, 1999), 57–86; Sam Lucy, *The Anglo-Saxon Way of Death* (Stroud, 2000), p. 152; Andrew Richardson, *The Anglo-Saxon Cemeteries of Kent* (Oxford, 2005), pp. 69–77.

50 Andy Boddington, 'Models of burial, settlement and worship: the final phase reviewed', in *Anglo-Saxon Cemeteries: A Reappraisal*, ed. E. Southworth (Stroud, 1990), 177–99; Morris, *Church in British Archaeology*, pp. 53–9; Geake, *Use of Grave-Goods*.

51 Sally Crawford, 'Anglo-Saxon women, furnished burial, and the Church', in *Women and Religion in Medieval England*, ed. Diana Wood (Oxford, 2003), 1–12; Sally Crawford, 'Votive deposition, religion and the Anglo-Saxon furnished burial rite', *World Archaeology* 36 (2004), 87–102; Hoggett, 'Charting conversion: burial as a barometer of belief', pp. 28–37.

52 Helen Geake, 'Persistent problems in the study of conversion-period burials in England', in *Burial in Early Medieval England and Wales*, eds Sam Lucy and Andrew Reynolds (London, 2002), 144–55, at pp. 144–8.

53 John Myres and Barbara Green, *The Anglo-Saxon Cemeteries of Caistor-by-Norwich and Markshall, Norfolk* (London, 1973).

Plate XI.3. *Venta Icenorum* looking north-east. Note the parish church within the town's walls. One Early Saxon cemetery lay in the wooded area to the right of the frame and another just to the left of the frame. Harford Farm lies *c.*1km to the north-west of the town. © and reproduced with the permission of Norfolk Museums and Archaeology Service

abandonment was not the cause of these cemeteries' disuse, for Middle Saxon settlement evidence has been discovered immediately outside the town wall and new cemeteries were founded in their place. It would seem that the coming of Christianity was the ultimate reason behind their demise.

Venta Icenorum was a walled Roman enclosure, albeit a much larger one than many of the examples considered here, and would have been attractive to newly arrived Christian missionaries, all the more so if any administrative capacity or residual occupation remained at the site.[54] The parish church still stands within the walls of the Roman town, in a position typical of a church founded as a part of the missionary process (Pl. XI.3). As we have seen, if the church were founded as a part of the conversion process then it should also have had a concomitant cemetery of Burgh Castle/Caister-on-Sea type. Here then would be one of the successors to the pre-Christian Early Saxon cemeteries. Yet, the churchyard within the walls is only a part of the story.

54 William Bowden and David Bescoby, 'The plan of *Venta Icenorum* (Caistor-by-Norwich): interpreting a new geophysical survey', *Journal of Roman Archaeology* 21 (2008), 324–35.

On a hilltop to the north-west of the Roman town a seventh-century 'Final Phase' cemetery has also been excavated at Harford Farm.[55] Some of the graves were richly furnished and contained artefacts which can be argued to display a Christian influence; it must be concluded that both of these seventh-century cemeteries were used simultaneously by the local population. A select few of the population were buried in the 'Final Phase' manner at Harford Farm, but most must have been buried in newly founded 'churchyard-type' cemeteries such as that presumed to lie within the walls of the town. Both of these new cemeteries would have been employed for a while, but the cemetery at Harford Farm fell out of use in the early years of the eighth century, while the churchyard survives within the town to this day.

This raises two significant points. First, rather than following a simple linear development, it would appear that the Early Saxon cemeteries were sometimes superseded by a choice of Middle Saxon cemeteries and that 'Final Phase' cemeteries and more conventional Christian 'churchyard' cemeteries existed side by side. Second, the *Venta Icenorum* example demonstrates that if a church founded in the seventh-century remains on its original site, all of the evidence for these earlier phases is likely to have been disturbed by and buried beneath up to 1400 years' worth of inhumations and ecclesiastical rebuilding.

Cemeteries within Settlements

Although several examples of certain and probable missionary stations have been discussed here, recognisable examples are not particularly numerous and they alone cannot have accommodated all of the Middle Saxon East Anglian dead. We are once again brought back to the fact that Middle Saxon inhumation cemeteries are not common archaeological discoveries. In seeking an explanation for this paucity, it is particularly telling that all of the excavated East Anglian Middle Saxon cemeteries were integrated into settlements of one kind or another. This indicates that the separation of settlement and cemetery which characterised the Early Saxon landscape had ceased to occur.

It is widely accepted that a great restructuring of the landscape occurred during the Middle Saxon period, not least the coalescence of the numerous, comparatively transitory Early Saxon settlements into more permanent settlements. A number of explanations for these changes, primarily of an economic, social or environmental nature, have been suggested and many commentators have also attributed the observed fusion of cemeteries and settlements to these same factors.[56] But where might the impetus for this change of attitude towards the placing of the dead have originated?

55 Kenneth Penn, *Excavations on the Norwich Southern Bypass, 1989–91. Part II: The Anglo-Saxon Cemetery at Harford Farm, Caistor St Edmund, Norfolk*, East Anglian Archaeology 92 (Gressenhall, 2000).

56 Chris Arnold and Peter Wardle, 'Early medieval settlement patterns in England', *Medieval Archaeology* 25 (1981), 145–9; Martin Welch, 'Rural settlement patterns in the Early

It is clear that the creation of seventh-century cemeteries was intimately bound up with the abandonment of the old cemeteries and this abandonment has, in turn, been argued to be a direct result of the conversion to Christianity. Therefore, the fusion of cemeteries and settlements during this period can also be argued to be attributable to the same process. This coming together of the living and the dead is a characteristic of Christian practice most commonly seen in the conjunction of church and churchyard, yet it is also seen in the incorporation of Christian inhumation cemeteries into Middle Saxon settlements.[57] It is difficult to identify the religious motivations behind this integration by archaeological means alone, but one explanation might be found in the Christian belief in intercession.[58] The integration of the Christian dead into a settlement is a physical reflection of the fact that, under Christianity, the dead remained an important part of the community and Christian cemeteries became a focus of remembrance and worship.[59]

The sites chosen for Middle Saxon execution cemeteries also emphasise the changing attitude towards the appropriate location of the dead in newly Christianised societies.[60] The reuse of extant prehistoric monuments as foci for Early Saxon burials is a trend which has long been recognised and the deliberate association of Early Saxon dead with these monuments is often interpreted as an attempt to forge a link with the past, thereby legitimising authority and defining territory in the present.[61] By the Middle Saxon period these same barrows had come to be regarded as unholy and liminal places, primarily, it seems, because

and Middle Anglo-Saxon periods', *Landscape History* 7 (1985), 13–25; Richard Hodges, *The Anglo-Saxon Achievement* (New York, 1989), pp. 43–68; Helena Hamerow, 'Settlement mobility and the "Middle Saxon Shift": rural settlements and settlement patterns in Anglo-Saxon England', *Anglo-Saxon England* 20 (1991), 1–17; Tom Williamson, *Shaping Medieval Landscapes* (Macclesfield, 2003).

57 Boddington, 'Models of burial'; Elisabeth Zadora-Rio, 'The making of churchyards and parish territories in the early-medieval landscape of France and England in the 7th–12th centuries: a reconsideration', *Medieval Archaeology* 47 (2003), 1–19; Victoria Thompson, *Dying and Death in Later Anglo-Saxon England* (Woodbridge, 2004), pp. 26–56; John Blair, *The Church in Anglo-Saxon Society* (Oxford, 2005), pp. 228–45; Sam Turner, *Making A Christian Landscape* (Exeter, 2006).

58 Phillipe Aries, *The Hour of Our Death* (London, 1981), pp. 29–40; Patrick Geary, *Living with the Dead in the Middle Ages* (London, 1994), pp. 77–87.

59 Donald Bullough, 'Burial, community and belief in the early medieval West', in *Ideal and Reality in Frankish and Anglo-Saxon Society*, ed. Patrick Wormald (Oxford, 1983), 177–201; Helen Gittos, 'Creating the sacred: Anglo-Saxon rites for consecrating cemeteries', in *Burial in Early Medieval England and Wales*, eds Sam Lucy and Andrew Reynolds (London, 2002), 195–208; Thompson, *Dying and Death*, pp. 170–206.

60 Helen Geake, 'Burial practice in seventh- and eighth-century England', in *The Age of Sutton Hoo*, ed. Martin Carver (Woodbridge, 1992), 83–94, at pp. 87–9; Andrew Reynolds, 'The definition and ideology of Anglo-Saxon execution sites and cemeteries', in *Death and Burial in Medieval Europe*, eds Guy De Boe and Frans Verhaeghe (Zellik, 1997) II, 33–41.

61 Sam Lucy, 'The significance of mortuary ritual in the political manipulation of the landscape', *Archaeological Review from Cambridge* 11.1 (1992), 93–103; Howard Williams, 'Monuments and the past in Early Anglo-Saxon England', *World Archaeology* 30 (1998), 90–108; Williams, 'Placing the dead'.

of their association with pagan burials.[62] Whereas the revered dead of the Early Saxon period had been buried in locations often at some remove from centres of population, the traditional cemeteries became places to be feared and were therefore considered to be suitable sites for executions, their peripheral location physically mirroring the social exclusion of the executed individuals. East Anglian examples have been found at South Acre in west Norfolk and also at Sutton Hoo.[63] This reversal again emphasises the fact that, as a direct consequence of the introduction of a Christian ideology, the appropriate location for the revered dead in the Middle Saxon period was considered to be 'closer to home', in a cemetery that formed an integral part of a settlement.

Finding the Evidence

Tellingly, all of the excavated examples of Middle Saxon settlements and cemeteries referred to here are from sites where the settlement subsequently faltered, was relocated or was abandoned, leaving the Middle Saxon phases undisturbed. At sites where such settlements continued to thrive we are unable to study the earlier phases directly because they are sealed beneath later buildings or have been badly disturbed by subsequent development. Such observations lead to the inevitable conclusion that the vast majority of the archaeological evidence for early Christianity lies beneath later settlements, and in particular beneath later churches and their churchyards. How, then, are we to study it?

Whereas the area immediately beneath a church is effectively reachable only via partial excavation of the interior of the building, the surrounding churchyard is at once both more accessible and considerably more disturbed. Stray finds from churchyards can provide a useful indication of Anglo-Saxon activity on the site, yet stray finds are just that – stray – and as such their presence or absence, while informative, is not necessarily representative of any wider pattern of occupation. Fortunately, in East Anglia we are able to cast our net more widely, as the changes in the settlement pattern that occurred during the medieval period mean that many East Anglian churches are not now hemmed in by development. Phenomena such as common-edge drift and settlement desertion have resulted in many churches now being surrounded by arable fields; in many instances these fields have been investigated as part of systematic field-walking surveys.[64]

A large number of church sites have been investigated in this manner, albeit often as parts of larger surveys, and the presence or absence of surface scatters

62 Sarah Semple, 'A fear of the past: the place of the prehistoric burial mound in the ideology of Middle and Later Anglo-Saxon England', *World Archaeology* 30 (1998), 109–26; Nicola Whyte, 'The deviant dead in the Norfolk landscape', *Landscapes* 4.1 (2003), 24–39; Andrew Reynolds, 'Definition and ideology', in *Sutton Hoo: A Seventh-Century Princely Burial Ground and its Context*, ed. Martin Carver (London, 2005), pp. 347–9.

63 *Sutton Hoo*, ed. Carver; John Wymer, *Barrow Excavations in Norfolk, 1984–88*, East Anglian Archaeology 77 (Gressenhall, 1996), pp. 58–92.

64 Williamson, *Shaping Medieval Landscapes*, pp. 167–71; Tom Williamson, *England's Landscape: East Anglia* (London, 2006), pp. 51–6.

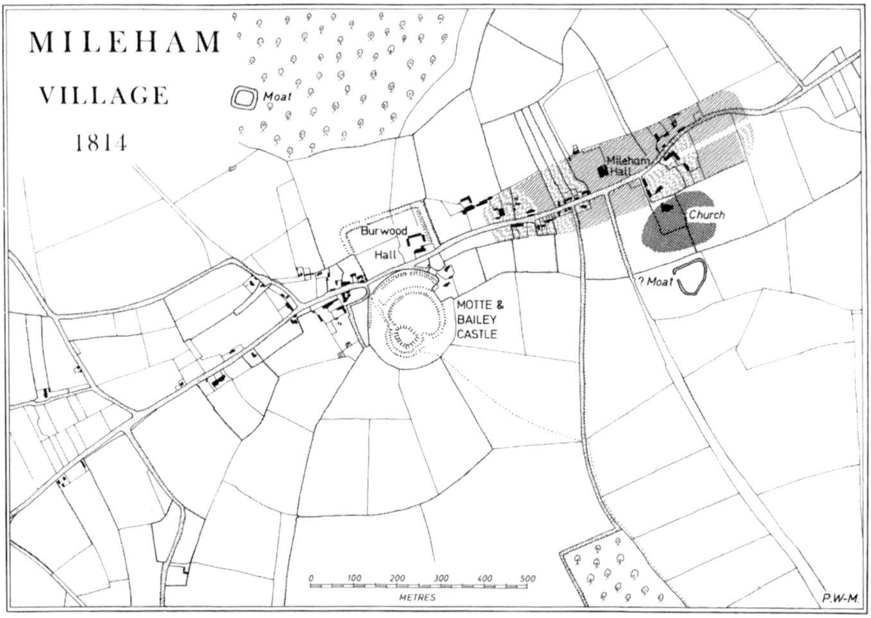

Figure 11.2. Mileham in 1814. Double hatching indicates the scatter of Middle Saxon Ipswich Ware surrounding the church; single hatching indicates the scatter of Late Saxon Thetford Ware to the north. (Reproduced from Wade-Martins, *Village Sites in Launditch Hundred* with the permission of Norfolk Museums and Archaeology Service)

of Middle Saxon Ipswich Ware and Late Saxon Thetford-type Ware can be used to draw conclusions about their foundation dates.[65] The evidence is dif-

65 Alan Davison, 'The distribution of medieval settlement in West Harling', *Norfolk Archaeology* 38 (1983), 329–36; Alan Davison, 'Little Hockham', *Norfolk Archaeology* 40 (1987), 84–93; Alan Davison, *The Evolution of Settlement in Three Parishes in South-East Norfolk*, East Anglian Archaeology 49 (Gressenhall, 1990); Alan Davison, 'The field archaeology of the Mannington and Wolterton estates', *Norfolk Archaeology* 42 (1995), 160–84; Alan Davison, 'The archaeology of the parish of West Acre. Part 1: field survey evidence', *Norfolk Archaeology* 44 (2003), 202–21; Alan Davison with Brian Cushion, 'The archaeology of the Hargham Estate', *Norfolk Archaeology* 43 (1999), 257–74; Alan Davison, Barbara Green and Bill Milligan, *Illington: A Study of a Breckland Parish and its Anglo-Saxon Cemetery*, East Anglian Archaeology 63 (Gressenhall, 1993); A. Lawson, *The Archaeology of Witton*, East Anglian Archaeology 18 (Gressenhall, 1983); John Newman, 'The Late Roman and Anglo-Saxon settlement pattern in the Sandlings of Suffolk', in *The Age of Sutton Hoo*, ed. Martin Carver (Woodbridge, 1992), 25–38; John Newman, 'Survey in the Deben Valley', in *Sutton Hoo: A Seventh-Century Princely Burial Ground and its Context*, ed. Martin Carver (London, 2005), 477–88; Andrew Rogerson, Alan Davison, David Pritchard and Robert Silvester, *Barton Bendish and Caldecote*, East Anglian Archaeology 80 (Gressenhall, 1997); Robert Silvester, *The Fenland Project Number 3: Marshland and the Nar Valley, Norfolk*, East Anglian Archaeology 45 (Gressenhall, 1988); Robert Silvester, *The Fenland Project Number 4: The Wissey Embayment and the Fen Causeway, Norfolk*, East Anglian Archaeology 52 (Gressenhall, 1991);

ficult to interpret, as many churches are associated with both Middle and Late Saxon scatters, but when this class of evidence is combined with others, such as topography or associations with existing sites, a more comprehensive picture emerges.

Churches solely associated with Late Saxon scatters can be argued to be Late Saxon foundations resulting from the recognised proliferation of parish churches in this period.[66] However, there are some churches that are only associated with Middle Saxon material, usually because the Late Saxon scatter lies elsewhere, and in these instances we can say with some certainty that the church itself must be a Middle Saxon foundation. Such examples are rare, but Wade-Martins' study of village sites in central Norfolk's Launditch hundred revealed that in the parish of Mileham the church stood within a distinct Ipswich Ware scatter, while the Late Saxon scatter lay to the north along the main road (Fig. 11.2).[67]

Many more of the churches are associated with both Middle and Late Saxon artefact scatters. In these instances the artefact scatters do not allow us to say whether the church was founded during the Middle or Late Saxon period, but the presence of the Middle Saxon material indicates that we are at least dealing with a settlement with seventh-century origins. Given the arguments developed here, it is extremely likely that these Middle Saxon settlements contained a Christian cemetery of some kind, possibly with an accompanying church.

Conclusions

The widespread landscape upheavals caused by the conversion indicate that the new religion had an impact on both the living and the dead. The nature and location of cemeteries changed dramatically, while the constituent parts of settlements were also altered by the introduction of a funerary element. Completely new classes of site were introduced to the Middle Saxon landscape in the form of missionary churches; islands and peninsulas were populated; and, for the first time in two centuries, Roman masonry structures were reoccupied.

The progress of the conversion can also be read in the changing landscape context of cemeteries and in particular in the changing relationship between cemeteries and settlements. Whereas pre-Christian settlements and cemeteries had remained separate landscape entities, under the influence of Christianity settlements and cemeteries converged to become a unified whole, providing us with a vivid material indication of the progress of the conversion.

Field-walking also gives us an insight into early Christian foundations which later became parish churches. If each of the church sites associated with a Middle Saxon scatter possessed a Middle Saxon Christian cemetery this would

Peter Wade-Martins, *Village Sites in Launditch Hundred*, East Anglian Archaeology 10 (Gressenhall, 1980).

66 Richard Morris, *Churches in the Landscape* (London, 1989), pp. 140–67.

67 Wade-Martins, *Village Sites in Launditch Hundred*, pp. 40–8.

suggest that much of the Middle Saxon population became wholly and actively Christian during the seventh century. If this interpretation is taken to its extreme and it is suggested that all of these sites might have had Middle Saxon churches as well, then we are confronted with the possibility of a very densely populated seventh-century ecclesiastical landscape indeed. Even a more moderate view which assumes that only some of these sites had churches suggests that the number of seventh-century foundations would still be higher than might traditionally have been expected.

All of which conclusions contradict many traditionally held views on the speed with which Christianity took hold in Anglo-Saxon East Anglia and the extent to which it spread through society. Far from supporting the notion of a nominal conversion on the part of the king which had little effect on the lower echelons of society, the archaeological evidence and the evidence of the landscape itself suggest that, even in the mid-seventh century, the conversion of East Anglia was already a significant and wide-reaching process which was widespread at a grassroots level and which changed the nature of the Anglo-Saxon landscape forever.

12

The Landscape and Economy of the Anglo-Saxon Coast: New Archaeological Evidence

PETER MURPHY

Introduction

Stephen Rippon has provided a helpful framework within which to consider land-use in coastal wetlands during the first millennium AD.[1] He distinguishes three types of land-use. *Exploitation* was simply making use of the available resources: salt itself, saltmarsh grazing, fisheries, wildfowl, sub-surface peat, and constructional materials. *Modification* involved increasing productivity and utility, primarily by controlling water, by drainage and limited embankment of grazing and settlement areas. *Transformation* – the construction of sea-walls to exclude tidal waters, with permanent drainage systems landwards, and conversion of the former intertidal zone to grazing and arable – marked a fundamental disjunction with previous land-use. The landscape was changed (it was thought) permanently, in a high-risk, high-cost but also high-return strategy.

There was never anything inevitable nor necessarily sequential about shifts from one of these forms of land-use to another: each represented an appropriate adaptation of human behaviour to prevailing circumstances in particular places. However, land-use in the second millennium AD tended towards transformation wherever that could be achieved, reaching its furthest extent in the nineteenth century. Indeed, some land-claim seems to have been undertaken then without very much thought, simply because agricultural 'improvement' was beyond question. The defence of reclaimed land was likewise scarcely questioned, well into the twentieth century. Formal economic appraisal to consider the value of the land defended in relation to the costs of its maintenance did not then figure.

In the first decade of the third millennium, the appropriate use of coastal wetlands is being reappraised, again in the light of changing circumstances.[2] The criteria now being applied differ: coastal land-use is no longer the exclusive pre-

1 Stephen Rippon, *The Transformation of Coastal Wetlands: Exploitation and Management of Marshland Landscapes in North-West Europe during the Roman and Medieval Periods* (Oxford, 2000).

2 Department for Environment, *Food and Rural Affairs, Shoreline Management Plan Guidance*: Volume 1: *Aims and requirements*; Volume 2: *Procedures* (London, 2006).

serve of private owners hoping for profit. State direction of what is now called Flood and Coastal Erosion Risk Management (FCERM) leads to other priorities, such as conservation of natural habitats (driven by the EU Species, Birds and Habitats Directives), and longer-term economic considerations about climate change and the sustainability of coasts. The earlier paradigm – in which land-claim to increase agricultural productivity was seen as the natural and obvious course of action, and reclaimed land was considered to be claimed for ever – has now been abandoned. In turn, coastal policy options such as 'managed realignment' or 'no active intervention' are already having adverse effects on coastal archaeological sites and the wider historic environment.

It is for this reason that English Heritage is funding a national programme of Rapid Coastal Zone Assessment Surveys (RCZAS), designed to enhance the National Monuments Record and local authority Historic Environment Records, in order to provide archaeological managers with the information they need to respond to these policy shifts.[3] Alongside this, and in the shorter term, other archaeological interventions are being undertaken, in response to specific threats to coastal archaeological sites, whether from natural processes of erosion or the impacts of FCERM schemes. Consequently, a huge amount of new archaeological information is being generated, but most of it remains unassimilated, in grey literature and internal reports. Several earlier surveys, undertaken for management purposes, have been published, for example the Fenland Management Project,[4] but the results, published in regional journals or monograph series, are not widely known.

To produce a complete appraisal of all these new data at this stage would be an enormous task. This paper has the much more modest aim of reviewing some of the latest evidence for just two aspects of Anglo-Saxon coastal land-use, principally in the East of England: early crop production and the use of fish traps. However, once the RCZAS programme is completed, the intention is to produce a review volume.[5]

Anglo-Saxon Coastal Arable Farming before Landscape Transformation

In Rippon's model, conversion of coastal wetlands to arable production is seen as closely related to construction of sea defences, and so was dependent on the most extreme category of intervention: landscape transformation. However,

3 English Heritage, *Shoreline Management Plan Review and the Historic Environment: English Heritage Guidance* (Swindon, 2006). Survey reports are available at <http://www.english-heritage.org.uk/>, and search for RCZAS.

4 *Fenland Management Project excavations 1991–1995*, eds Andrew Crowson, Tom Lane and Jez Reeve, Lincolnshire Archaeology and Heritage Reports Series, 3 (2000), 10–14 and passim.

5 This will replace *England's Coastal Heritage: a Survey for English Heritage and the RCHME*, eds Michael Fulford, Timothy Champion and Andrew Long, English Heritage Archaeological Report 15 (London, 1997).

there is now evidence from Eastern England for arable production on undefended coasts.

As part of the Fenland Management Project, small-scale excavations were undertaken at sites of Anglo-Saxon date: three in Norfolk, at West Walton (WNW 42/18943), Rose Hall Farm, Walpole St Andrew (WPA 23/22145) and Hay Green, Terrington St Clement (TSC 17/22275 and TSC 23/22576), and three in Lincolnshire, at Third Drove, Gosberton (GOS 16(GBT93)/23470), Chopdike Drove, Gosberton (GOS 22(GOS92)/23477) and Mornington House, Gosberton (GOS37(GOS93)/23495). Most of the samples collected from sites excavated during this project were of Middle Saxon date, but there were some Late Saxon and probably Early Post-Conquest ones.

Palaeoecological data from these sites illustrate, initially, human responses to coastal change and, subsequently, transformation of the coastal environment through construction of the fenland Sea Bank in the Late Saxon period. The Lincolnshire and Norfolk sites were widely separated geographically, and show somewhat different conditions.[6]

At Third Drove, Gosberton, the basal fills of a Roman ditch included cockles and oysters in life position, and a foraminiferal assemblage indicating low current velocities and salinity levels at around 20–30ppt.[7] By contrast foraminifers from the upper fills indicated shallowing of the environment and low salinity levels (0–15ppt). In Early Saxon features at the site, shells of freshwater molluscs, stonewort remains and seeds of duckweed were abundant, indicating freshwater conditions. A marked shift from intertidal to freshwater conditions is indicated. These results support palaeogeographic data indicating an eastwards expansion of freshwater fen over marine silts in this area during Early–Middle Saxon times.

Middle Saxon features at Chopdike Drove, Gosberton, included mixed mollusc assemblages, mainly of land and freshwater species, but including some intertidal molluscs. Foraminifera from a pit indicate a marine flood event: subtidal and marine species were present. The fills from a sequence of ditch cuts also produced assemblages indicating marine flooding. Mollusc shell assemblages from Mornington House, Gosberton, were again mainly of freshwater and land species, but the foraminifers from a Middle Saxon ditch fill indicated a complex sequence of events. The basal fill included microfossils indicating a marine flood event, similar to those at Chopdike Drove, but in general tidal channel conditions were indicated, with one phase of freshwater flooding. At these sites relatively minor variations in topography and in the depth of ditch

6 Peter Murphy, 'Mollusca; environment and economy: a summary', and Mike Godwin, 'Foraminifera', in *Anglo-Saxon Settlement on the Siltland of Eastern England*, eds A. Crowson, T. Lane, K. Penn and D.Trimble, Lincolnshire Archaeology and Heritage Report Series, 7 (2005), 228–63.

7 ppt is short for parts per thousand. Foraminifera, or foraminifers, are single-celled marine to brackish-water organisms with resistant, identifiable outer 'shells' known as tests. The range and relative abundance of species present in sediments and archaeological deposits gives a proxy indication of water depth and salinity.

cuts would have affected salinity levels within features, but it is plain that they were subject to flood events – both marine and freshwater.

At the Norfolk sites, only sparse and mixed mollusc shell assemblages were recovered, but the micro- and meio-fossils are more informative. Foraminifera from the 'post-Roman silt' at Ingleborough, West Walton, showed it to be an overbank flood deposit from the adjacent roddon, and are interpreted as indicating that this was an area of lower salt marsh with creeks prior to Middle Saxon settlement. Middle Saxon ditches at Rose Hall Farm, Walpole St Andrew, and Hay Green, Terrington St Clement, included assemblages indicating that the ditches functioned as marsh creeks. At Walpole, the locations sampled showed similarities, at some levels, to the terminal ends of natural creek systems, where they join high intertidal flats, but the watercourses were also directly connected to the Wash and North Sea.

A Late Saxon ditch at Terrington showed a very different assemblage, indicating lowered salinity and protection from direct marine influence, whilst at West Walton foraminifers were virtually absent in ditch fills, again implying isolation from marine conditions, though perhaps with occasional marine flooding. Isolation of sites from marine influence in the Late Saxon period can probably be attributed to construction of the Sea Bank.

Charred and mineral-replaced crop plant remains were recovered at all sites.[8] Barley was the most frequent cereal crop: a hulled lax-eared variety with three fertile florets per rachis node (*Hordeum vulgare* var. *vulgare* forma. *tetrastichum*). Charred macrofossils of *Avena* (oats) also occurred, with grains and rachis fragments of *Secale cereale* (rye) and *Triticum aestivum*-type (bread wheat). At Gosberton 16 and 37, remains of *Triticum spelta* (spelt) and perhaps *T. dicoccum* (emmer, or another tetraploid species) were present. These either came from Roman contexts (at GOS 16) or probably represent residual Roman material in Anglo-Saxon features (GOS 37). Pulses were common, though often represented by indeterminate cotyledons or fragments. Large, elongate seeds and cotyledons of *Vicia faba* var. *minor* (horsebean) were distinctive, but separation of smaller-seeded *Vicia* spp. from *Pisum* (pea) was problematic. Only one definite seed of *Pisum sativum* var. *arvense*, with its distinctive short oval hilum, was identified: from Gosberton 22. *Linum usitatissimum* (flax/linseed) was represented mainly by seeds and occasional capsule fragments. The fruits of *Cannabis sativa* (hemp) from Gosberton 22 were all mineral-replaced: no charred specimens were noted.

Seeds of *Brassica* sp. (cabbage family) were common in several samples from West Walton. Specific identification depends mainly upon metrical studies of testa patterning,[9] and has not been attempted here; shrinkage and deformation may well have occurred during charring. However, these seeds could represent a cultivated plant.

The first and most obvious point to emphasise is the abundance of six-row hulled barley, the main crop in Middle Saxon to probably eleventh-century

8 Murphy, 'Plant macrofossils', pp. 238–60.

9 Greta Berggren, 'Reviews on the taxonomy of some species of Brassica based on their seeds', *Svensk. Botanisker Tidskrift* 56 (1962), 65–133.

phases at all sites. Total counts of grains and rachis nodes (components of the central 'stem' of the cereal ear: the 'chaff') for each site or site group respectively were:

- Norfolk sites (total) – 653 grains: 454 rachis nodes (1.43:1),
- Chopdike Drove, Gosberton (GOS 22) – 611 grains: 127 rachis nodes (4.8:1)
- Mornington House, Gosberton (GOS 37) – 471 grains: 65 rachis nodes (7.2:1).

Assuming that only six-row barley is represented, a ratio of approximately 3:1 would be expected in an unprocessed crop. It is therefore apparent that at the Norfolk sites there is a definite excess of rachis nodes over grains (notably in the Late Saxon samples, but also in many Middle Saxon ones), whereas at the Lincolnshire sites grains occur in excess. It is possible that this variation might relate to the generally poorer preservation of material and greater degree of sediment encrustation, particularly at Mornington House. At all sites and phases, however, the relative abundance of rachis nodes indicates local processing and, by inference, local production.

The predominance of barley at these coastal sites is thought to have been related to its salt-tolerance compared to other crops.[10] Experimental work in the Netherlands has shown that barley is the only cereal capable of producing acceptable yields in highly saline environments.[11] The siting of Fenland Anglo-Saxon settlements on roddons (elevated sinuous silt ridges, which in the Fens mark the channels of much earlier, commonly Iron Age, creeks[12]) meant that arable production was possible. However, it was still hazardous, due to potential marine flooding during storm surges, and salt-spray would have restricted yields from crops less able to tolerate salinity.

The general similarity of these Fenland assemblages to those from late prehistoric to early medieval coastal sites in the Netherlands is striking,[13] and it seems likely that, faced with common problems, early farmers on the fen siltlands and on the Dutch coast developed similar agricultural systems independently, relying primarily on salt-tolerant crops.

In short, the evidence now is that permanently occupied farms were established on the highest ground available – mainly on roddons – in a very haz-

[10] S. Baykal, 'Effect of NaCl on the germination and development of Hordeum distichum L., Hordeum vulgare L., Triticum aestivum L. and Triticum durum Desf.', *Fen Fakultesi Mecmausi* (Istanbul University), Series B, 44 (1979), 49–96.

[11] S. Bottema, T. C. van Hoorn, H. Woldring and W. H. E. Gremmen, 'An agricultural experiment in the unprotected salt marsh, Part II', *Palaeohistoria* 22 (1980), 127–40. W. Van Zeist, T. C. van Hoorn, S. Bottema and H. Woldring, 'An agricultural experiment in the unprotected salt marsh', *Palaeohistoria* 18 (1977), 111–53.

[12] Martin Waller, *The Fenland Project No. 9: Flandrian Environmental Change in Fenland*, East Anglian Archaeology 70 (1994), pp. 45–6.

[13] Karl-Ernst Behre and Stefanie Jacomet, 'The ecological interpretation of archaeobotanical data', in *Progress in Old World Palaeoethnobotany*, eds W. Van Zeist, K. Wasylikowa and K-E. Behre (Rotterdam/Brookfield, 1991), pp. 81–108.

ardous environment subject to marine (and sometimes freshwater) flooding from the Middle Saxon period onwards. The productivity of the silt fenlands evidently provided sufficient incentive for Anglo-Saxon farmers to accept the risks of living there all year round, even before construction of the Sea Bank.

Fish Traps

The Romans were obsessed with fish and seafood;[14] this is represented archaeologically at coastal and inland sites in Britain. Mollusc shell assemblages from Roman sites are commonly dominated by oysters (*Ostrea edulis*), but a more specifically Mediterranean taste is indicated by the presence of carpet shells (*Venerupis* spp.).[15] Shellfish of this genus are widely eaten in the Mediterranean area today though rarely, for obscure reasons, in England (except at Italian restaurants). Roman deposits at Culver Street, Colchester, also produced a substantial fish-bone assemblage of 21 taxa, dominated by eel (*Anguilla anguilla*), herring (*Clupea harengus*), plaice (*Pleuronectes platessa*) and flounder (*Platichthys flesus*).[16] There were obviously large-scale commercial fisheries and, potentially, aquaculture. However, at this site, as elsewhere, medieval deposits produced much higher densities of fish-bones than Roman ones: mean values of 1.82 and 5.50 bones/litre of soil respectively. This pattern has generally been interpreted as indicating a trend towards an increasing importance of fish in the diet (at least in towns) through time. Associated with this trend was the construction of large timber and stone fish traps in estuaries and on some open coasts.[17]

Anglo-Saxon and later fish weirs are abundant in the Severn Estuary and North Devon. There was a distinction between the 'hedge-weir' (*haecwer*) and 'basket-weir' (*cytwer*). In the Domesday record for the Severn and Wye valleys there were ninety-one *cytweras* and four *haecwers*.[18] 'Basket-weirs' involved use of conical baskets of wicker, placed behind V-shaped arrays of hurdle panels. These were termed weirs in Somerset, but *kidells* in Shropshire. In Minehead, Blue Anchor and Bridgwater Bays there are the remains of hundreds of weirs.[19]

14 See Tom Holland, *Rubicon: The Triumph and Tragedy of the Roman Republic* (London, 2004), p. 187.

15 Peter Murphy, 'Environmental studies: Culver Street', in *Excavations at Culver Street, the Gilberd School and Other Sites in Colchester 1971–85*, ed. Philip Crummy, Colchester Archaeological Report 6 (Colchester, 1992), pp. 273–87.

16 Alison Locker, 'The Fish Bones', in *Excavations at Culver Street*, ed. Crummy, pp. 287–80.

17 *England's Coastal Heritage*, eds Fulford, Champion and Long; Rippon, Transformation of Coastal Wetlands, pp. 221–3; David Strachan, 'Intertidal stationary fishing structures in Essex: some C14 dates', *Essex Archaeology and History* 29 (1998), 274–82.

18 C. James Bond, 'Monastic fisheries', in *Medieval Fish, Fisheries and Fishponds in England*, ed. Mick Aston British Archaeological Reports (British Series) 182 (Oxford, 1998), pp. 69–112.

19 A. Dickson and S. Crowther, *Rapid Coastal Zone Assessment for the Severn Estuary, Archaeological Aerial Survey, National Mapping Programme Interim Report* (Swindon,

The latter have provided the only scientific dates for fishing structures in the Severn, though of timber samples submitted from 15 structures only 2 could be dated by dendrochronology, with felling dates for the wood of 932AD and 966AD.[20] Some stone fish weirs and composite stone/timber traps also survive, most of which appear to be of medieval date. The current method of using baskets called 'putts' or 'putchers', arrayed in rows on wooden frames, appears to have originated in the post-medieval period. Waterlogged intertidal deposits investigated prior to construction of the Second Severn Crossing produced a woven rectangular fish basket, dated to 590 ± 70 BP,[21] though in form it does not exactly match the baskets used in 'putcher' weirs.

'Hedge-weirs' occur everywhere, but are virtually the only type of trap known from the east coast. They are typically large V-shaped lines of posts, which supported vertical hurdle panels (or in the west and south, boulder walls) and they funnelled fish within the tidal prism enclosed towards a basket, or other means of trapping, at the apex of the V. There are frequently horizontal hurdle walkways parallel to the walls, presumably used both for maintenance and to collect any fish which became trapped away from the apex. New archaeological survey is extending the geographical range and known density of these traps. In the East of England, for example, traps have been recorded at Holme-next-the-Sea, Norfolk, and Holbrook Bay and Barber's Point in Suffolk. Others have been reported from North Kent.[22] Further recording work is currently being undertaken on the previously known traps at Collins Creek, Mersea, The Nass, Pewet Island and Sales Point, all in Essex.[23]

There have been few studies of the wood and timber of which these traps were constructed. A very small sub-sample of seven hurdle panels has been examined from the trap at Collins Creek, Essex.[24] They were made of oak, willow, birch and hazel roundwood. The distribution of stem age/size did not show any clear clustering, as would be expected in managed woodland: presumably this relates to the enormous amounts of wood required, so that roundwood from many woodlands managed in different ways was stockpiled and became mixed

2007); M. McDonnell, 'Bridgwater Bay: a summary of its geomorphology, tidal characteristics and intertidal cultural resource', *Severn Estuary Levels Research Committee Annual Report 1994*, 87–114.

20 C. Groves, C. Locatelli and N. Nayling, 'Tree-ring analysis of oak samples from Stert Flats fish weirs, Bridgwater Bay, Somerset', *Centre for Archaeology Report* 43 (2004).

21 Steve Goldbold and Rick Turner, 'Second Severn Crossing 1991', *Welsh Intertidal Zone, Severn Estuary Levels Research Committee Annual Report* (1992), 45–55.

22 Norfolk Archaeological Unit, 'An Archaeological Walkover Survey of Holme Beach, Holme-next-the-Sea, Norfolk. Assessment Report and Updated Project Design' (unpublished report for English Heritage, Norwich, 2003); Linzi Everett, ed., *Targeted Intertidal Survey*, Suffolk County Council Archaeological Service Report 192 (Ipswich, 2007); Wessex Archaeology, *North Kent Coast Rapid Coastal Zone Assessment Survey. Phase II: Field Assessment*. Year 2 Report, Ref. 56751.01, Wessex Archaeology, for English Heritage and Kent County Council (Salisbury, 2006).

23 Ellen Heppell, pers. comm.

24 Peter Murphy, 'Anglo-Saxon hurdles and basketry: Collins Creek, Blackwater Estuary, Essex', *Ancient Monuments Laboratory Report* 5/95 (1995), 17.

Table 12.1 Radiocarbon determinations from fish traps at Holme-next-the-Sea, Norfolk; Barber's Point, Alde Estuary, Holbrook Bay, Stour Estuary, the Blackwater Estuary and Sales Point Essex. See note 25 for full references to sources.

Laboratory Code	Feature Identification	Material	δ^{13}C (‰)	Radiocarbon Age (BP)	Calibrated Date (95% confidence)
GU-5800	Holme fish trap I: HER38042	wood, *Alnus* sp. with bark	-28.2	1250 ±50	cal AD 660–900
GU-5801	Holme fish trap I: HER38042	wood, *Alnus* sp. with bark	-22.6	1510 ±50	cal AD 420–650
GU-5802	Holme fish trap II: HER38043	wood, *Pomoideae* with bark	-28.2	1650 ±50	cal AD 250–540
GU-5803	Holme fish trap II: HER38043	wood, *Acer* sp.	-30.5	1280 ±50	cal AD 650–890
GU-6012	Holme fish trap I: HER38042	wood, *Salix* sp./*Populus* sp.	-28.0	1210 ±50	cal AD 670–970
GU-6013	Holme fish trap I: HER38042	wood, *Betula* sp.	-28.1	1260 ±50	cal AD 650–890
GU-6028	Holme fish trap III: HER39586	wood, *Alnus glutinosa*	-28.0	1310 ±50	cal AD 640–810
GU-6029	Holme fish trap III: HER39586	wood, *Alnus glutinosa/ Corylus avallana*	-28.5	1310 ±50	cal AD 640–810
GU-6030	Holme fish trap IV: HER37613	wood, *Quercus* sp., squashed roundwood	-25.9	1480 ±50	cal AD 430–660
GU-6031	Holme fish trap IV: HER37613	wood, *Quercus* sp., roundwood and sapwood	-24.2	1450 ±50	cal AD 530–670
GU-6034	Holme fish trap V: HER38222	wood, *Alnus glutinosa/ Corylus avallana*	-26.6	1090 ±50	cal AD 820–1030
GU-6035	Holme fish trap V: HER38222	wood, *Alnus glutinosa*	-30.9	1170 ±50	cal AD 690–990
GrN-30512	Barber's Point, Alde Estuary	*Ulex* or *Sarothamnus* stems	-25.6	1455 ± 25	cal AD 550–650
GrN-30513	Barber's Point, Alde Estuary	cf. *Sambucus* stem	-25.7	1370 ± 25	cal AD 640–680
GrN-30514	Barber's Point, Alde Estuary	*Quercus* sp. sapwood	-27.3	1310 ± 40	cal AD 650–780
GrN-30515	Barber's Point, Alde Estuary	*Ulex* or *Sarothamnus* stems	-27.9	1360 ± 35	cal AD 630–760
GrN-30516	Barber's Point, Alde Estuary	*Ulex* or *Sarothamnus* stems	-26.6	1435 ± 30	cal AD 560–660
GrN-30517	Barber's Point, Alde Estuary	*Quercus* sp. roundwood	-27.5	1350 + 20	cal AD 645–685
UB-5224	Holbrook Bay, Stour Estuary	*Alnus* roundwood	-28.2	1135 ± 17	cal AD 880–975
UB-5225	Holbrook Bay, Stour Estuary	*Alnus* roundwood	-29.1	1029 ± 17	cal AD 985–1025
UB-5227	Holbrook Bay, Stour Estuary	*Corylus* roundwood	-28.6	1312 ± 16	cal AD 660–765
UB-5228	Holbrook Bay, Stour Estuary	*Corylus* roundwood	-29.5	1260 ± 20	cal AD 675–805
UB-5229	Holbrook Bay, Stour Estuary	*Fraxinus* sapwood	-27.7	1269 ± 16	cal AD 675–780
UB-5230	Holbrook Bay, Stour Estuary	*Fraxinus* sapwood	-28.4	1287 ± 20	cal AD 665–775

UB-5231	Holbrook Bay, Stour Estuary	*Salix/Populus* roundwood	-27.2	1323 ± 16	cal AD 655–765
Not specified	Collins Creek	wood, species not specified		1364 ± 48	cal AD 603–761
Not specified	Collins Creek	wood, species not specified		1140 ± 33	cal AD 789–980
UB-4139	Collins Creek	wood, *Quercus* sp.		1300 ± 45	cal AD 650–797
UB-4140	Collins Creek	wood, *Corylus* sp.		1286 ± 45	cal AD 654–858
UB-4141	Collins Creek	wood, *Quercus* sp		1261 ± 45	cal AD 662–883
UB-4177	The Nass, Tollesbury.	wood, *Corylus* sp.		1268 ± 39	cal AD 664–862
UB-4178	The Nass, Tollesbury.	wood, *Quercus* sp.		1227 ± 24	cal AD 690–882
UB-4113	Sales Point	wood, *Alnus* sp.		1144 ± 16	cal AD 873–957
UB-4114	Sales Point	wood, *Alnus* sp.		1214 ± 16	cal AD 772–881
UB-4115	Sales Point	wood, *Alnus* sp.		1251 ± 21	cal AD 682–800
UB-4116	Sales Point	wood, *Alnus* sp.		1277 ± 43	cal AD 659–860

together before final use. The use of broom or gorse stems at Barber's Point indicates that coastal heathland areas also provided roundwood.

Previous discussions of these structures have tended to focus on when, why, and by whom, they began to be constructed. It is perfectly plain that to obtain the necessary supplies of wood and timber, and to oversee the construction project, some central authority would have been required. Strachan and Rippon argue for monastic direction. The religious were not, of course, the only people who ate fish, but the fish traps could be seen as precursors of later monastic fishponds.

Several groups of traps on the east coast have now been dated by radiocarbon (see Table 12.1), at Holme-next-the-Sea and in estuaries off Suffolk and Essex.[25] Intertidal fish traps certainly remained in use into recent times but inspection of the dates presented reveals a distinct clustering of the probability ranges. The majority of determinations fall between 600 and 900 AD, apart from the 'early' outliers from Holme. There are several structures of later Saxon date, but fewer than for the earlier period. At present the evidence suggests an intense phase of activity in the seventh to ninth centuries, and reduced activity thereafter. Why should this be? Several possible explanations occur:

1. The traps were so effective that they depleted estuarine fish-stocks to below economic levels – an early example of the fish-stock depletion that now threatens the world's fisheries. Assessing the impact of these structures on stocks is difficult, however, for we do not know how many traps there were originally. Some,

25 Strachan, 'Intertidal stationary fishing structures'; D. Hamilton, D. Robertson and G. Cook, 'Radiocarbon dating: Holme-next-the Sea 'Seahenge' Environs 1999 and Walkover Survey 2003' (unpublished report for English Heritage, Swindon, 2003); D. Hamilton, P. Manhall, J. van der Plicht and G. McCormac, 'Radiocarbon dating: Norfolk/Suffolk Coastal Survey Project, Appendix 1', in Targeted Inter-tidal Survey, ed. Linzi Everett, Suffolk County Council Archaeological Service Report 192 (Ipswich, 2007).

XII.1 Anglo-Saxon V-shaped fish trap at Holbrook Bay, Stour estuary, Suffolk. © and supplied courtesy of Essex County Council.

in the Stour Estuary (Pl. XII.1), are recorded as having been destroyed for navigational dredging in the nineteenth century and others may have been destroyed by natural processes of erosion and biodegradation without any record. Nor is the radiocarbon chronology sufficiently precise to indicate how many were in operation contemporaneously.

2. If the traps were under monastic control and direction, then the economic and social disruption related to the ninth-century Anglo-Scandinavian conflicts, and the incorporation of Eastern England in the Danelaw, might have meant that levels of construction were reduced in the east, at least for a time.

3. There is abundant evidence in the form of fish-bones from urban archaeology for increasing exploitation of cod, herring and other fisheries in the North Sea and beyond from around the tenth century. These new sources of supply might have reduced the profitability of estuarine fish traps.

These suggestions do not have to be mutually exclusive, and none of them is directly testable. However, compared to the East of England, few radiocarbon or dendrochronological dates are currently available from fish traps in the west, in the Severn Estuary and elsewhere. It remains to be seen whether a comparable chronological distribution will emerge for the west of England, but if new results demonstrate that construction there continued on a large scale beyond the ninth century there would be some support for the second suggestion – that reduced construction in the east was a consequence of conflict.

Conclusion

In conclusion, the two lines of evidence outlined briefly in this paper – for the earliest post-Roman expansion of arable farming onto coastal wetlands, and for a major phase of fish trap construction – indicate more intensive use of coastal resources in the seventh to ninth centuries AD than occurred either earlier or later. This fits well with other evidence discussed elsewhere in this volume for agricultural intensification in England at this time.

Index